MY OTHER LIFE
by
Terry Moore

"Why do we do these things to each other? In the end, after all the reasons that seem to die with us, what's the point? I can't help feeling we're all being used. That somebody, somewhere, has set us all up and they're laughing at us as we fall, taking each other out, one by one... until there are none."

-Katchoo

Strangers in Paradise: **MY OTHER LIFE**

First Edition: July 2000
Second Printing: July 2001
ISBN 1-892597-11-X

Printed in Canada by Quebecor Printing

Published by
Abstract Studio, Inc.
P. O. Box 271487
Houston, Texas 77277
www.StrangersInParadise.com
email: sipnet@StrangersInParadise.com

CONTENTS

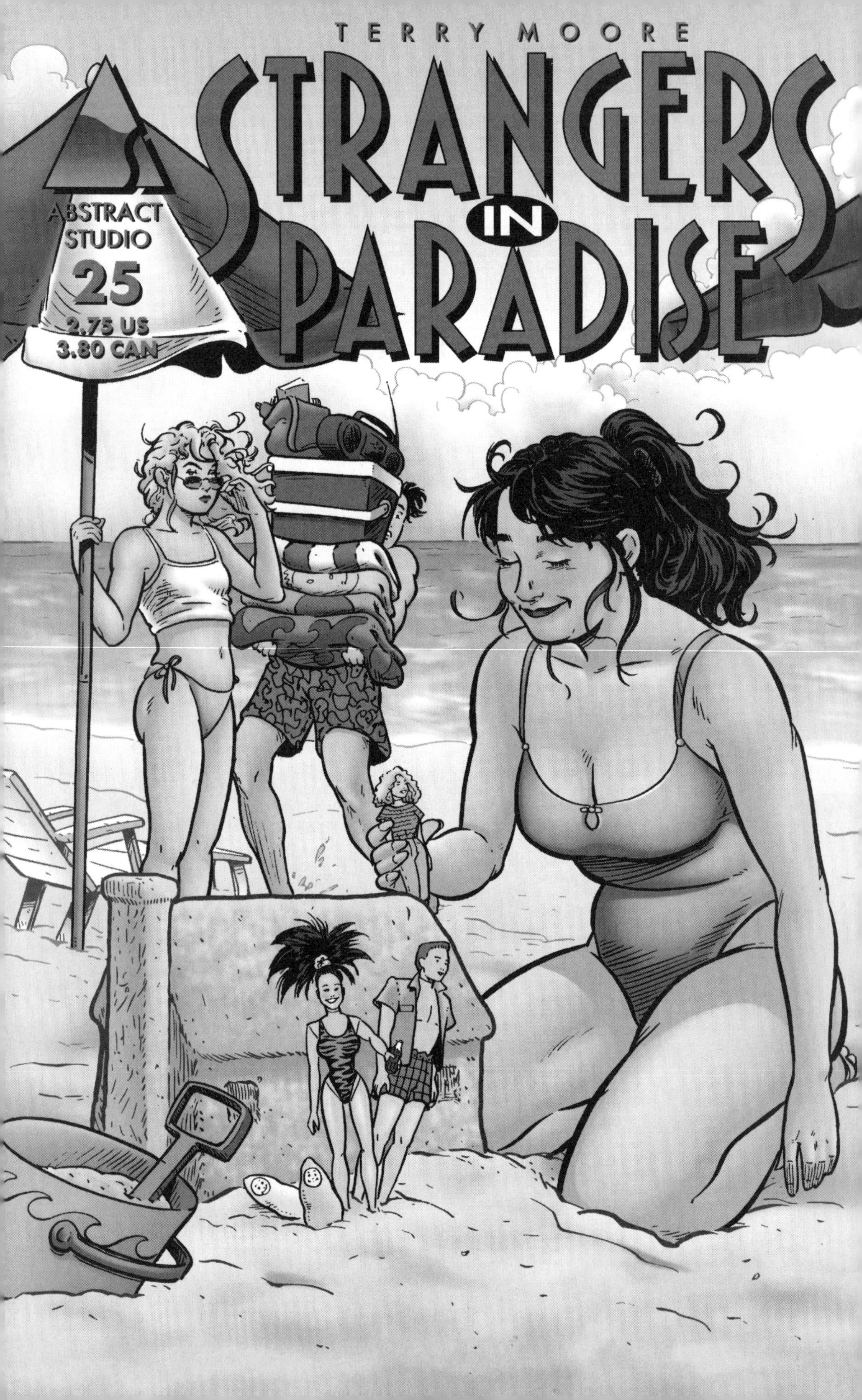
TERRY MOORE
STRANGERS IN PARADISE
ABSTRACT STUDIO
25
2.75 US
3.80 CAN

Three weeks ago David Qin buried his sister, Darcy Parker. Her sudden death brought an end to the infamous Parker Girl operation. This brings new hope for David and the love of his life, Katchoo, both of whom were on the verge of being destroyed by Darcy's wicked machine.

Now it's time to relax, recuperate and . . . *HIT THE BEACH!*

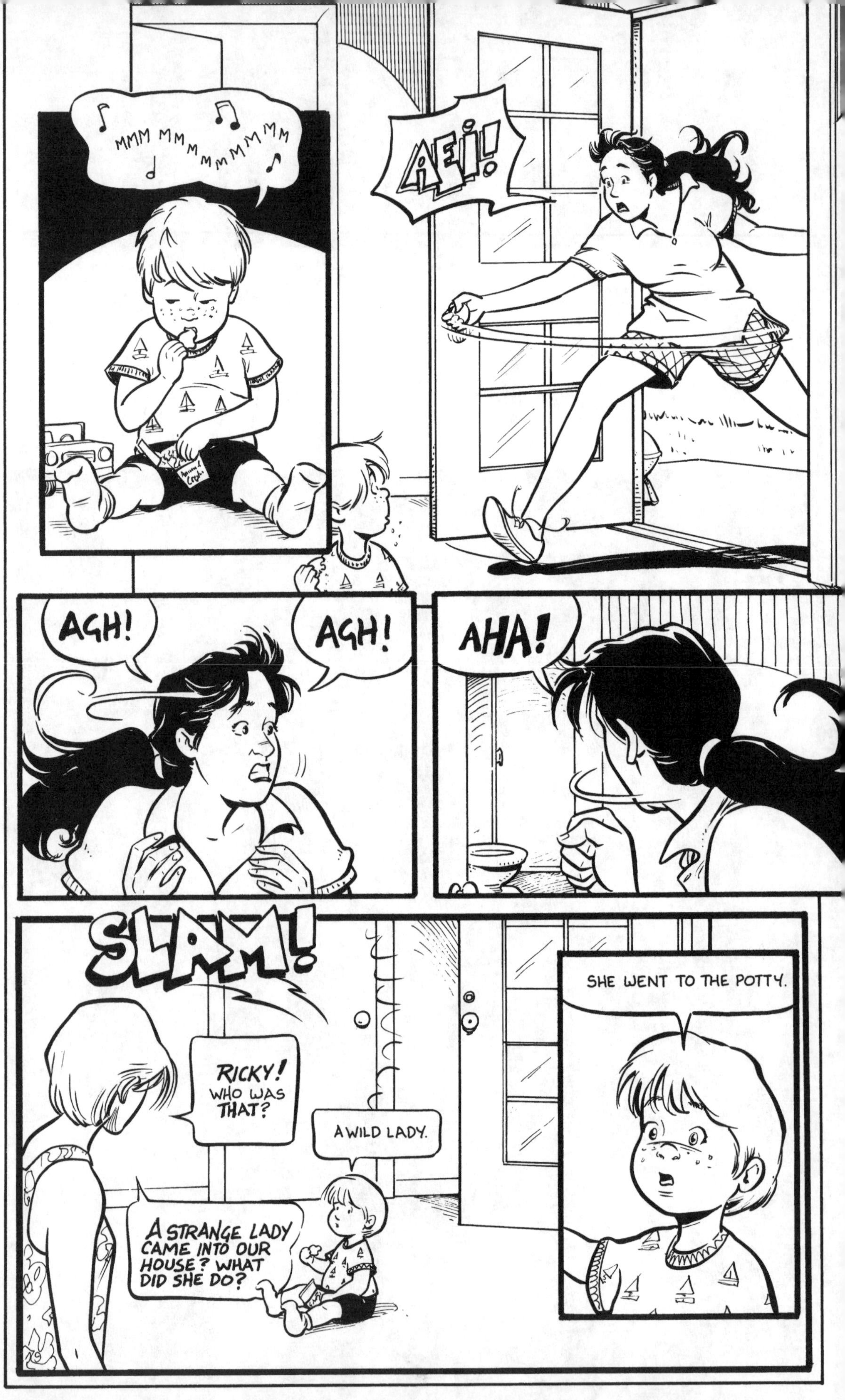

MMM MMMMMMMMMMMM
AEI!
AGH!
AGH!
AHA!
SLAM!
RICKY! WHO WAS THAT?
A WILD LADY.
A STRANGE LADY CAME INTO OUR HOUSE? WHAT DID SHE DO?
SHE WENT TO THE POTTY.

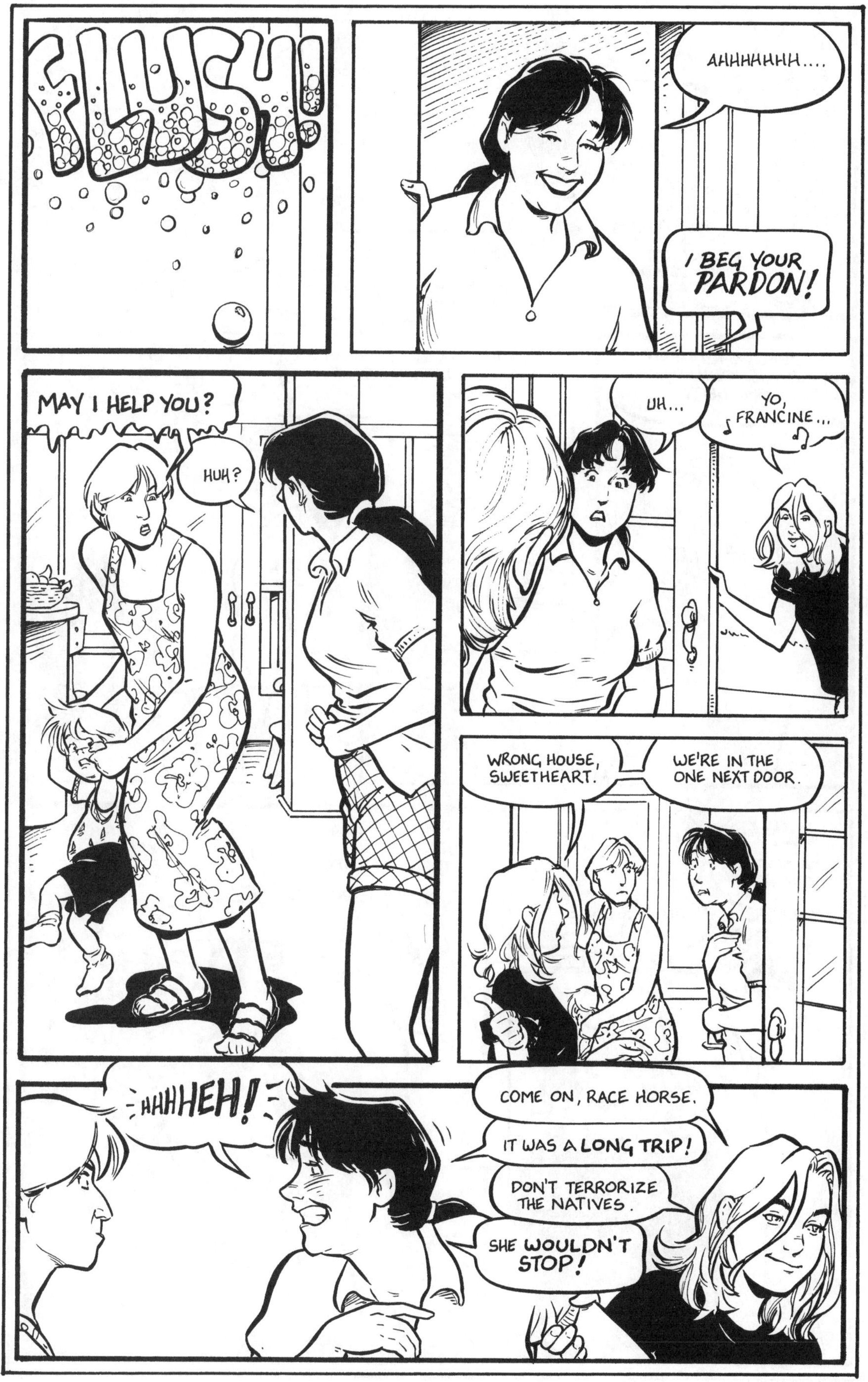
FLUSH!
AHHHHHHH....
I BEG YOUR PARDON!
MAY I HELP YOU?
HUH?
UH...
YO, FRANCINE...
WRONG HOUSE, SWEETHEART.
WE'RE IN THE ONE NEXT DOOR.
HHHHEH!
COME ON, RACE HORSE.
IT WAS A LONG TRIP!
DON'T TERRORIZE THE NATIVES.
SHE WOULDN'T STOP!

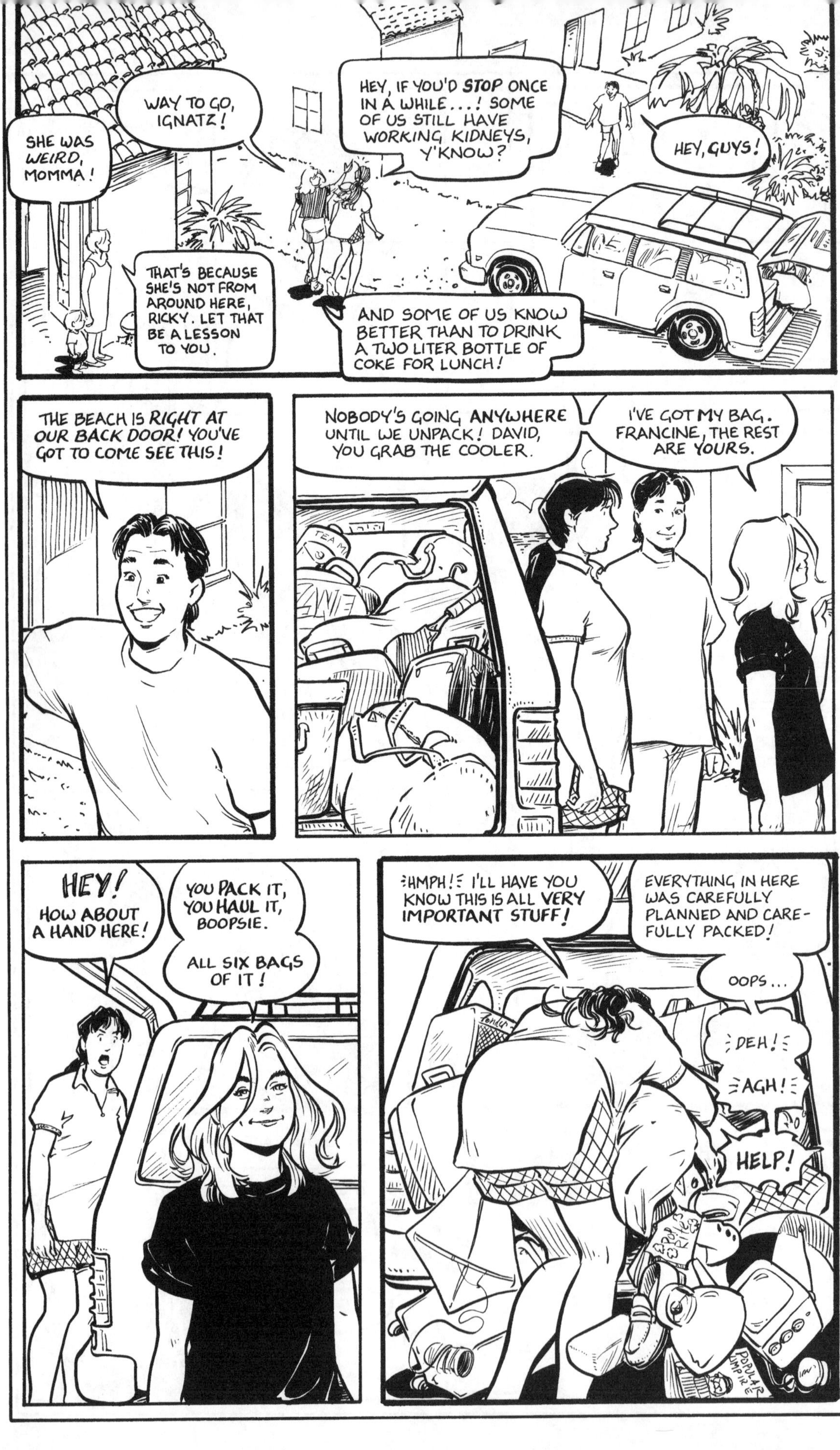
SHE WAS WEIRD, MOMMA!
WAY TO GO, IGNATZ!
HEY, IF YOU'D STOP ONCE IN A WHILE...! SOME OF US STILL HAVE WORKING KIDNEYS, Y'KNOW?
HEY, GUYS!
THAT'S BECAUSE SHE'S NOT FROM AROUND HERE, RICKY. LET THAT BE A LESSON TO YOU.
AND SOME OF US KNOW BETTER THAN TO DRINK A TWO LITER BOTTLE OF COKE FOR LUNCH!
THE BEACH IS RIGHT AT OUR BACK DOOR! YOU'VE GOT TO COME SEE THIS!
NOBODY'S GOING ANYWHERE UNTIL WE UNPACK! DAVID, YOU GRAB THE COOLER.
I'VE GOT MY BAG. FRANCINE, THE REST ARE YOURS.
HEY! HOW ABOUT A HAND HERE!
YOU PACK IT, YOU HAUL IT, BOOPSIE.
ALL SIX BAGS OF IT!
HMPH! I'LL HAVE YOU KNOW THIS IS ALL VERY IMPORTANT STUFF!
EVERYTHING IN HERE WAS CAREFULLY PLANNED AND CAREFULLY PACKED!
OOPS...
DEH!
AGH!
HELP!
POPULAR VAMPIRE

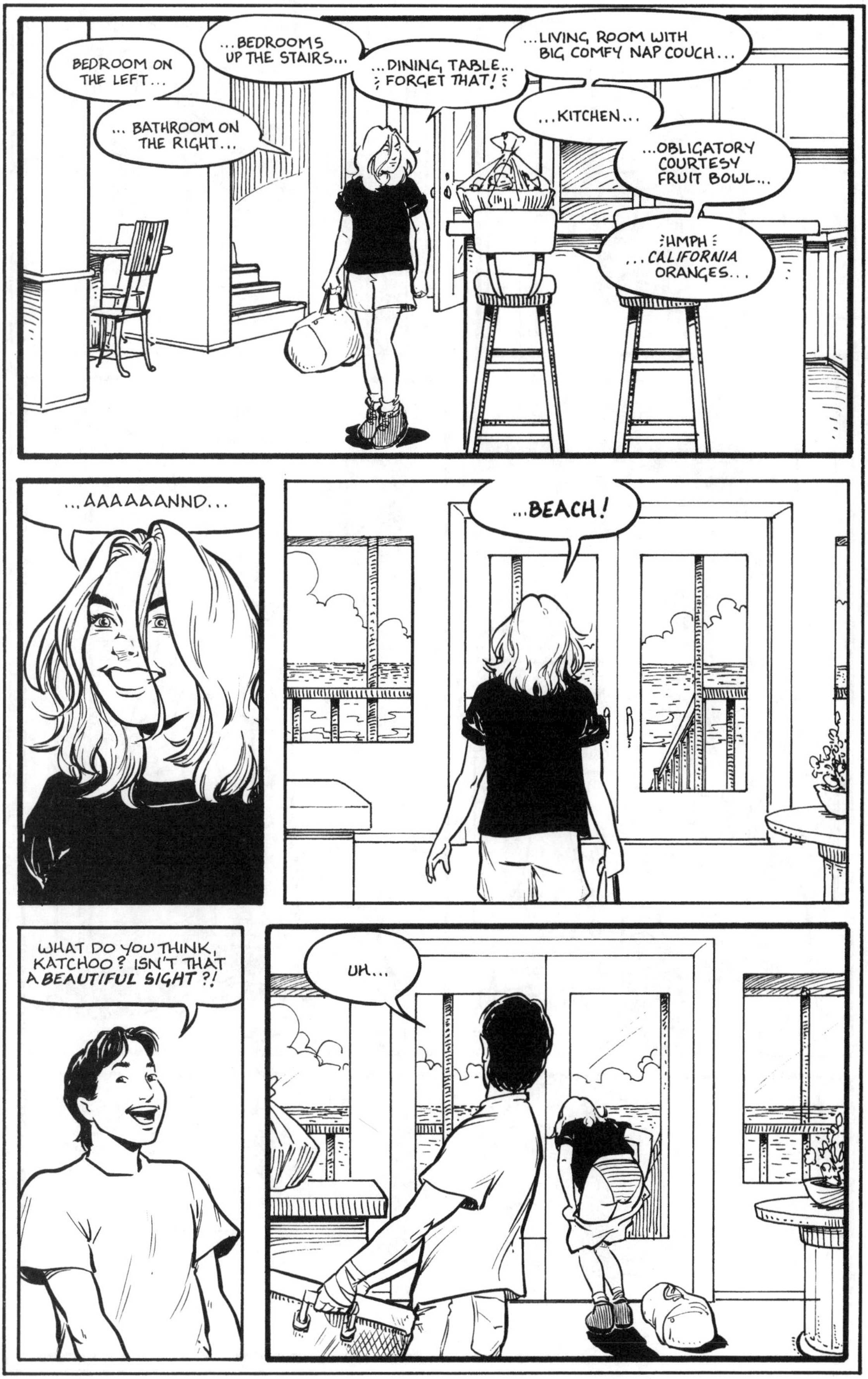
BEDROOM ON THE LEFT...
... BATHROOM ON THE RIGHT...
...BEDROOMS UP THE STAIRS...
...DINING TABLE... FORGET THAT!
...LIVING ROOM WITH BIG COMFY NAP COUCH...
...KITCHEN...
...OBLIGATORY COURTESY FRUIT BOWL...
HMPH ...CALIFORNIA ORANGES...
...AAAAAANND...
...BEACH!
WHAT DO YOU THINK, KATCHOO? ISN'T THAT A BEAUTIFUL SIGHT?!
UH...

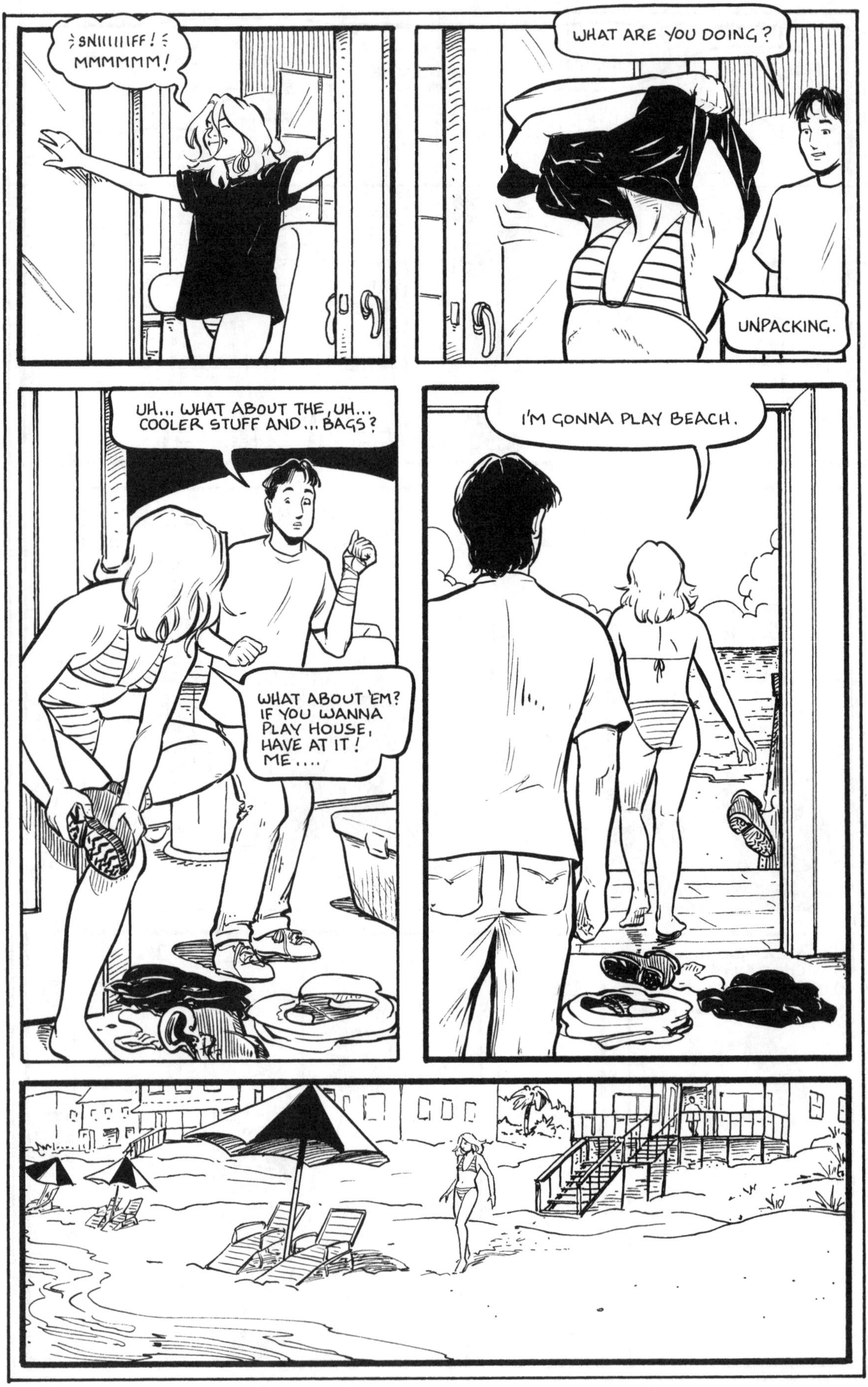
SNIIIIIIFF! MMMMMM!
WHAT ARE YOU DOING?
UNPACKING.
UH... WHAT ABOUT THE, UH... COOLER STUFF AND... BAGS?
WHAT ABOUT 'EM? IF YOU WANNA PLAY HOUSE, HAVE AT IT! ME....
I'M GONNA PLAY BEACH.

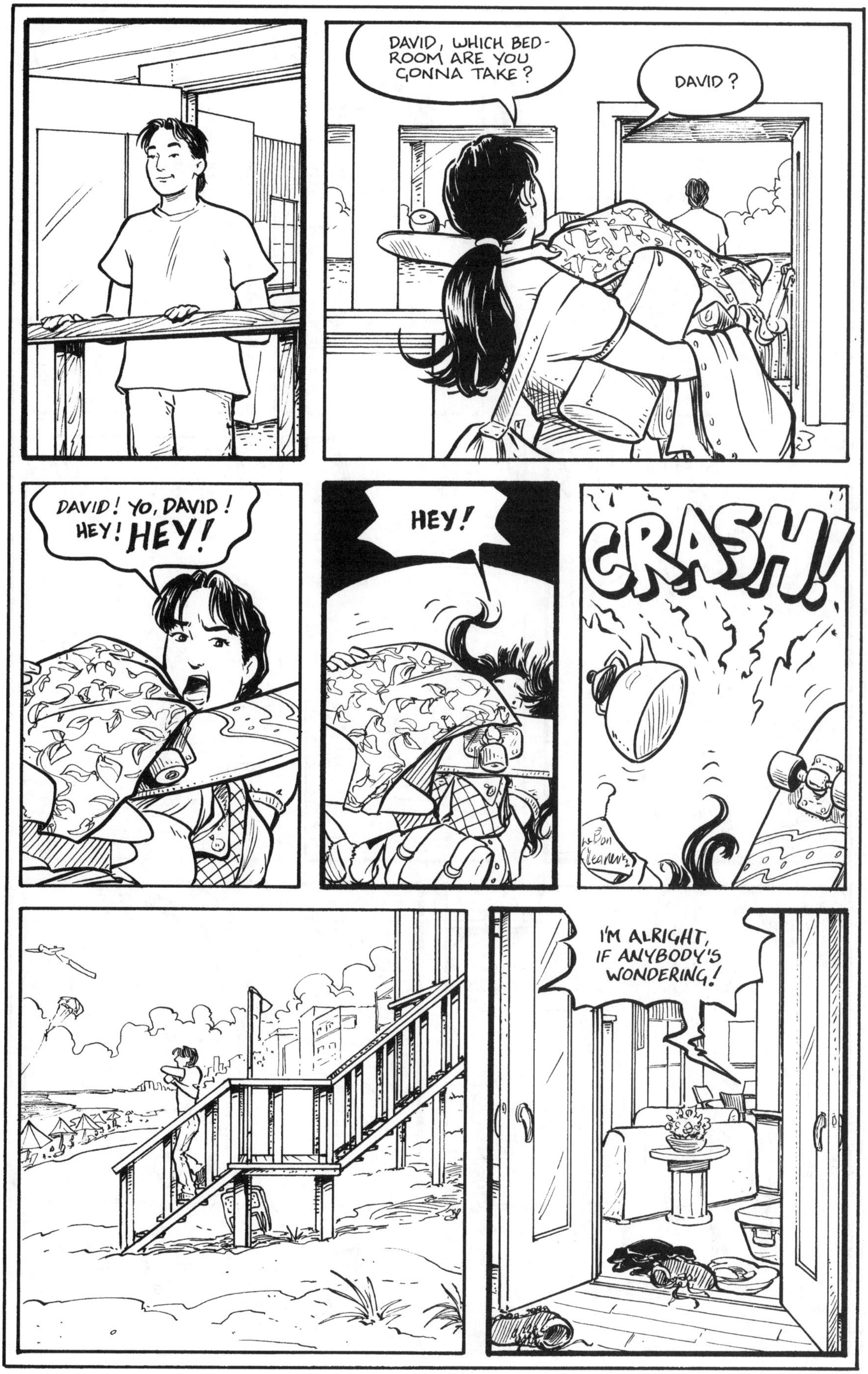
DAVID, WHICH BED-ROOM ARE YOU GONNA TAKE?
DAVID?
DAVID! YO, DAVID! HEY! HEY!
HEY!
CRASH!
I'M ALRIGHT, IF ANYBODY'S WONDERING!

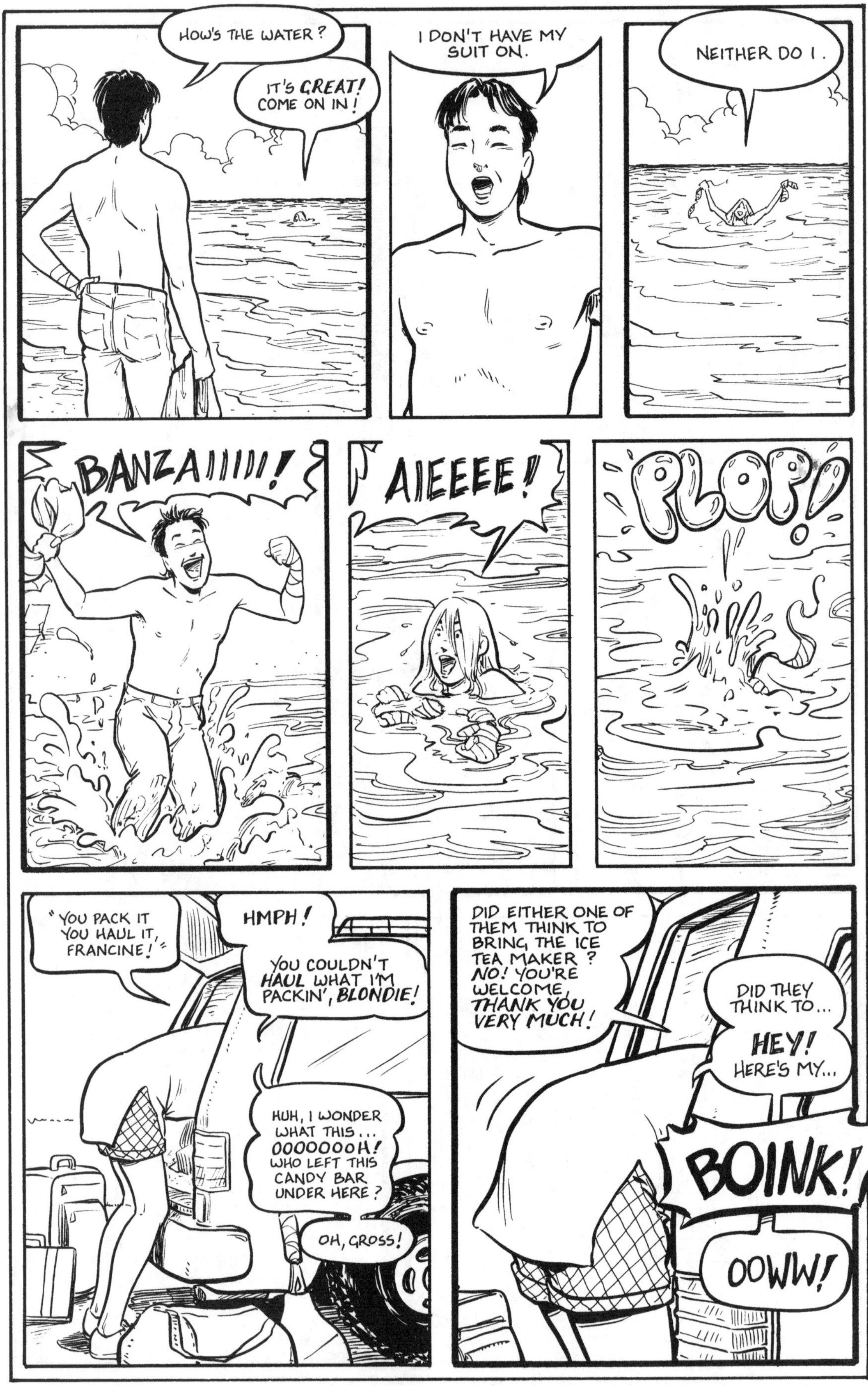
HOW'S THE WATER?
IT'S GREAT! COME ON IN!
I DON'T HAVE MY SUIT ON.
NEITHER DO I.
BANZAIIIIII!
AIEEEE!
PLOP!
"YOU PACK IT YOU HAUL IT, FRANCINE!"
HMPH!
YOU COULDN'T HAUL WHAT I'M PACKIN', BLONDIE!
HUH, I WONDER WHAT THIS... OOOOOOOH! WHO LEFT THIS CANDY BAR UNDER HERE?
OH, GROSS!
DID EITHER ONE OF THEM THINK TO BRING THE ICE TEA MAKER? NO! YOU'RE WELCOME, THANK YOU VERY MUCH!
DID THEY THINK TO...
HEY! HERE'S MY...
BOINK!
OOWW!

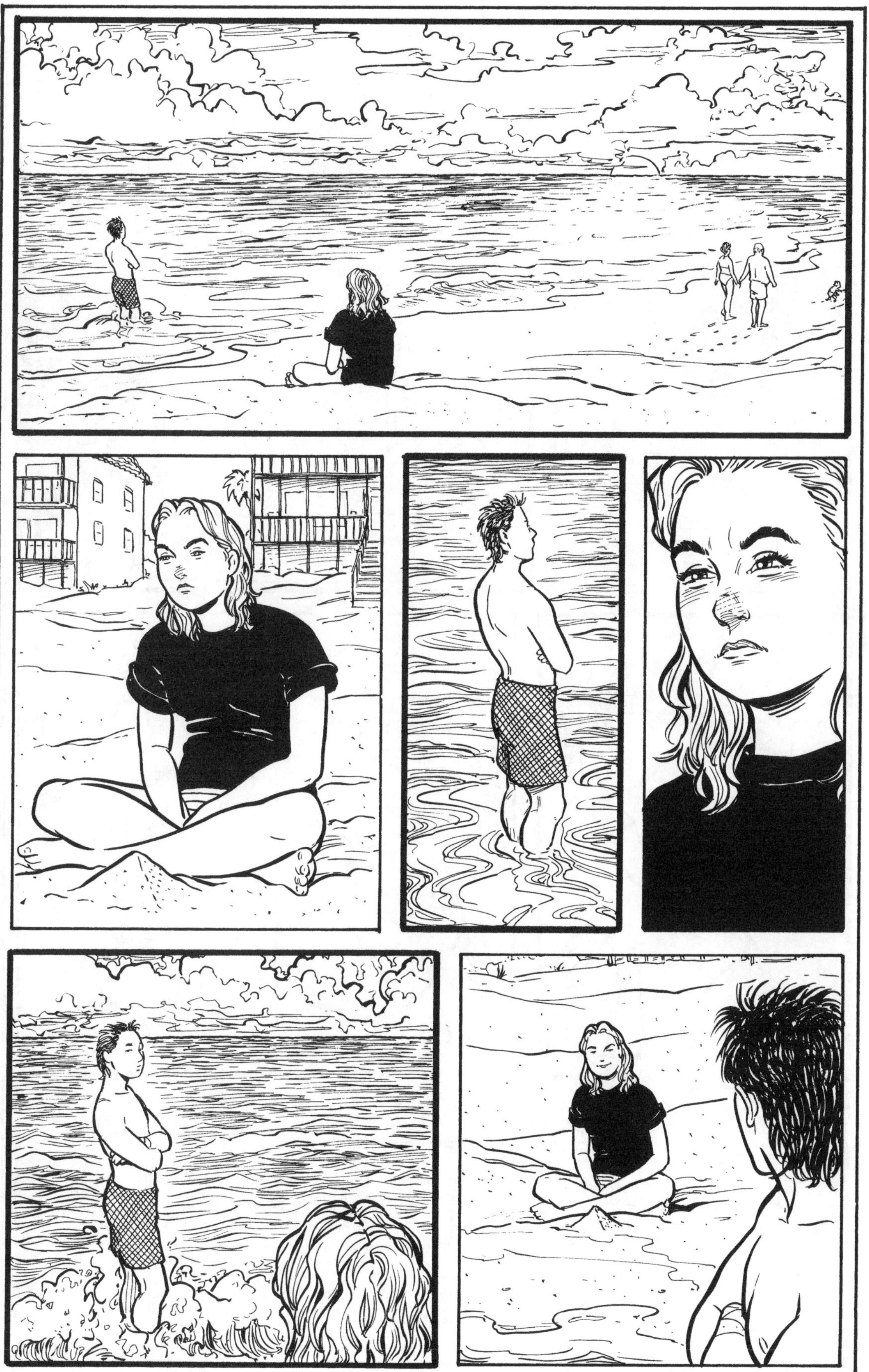

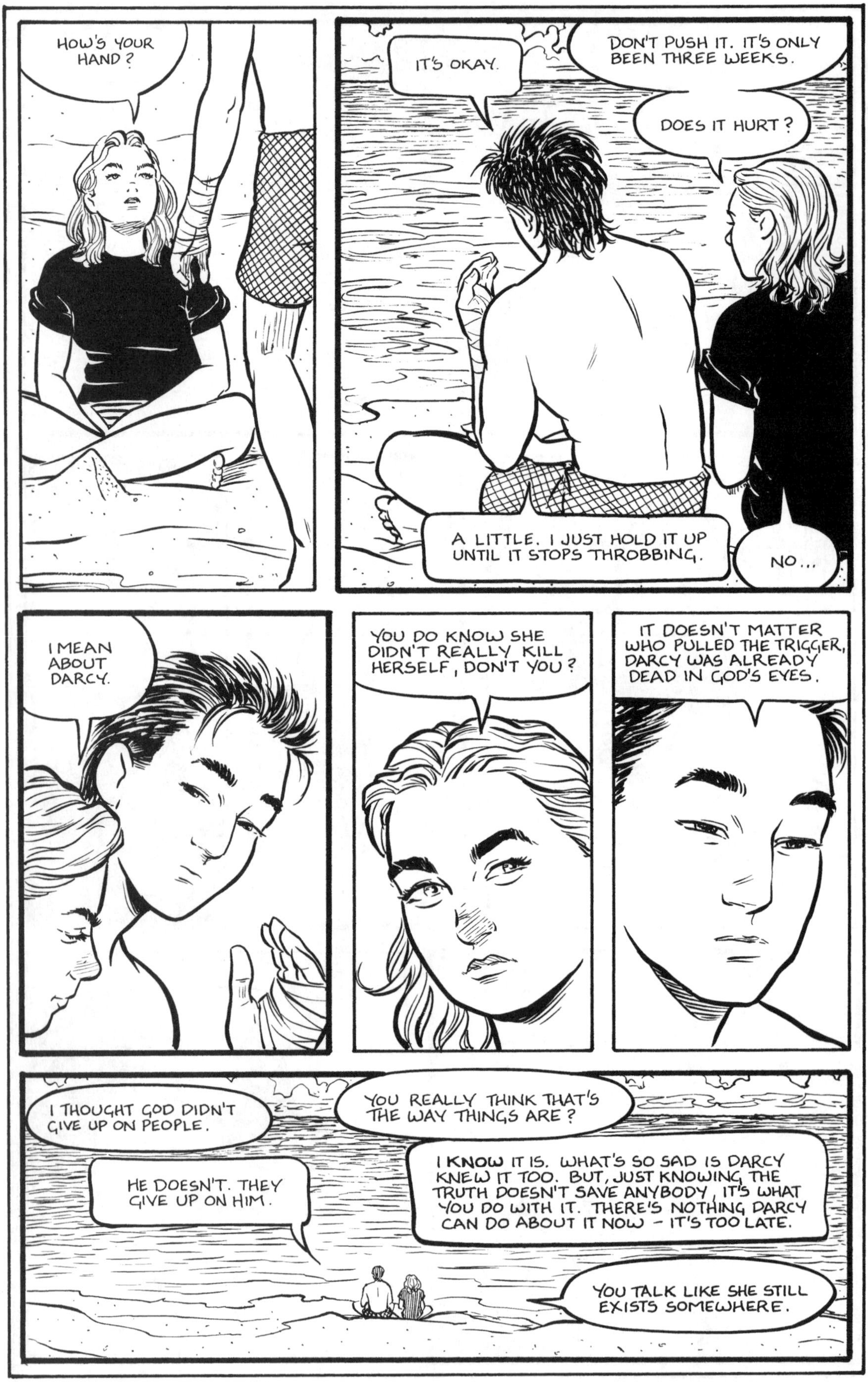
HOW'S YOUR HAND?
IT'S OKAY.
DON'T PUSH IT. IT'S ONLY BEEN THREE WEEKS.
DOES IT HURT?
A LITTLE. I JUST HOLD IT UP UNTIL IT STOPS THROBBING.
NO...
I MEAN ABOUT DARCY.
YOU DO KNOW SHE DIDN'T REALLY KILL HERSELF, DON'T YOU?
IT DOESN'T MATTER WHO PULLED THE TRIGGER, DARCY WAS ALREADY DEAD IN GOD'S EYES.
I THOUGHT GOD DIDN'T GIVE UP ON PEOPLE.
YOU REALLY THINK THAT'S THE WAY THINGS ARE?
HE DOESN'T. THEY GIVE UP ON HIM.
I KNOW IT IS. WHAT'S SO SAD IS DARCY KNEW IT TOO. BUT, JUST KNOWING THE TRUTH DOESN'T SAVE ANYBODY, IT'S WHAT YOU DO WITH IT. THERE'S NOTHING DARCY CAN DO ABOUT IT NOW - IT'S TOO LATE.
YOU TALK LIKE SHE STILL EXISTS SOMEWHERE.

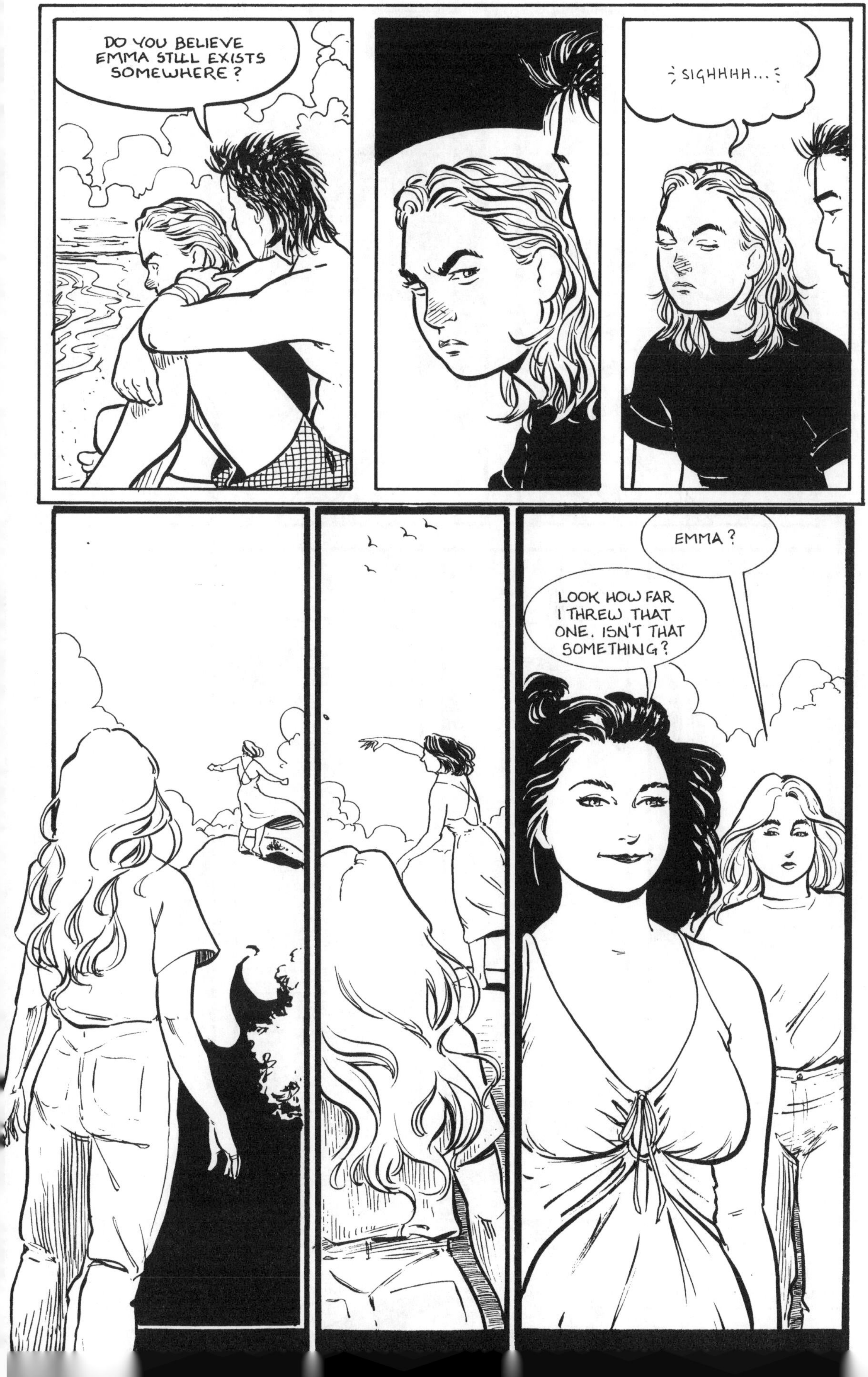
DO YOU BELIEVE EMMA STILL EXISTS SOMEWHERE?
SIGHHHH...
EMMA?
LOOK HOW FAR I THREW THAT ONE. ISN'T THAT SOMETHING?

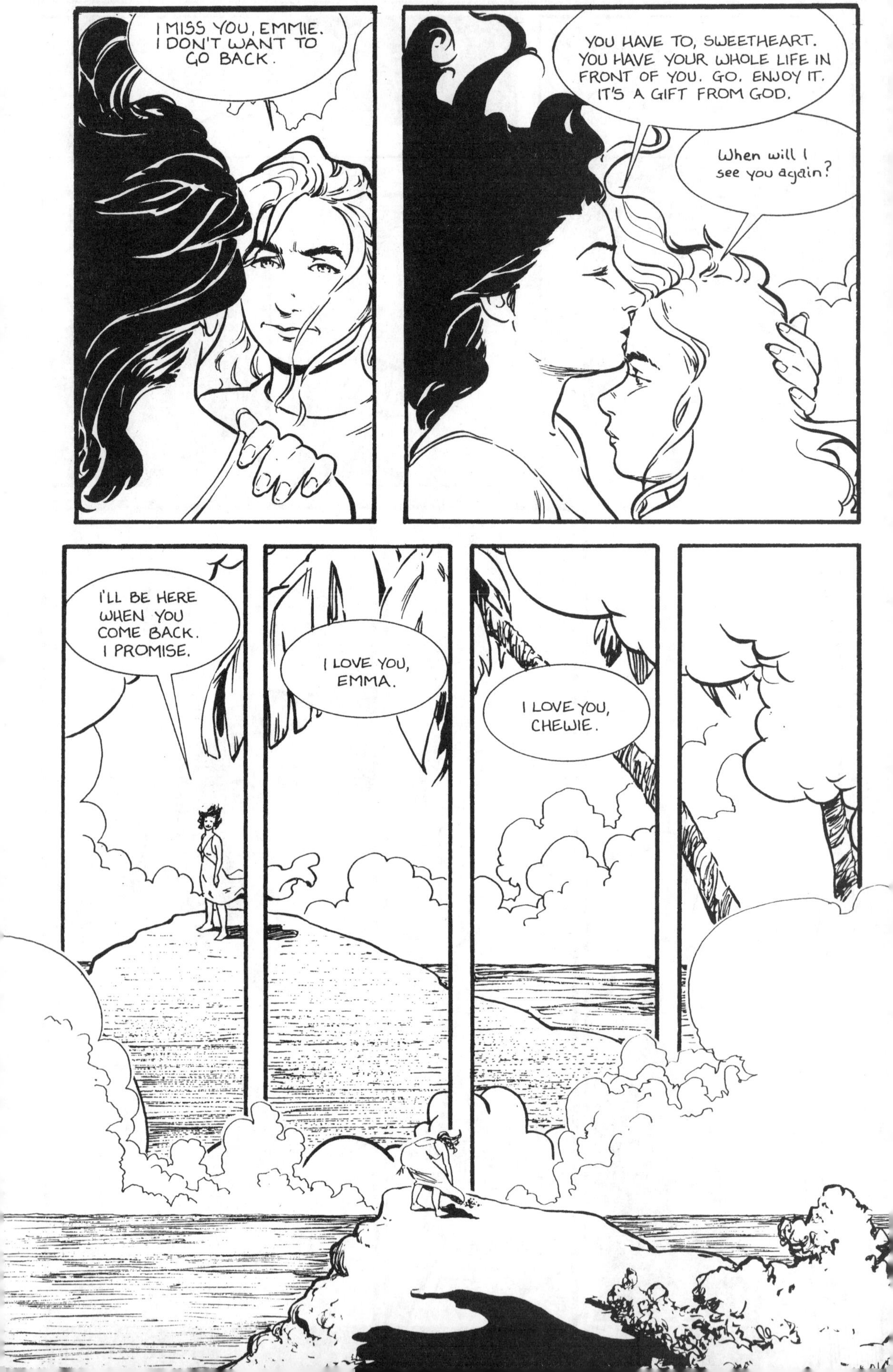
I MISS YOU, EMMIE. I DON'T WANT TO GO BACK.
YOU HAVE TO, SWEETHEART. YOU HAVE YOUR WHOLE LIFE IN FRONT OF YOU. GO. ENJOY IT. IT'S A GIFT FROM GOD.
When will I see you again?
I'LL BE HERE WHEN YOU COME BACK. I PROMISE.
I LOVE YOU, EMMA.
I LOVE YOU, CHEWIE.

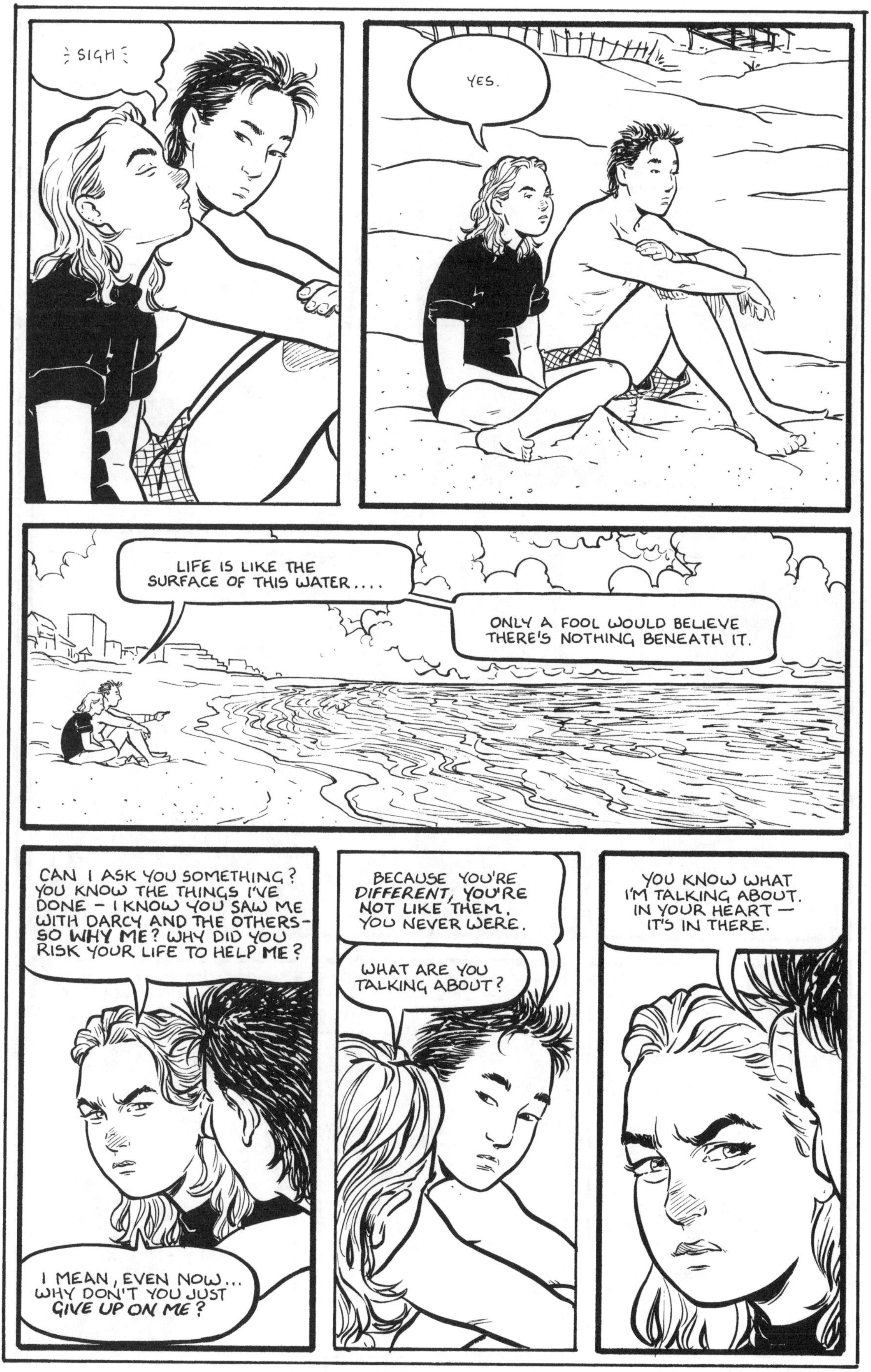
SIGH
YES.
LIFE IS LIKE THE SURFACE OF THIS WATER....
ONLY A FOOL WOULD BELIEVE THERE'S NOTHING BENEATH IT.
CAN I ASK YOU SOMETHING? YOU KNOW THE THINGS I'VE DONE – I KNOW YOU SAW ME WITH DARCY AND THE OTHERS– SO WHY ME? WHY DID YOU RISK YOUR LIFE TO HELP ME?
I MEAN, EVEN NOW... WHY DON'T YOU JUST GIVE UP ON ME?
BECAUSE YOU'RE DIFFERENT, YOU'RE NOT LIKE THEM. YOU NEVER WERE.
WHAT ARE YOU TALKING ABOUT?
YOU KNOW WHAT I'M TALKING ABOUT. IN YOUR HEART – IT'S IN THERE.

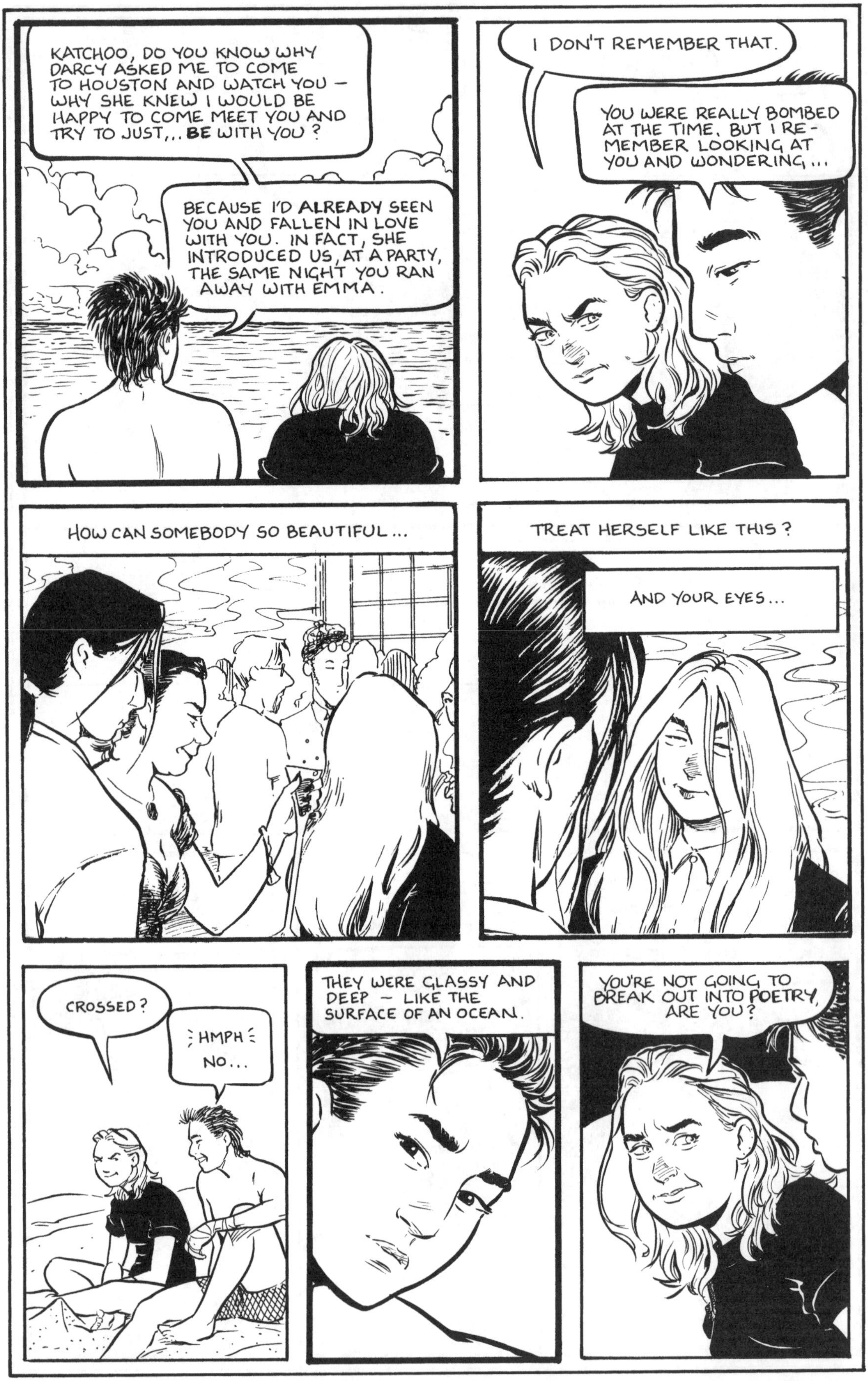
KATCHOO, DO YOU KNOW WHY DARCY ASKED ME TO COME TO HOUSTON AND WATCH YOU – WHY SHE KNEW I WOULD BE HAPPY TO COME MEET YOU AND TRY TO JUST,.. BE WITH YOU?
BECAUSE I'D ALREADY SEEN YOU AND FALLEN IN LOVE WITH YOU. IN FACT, SHE INTRODUCED US, AT A PARTY, THE SAME NIGHT YOU RAN AWAY WITH EMMA.
I DON'T REMEMBER THAT.
YOU WERE REALLY BOMBED AT THE TIME, BUT I REMEMBER LOOKING AT YOU AND WONDERING...
HOW CAN SOMEBODY SO BEAUTIFUL...
TREAT HERSELF LIKE THIS?
AND YOUR EYES...
CROSSED?
HMPH NO...
THEY WERE GLASSY AND DEEP – LIKE THE SURFACE OF AN OCEAN.
YOU'RE NOT GOING TO BREAK OUT INTO POETRY, ARE YOU?

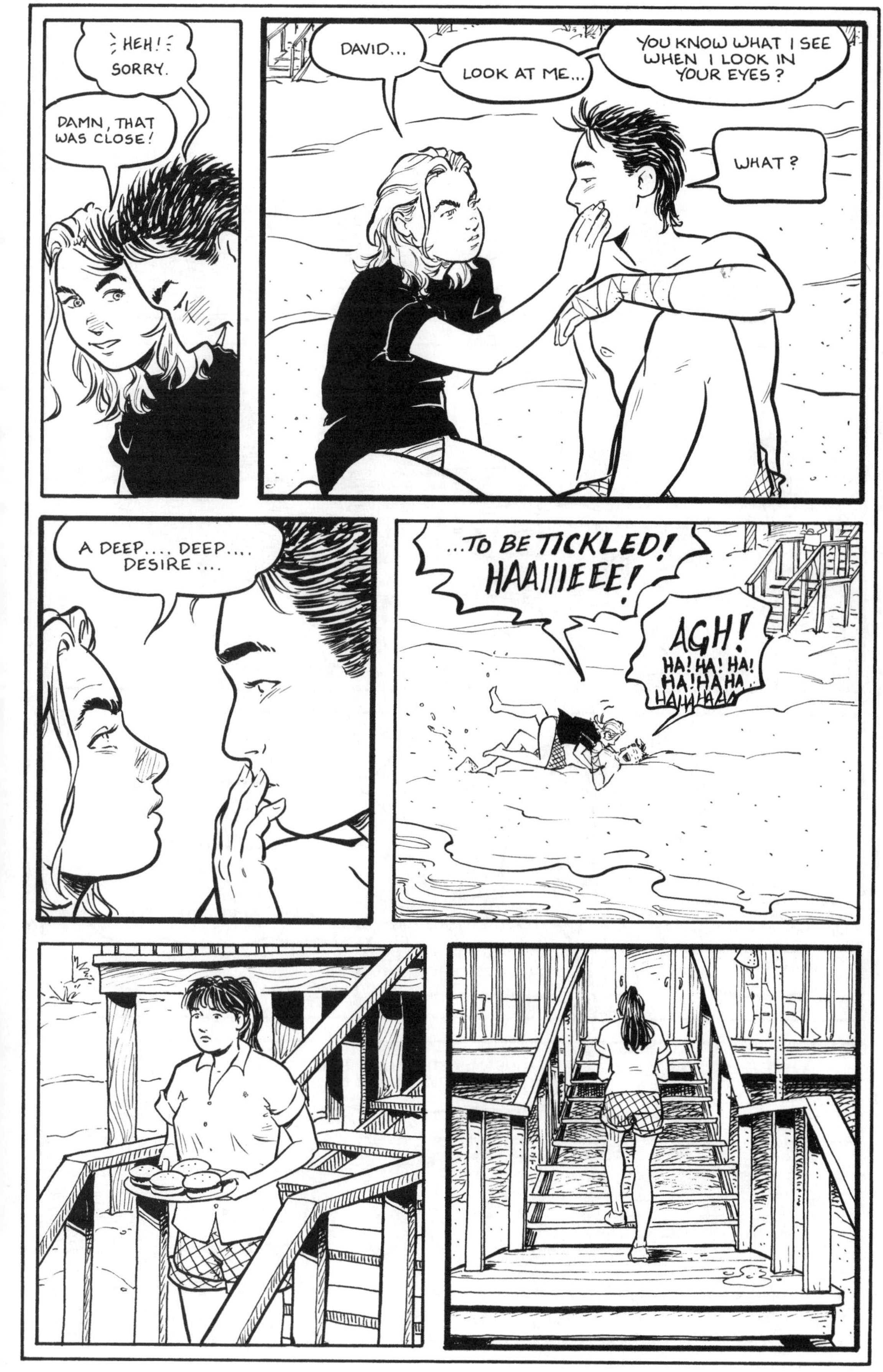
HEH! SORRY.
DAMN, THAT WAS CLOSE!
DAVID...
LOOK AT ME...
YOU KNOW WHAT I SEE WHEN I LOOK IN YOUR EYES?
WHAT?
A DEEP.... DEEP.... DESIRE....
...TO BE TICKLED! HAAIIIEEE!
AGH! HA! HA! HA! HA! HA HA HAHAHAHA

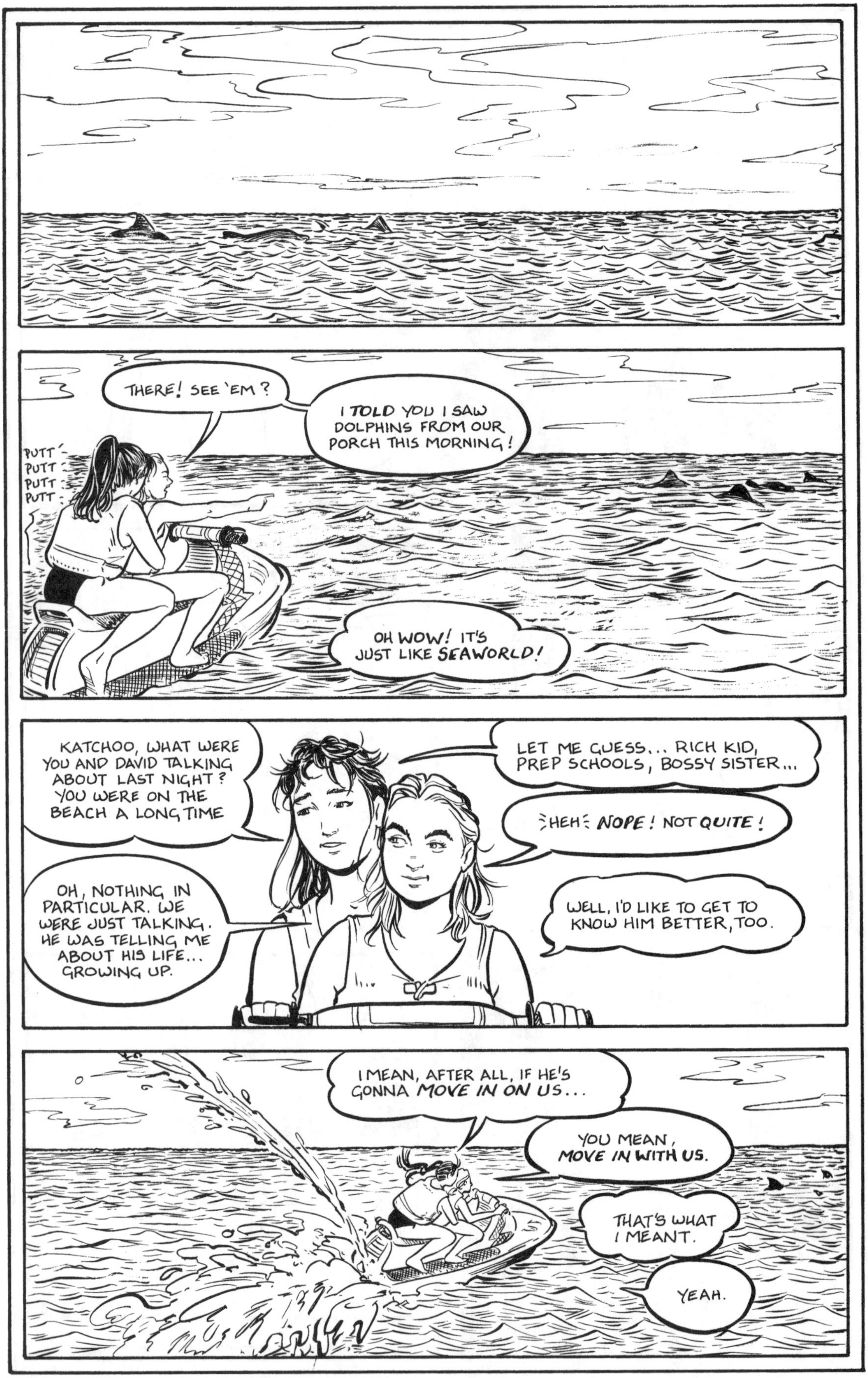

THERE! SEE 'EM?
I TOLD YOU I SAW DOLPHINS FROM OUR PORCH THIS MORNING!
PUTT PUTT PUTT PUTT
OH WOW! IT'S JUST LIKE SEAWORLD!
KATCHOO, WHAT WERE YOU AND DAVID TALKING ABOUT LAST NIGHT? YOU WERE ON THE BEACH A LONG TIME
LET ME GUESS... RICH KID, PREP SCHOOLS, BOSSY SISTER...
HEH NOPE! NOT QUITE!
OH, NOTHING IN PARTICULAR. WE WERE JUST TALKING. HE WAS TELLING ME ABOUT HIS LIFE... GROWING UP.
WELL, I'D LIKE TO GET TO KNOW HIM BETTER, TOO.
I MEAN, AFTER ALL, IF HE'S GONNA MOVE IN ON US...
YOU MEAN, MOVE IN WITH US.
THAT'S WHAT I MEANT.
YEAH.

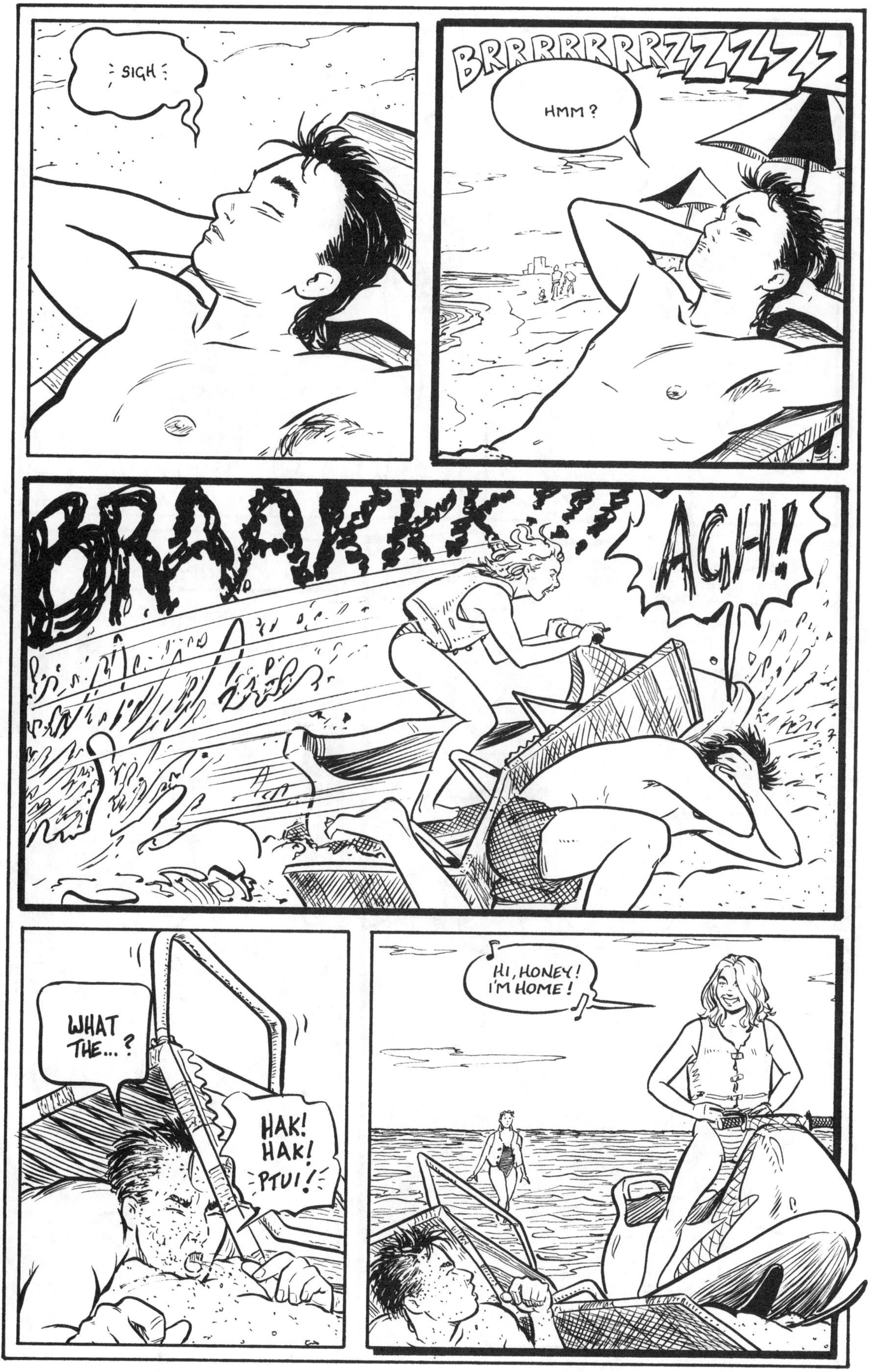
SIGH
BRRRRRRRRZZZZZZ
HMM?
BRAKKK!!!
AGH!
WHAT THE...?
HAK! HAK! PTUI!
HI, HONEY! I'M HOME!

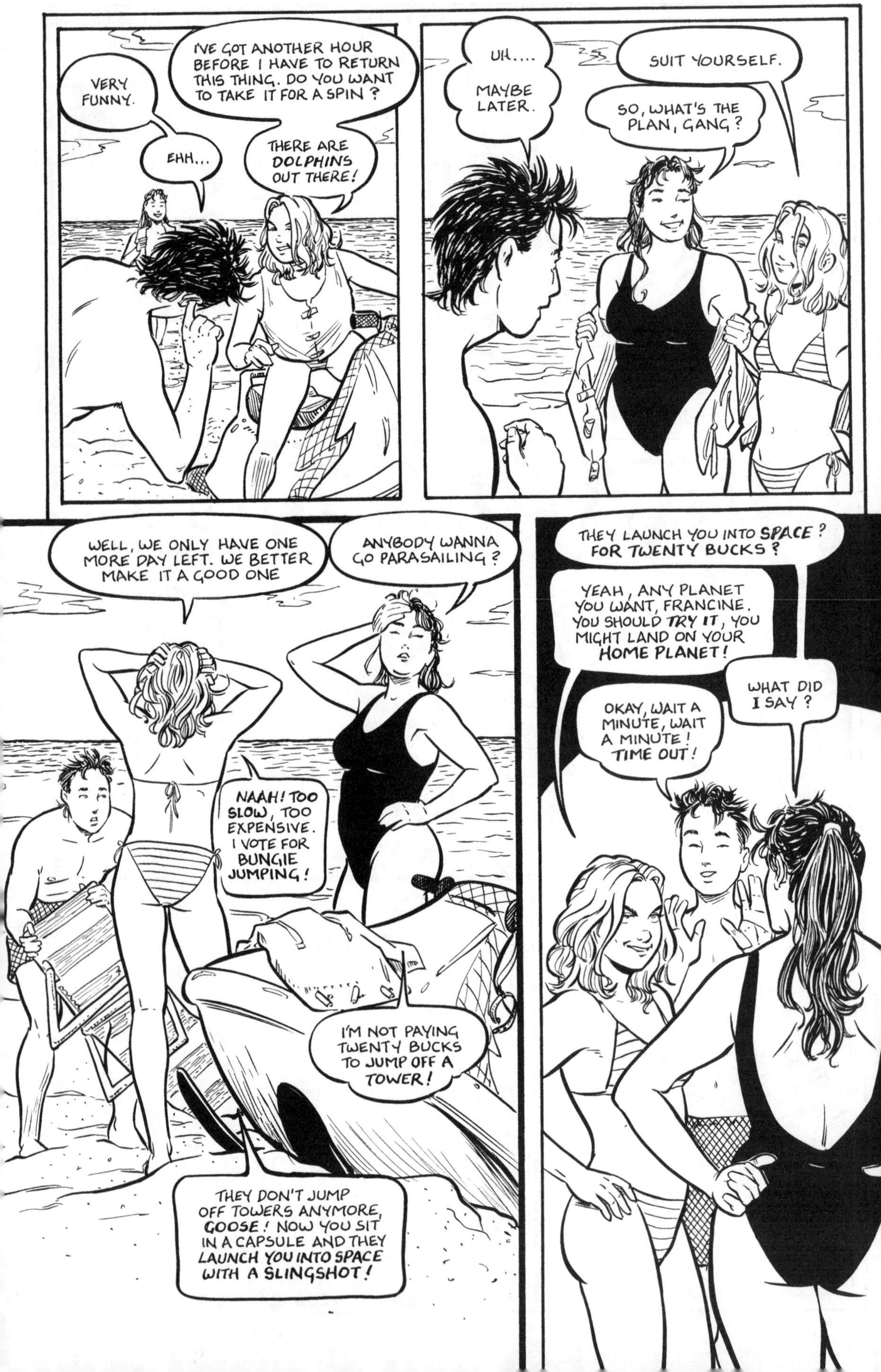
I'VE GOT ANOTHER HOUR BEFORE I HAVE TO RETURN THIS THING. DO YOU WANT TO TAKE IT FOR A SPIN ?
VERY FUNNY.
EHH...
THERE ARE DOLPHINS OUT THERE!
UH....
MAYBE LATER.
SUIT YOURSELF.
SO, WHAT'S THE PLAN, GANG ?
WELL, WE ONLY HAVE ONE MORE DAY LEFT. WE BETTER MAKE IT A GOOD ONE
ANYBODY WANNA GO PARASAILING ?
NAAH! TOO SLOW, TOO EXPENSIVE. I VOTE FOR BUNGIE JUMPING!
I'M NOT PAYING TWENTY BUCKS TO JUMP OFF A TOWER!
THEY DON'T JUMP OFF TOWERS ANYMORE, GOOSE! NOW YOU SIT IN A CAPSULE AND THEY LAUNCH YOU INTO SPACE WITH A SLINGSHOT!
THEY LAUNCH YOU INTO SPACE? FOR TWENTY BUCKS?
YEAH, ANY PLANET YOU WANT, FRANCINE. YOU SHOULD TRY IT, YOU MIGHT LAND ON YOUR HOME PLANET!
WHAT DID I SAY?
OKAY, WAIT A MINUTE, WAIT A MINUTE! TIME OUT!

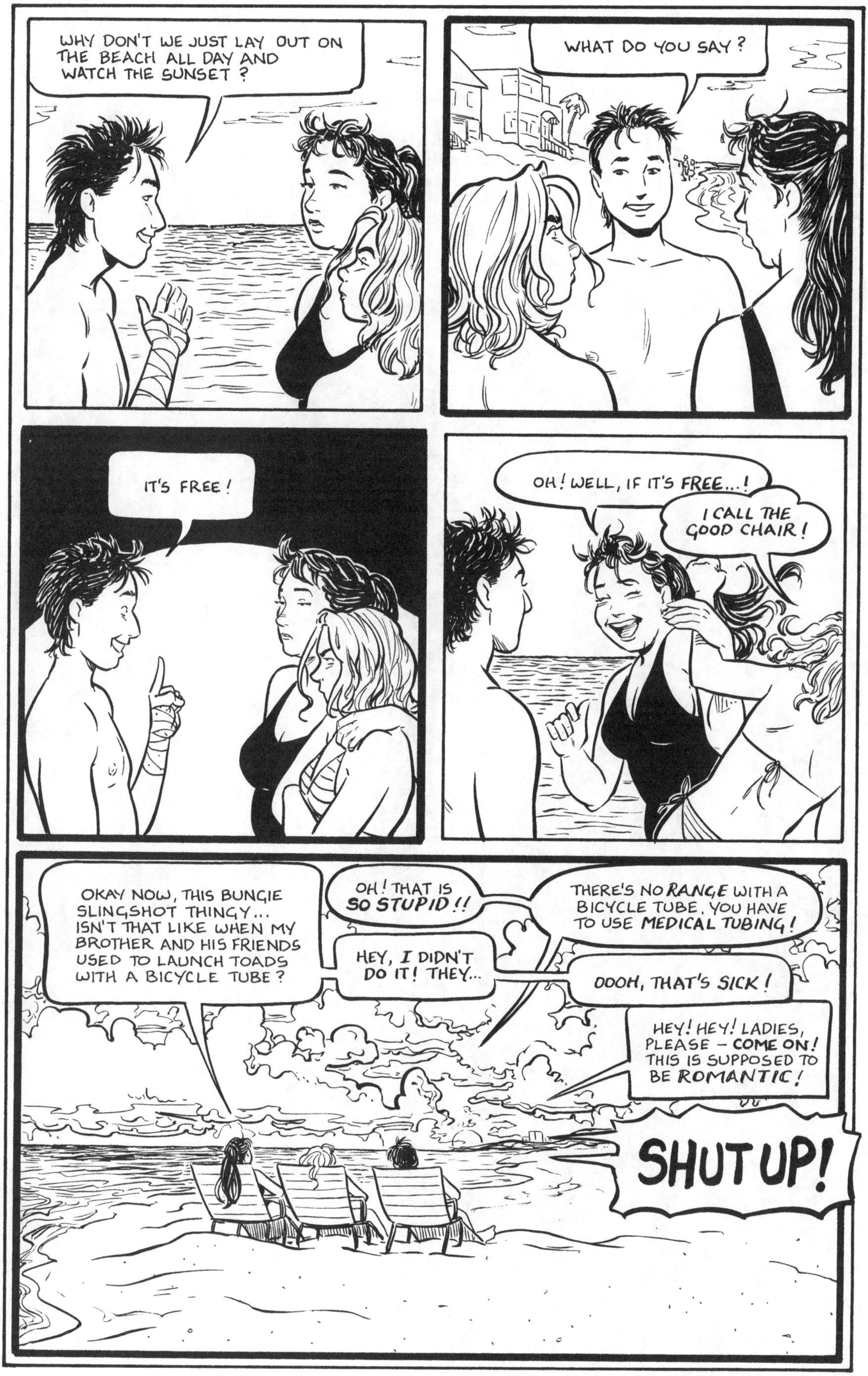
WHY DON'T WE JUST LAY OUT ON THE BEACH ALL DAY AND WATCH THE SUNSET ?
WHAT DO YOU SAY ?
IT'S FREE !
OH! WELL, IF IT'S FREE...!
I CALL THE GOOD CHAIR!
OKAY NOW, THIS BUNGIE SLINGSHOT THINGY... ISN'T THAT LIKE WHEN MY BROTHER AND HIS FRIENDS USED TO LAUNCH TOADS WITH A BICYCLE TUBE ?
OH! THAT IS SO STUPID!!
THERE'S NO RANGE WITH A BICYCLE TUBE, YOU HAVE TO USE MEDICAL TUBING!
HEY, I DIDN'T DO IT! THEY...
OOOH, THAT'S SICK!
HEY! HEY! LADIES, PLEASE - COME ON! THIS IS SUPPOSED TO BE ROMANTIC!
SHUT UP!

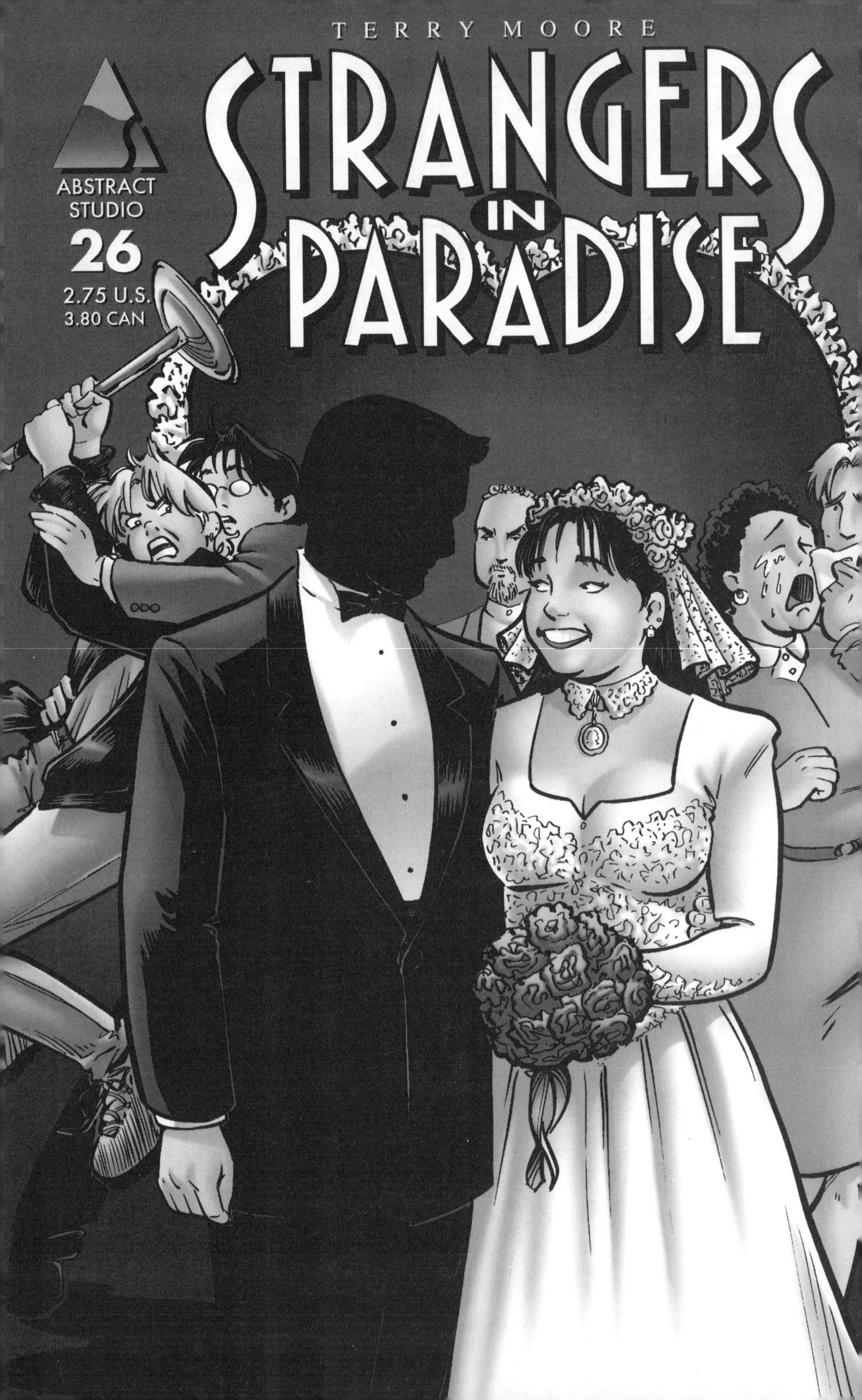

TERRY MOORE
STRANGERS IN PARADISE
ABSTRACT STUDIO
26
2.75 U.S.
3.80 CAN

I am waiting for you to see
What you do to me and to stop it
　　Running late

I am waiting for you to love me
Please come and touch me
　I'll thank you
　　Running late

Desperate running to
Catch you briefly to
Let you see me
When I can be wrong

Count the pennies you give to me
Days I dare to say what I'm thinking
　　Running late

I hold wonders in dreams and slumbers
I work to want to release them
　　Running late

Blazed and blasting they swear it's lasting to
Hear the footsteps behind me
　　Running late

Desperate running to
Catch my dream globe I
See my heart in
The middle on fire

　　Running late

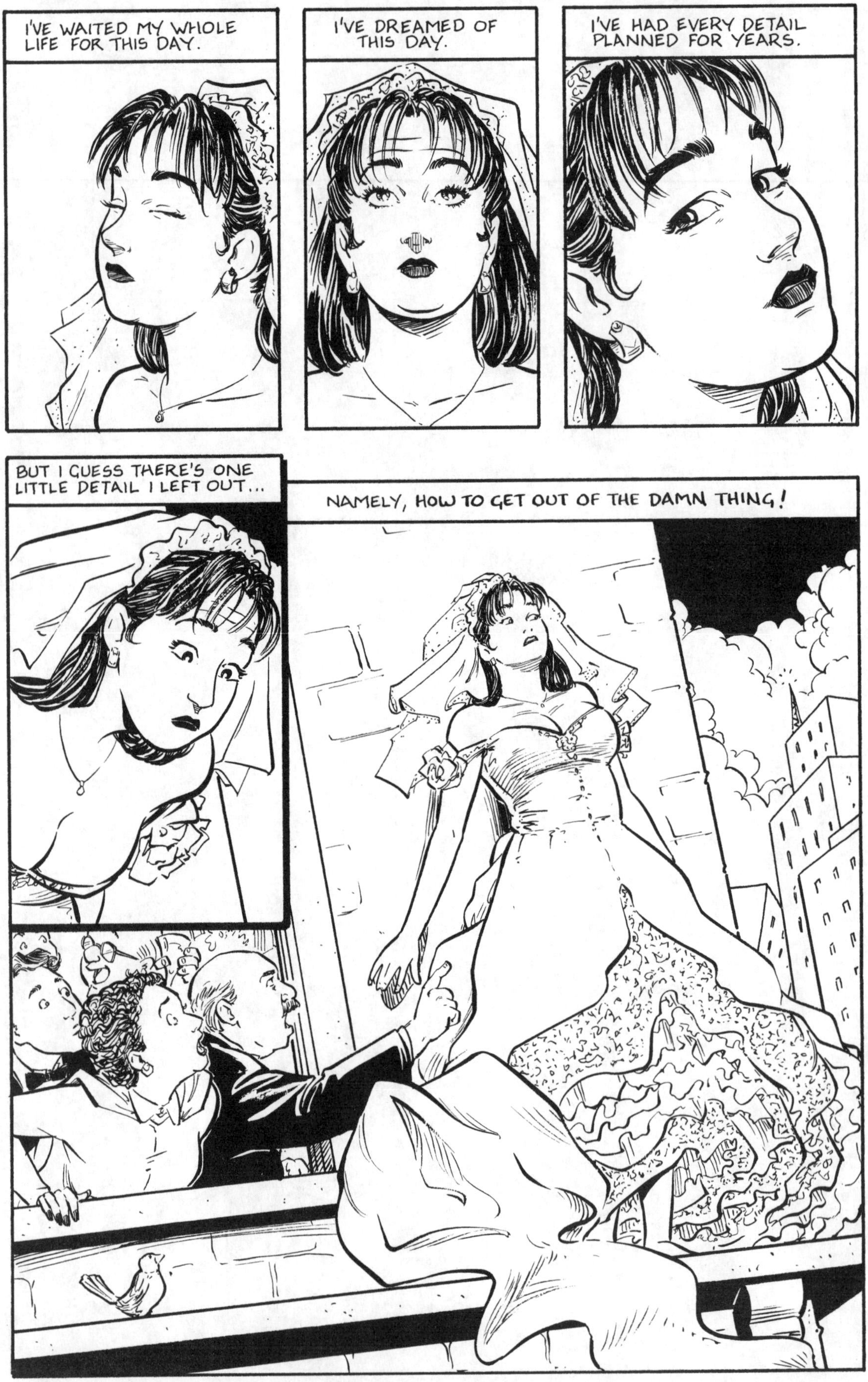
I'VE WAITED MY WHOLE LIFE FOR THIS DAY.
I'VE DREAMED OF THIS DAY.
I'VE HAD EVERY DETAIL PLANNED FOR YEARS.
BUT I GUESS THERE'S ONE LITTLE DETAIL I LEFT OUT...
NAMELY, HOW TO GET OUT OF THE DAMN THING!

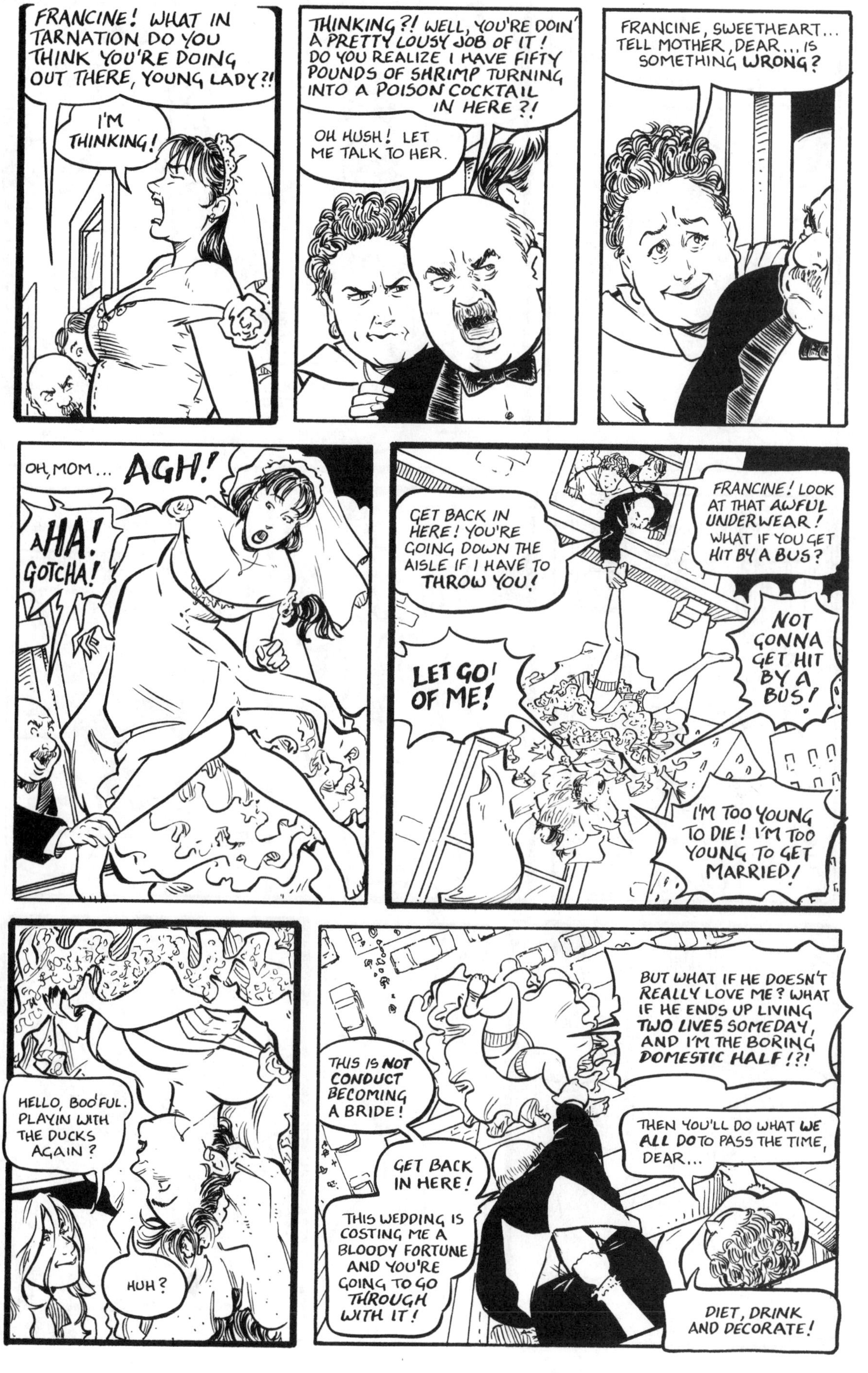
FRANCINE! WHAT IN TARNATION DO YOU THINK YOU'RE DOING OUT THERE, YOUNG LADY?!
I'M THINKING!
THINKING?! WELL, YOU'RE DOIN' A PRETTY LOUSY JOB OF IT! DO YOU REALIZE I HAVE FIFTY POUNDS OF SHRIMP TURNING INTO A POISON COCKTAIL IN HERE?!
OH HUSH! LET ME TALK TO HER.
FRANCINE, SWEETHEART... TELL MOTHER, DEAR... IS SOMETHING WRONG?
OH, MOM... AGH!
AHA! GOTCHA!
GET BACK IN HERE! YOU'RE GOING DOWN THE AISLE IF I HAVE TO THROW YOU!
FRANCINE! LOOK AT THAT AWFUL UNDERWEAR! WHAT IF YOU GET HIT BY A BUS?
LET GO OF ME!
NOT GONNA GET HIT BY A BUS!
I'M TOO YOUNG TO DIE! I'M TOO YOUNG TO GET MARRIED!
HELLO, BOO'FUL. PLAYIN WITH THE DUCKS AGAIN?
HUH?
THIS IS NOT CONDUCT BECOMING A BRIDE!
BUT WHAT IF HE DOESN'T REALLY LOVE ME? WHAT IF HE ENDS UP LIVING TWO LIVES SOMEDAY, AND I'M THE BORING DOMESTIC HALF!?!
GET BACK IN HERE!
THIS WEDDING IS COSTING ME A BLOODY FORTUNE AND YOU'RE GOING TO GO THROUGH WITH IT!
THEN YOU'LL DO WHAT WE ALL DO TO PASS THE TIME, DEAR...
DIET, DRINK AND DECORATE!

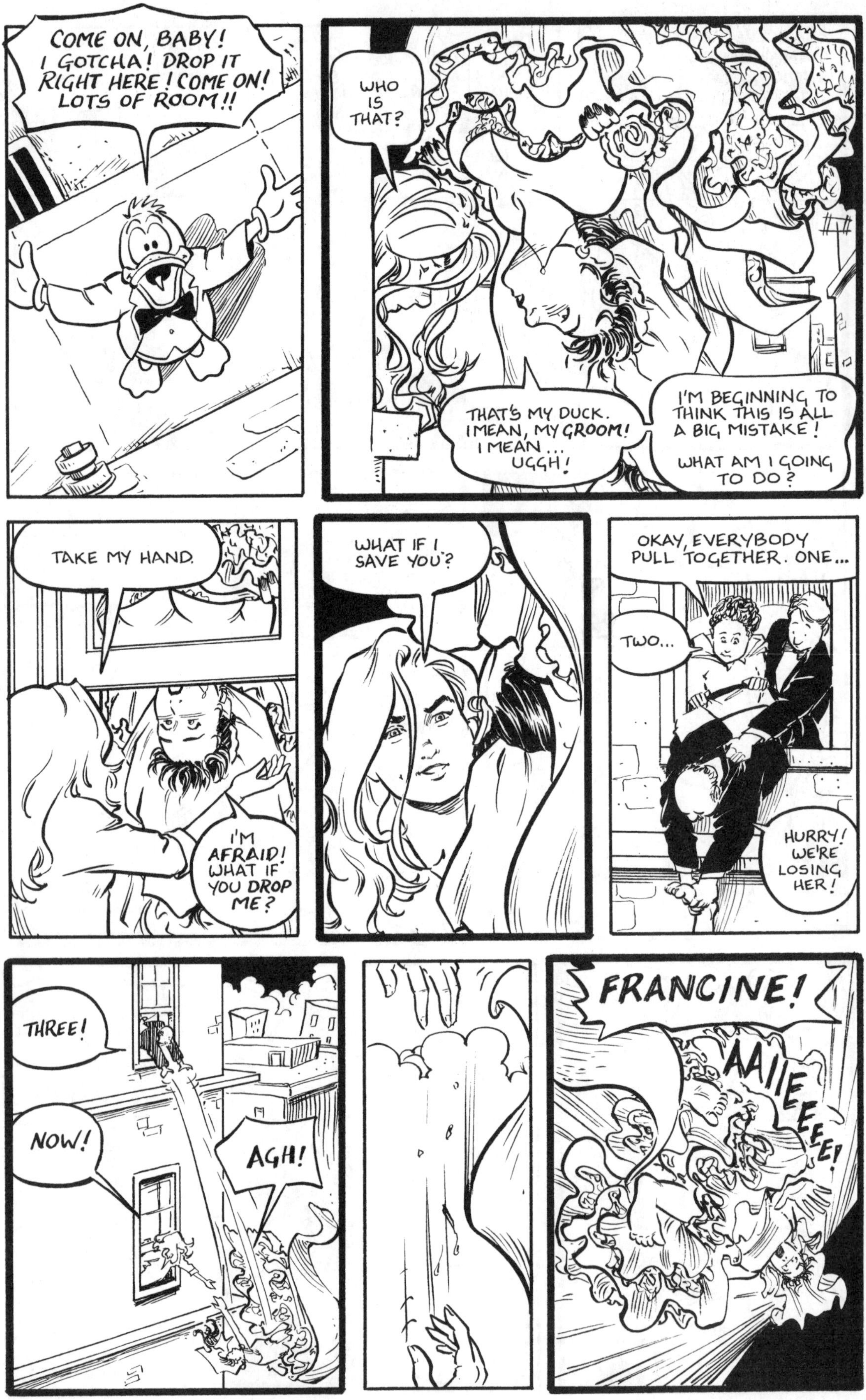
COME ON, BABY! I GOTCHA! DROP IT RIGHT HERE! COME ON! LOTS OF ROOM!!
WHO IS THAT?
THAT'S MY DUCK. I MEAN, MY GROOM! I MEAN... UGGH!
I'M BEGINNING TO THINK THIS IS ALL A BIG MISTAKE!
WHAT AM I GOING TO DO?
TAKE MY HAND.
I'M AFRAID! WHAT IF YOU DROP ME?
WHAT IF I SAVE YOU?
OKAY, EVERYBODY PULL TOGETHER. ONE...
TWO...
HURRY! WE'RE LOSING HER!
THREE!
NOW!
AGH!
FRANCINE!
AAIIEEEEE!

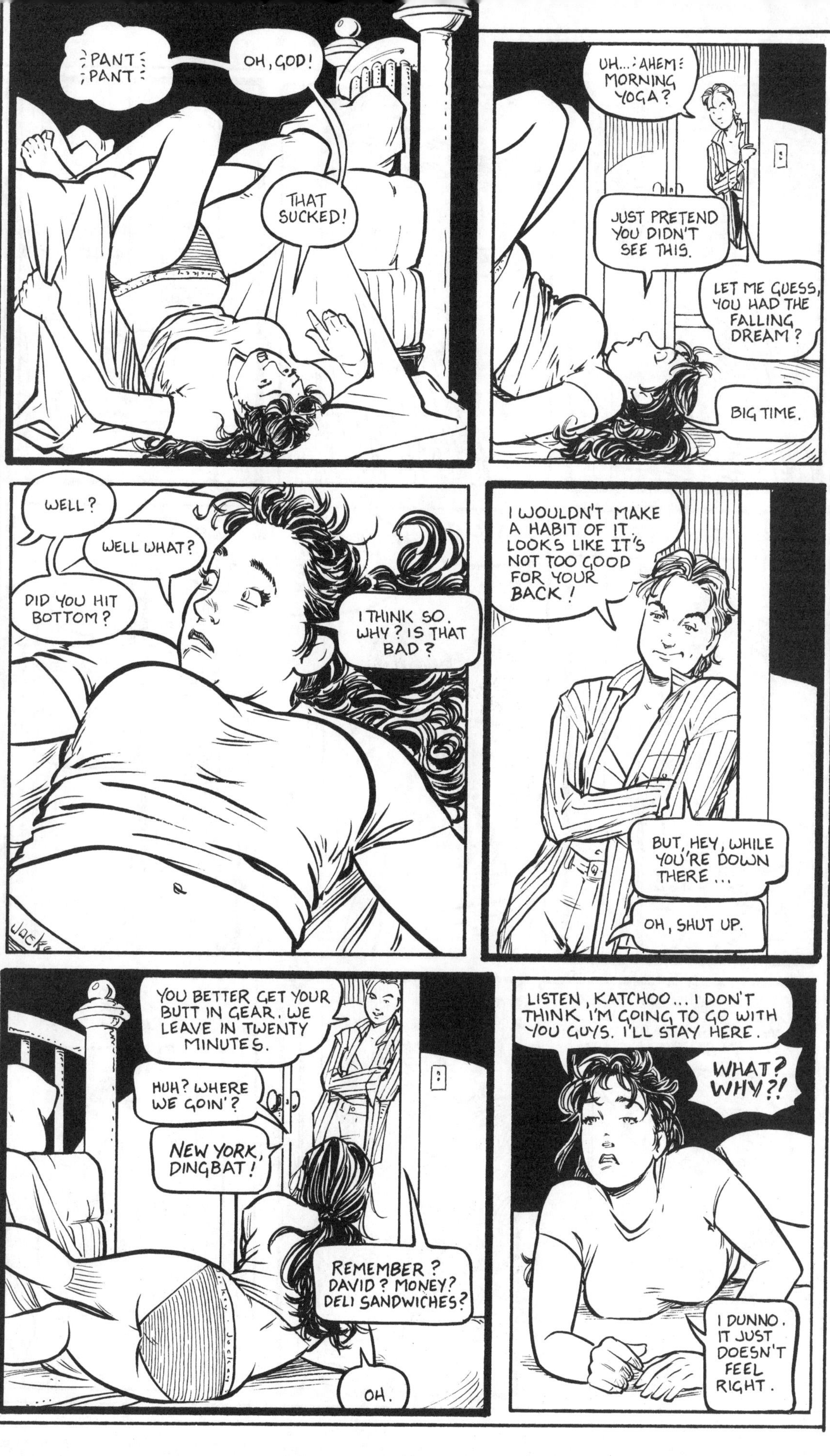
PANT PANT
OH, GOD!
THAT SUCKED!
UH... AHEM MORNING YOGA?
JUST PRETEND YOU DIDN'T SEE THIS.
LET ME GUESS, YOU HAD THE FALLING DREAM?
BIG TIME.
WELL?
WELL WHAT?
DID YOU HIT BOTTOM?
I THINK SO. WHY? IS THAT BAD?
I WOULDN'T MAKE A HABIT OF IT. LOOKS LIKE IT'S NOT TOO GOOD FOR YOUR BACK!
BUT, HEY, WHILE YOU'RE DOWN THERE...
OH, SHUT UP.
YOU BETTER GET YOUR BUTT IN GEAR. WE LEAVE IN TWENTY MINUTES.
HUH? WHERE WE GOIN'?
NEW YORK, DINGBAT!
REMEMBER? DAVID? MONEY? DELI SANDWICHES?
OH.
LISTEN, KATCHOO... I DON'T THINK I'M GOING TO GO WITH YOU GUYS. I'LL STAY HERE.
WHAT? WHY?!
I DUNNO. IT JUST DOESN'T FEEL RIGHT.

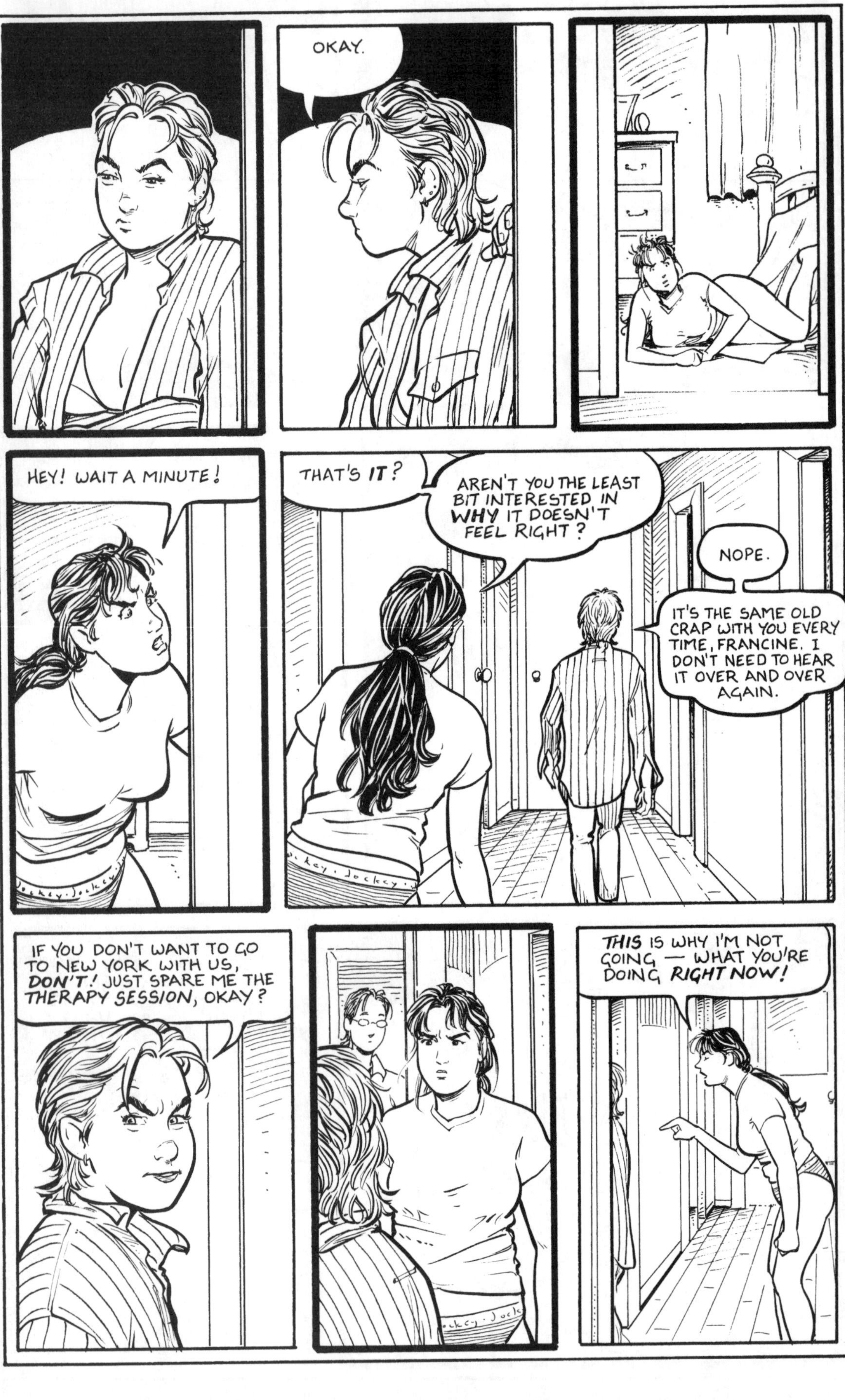
OKAY.
HEY! WAIT A MINUTE!
THAT'S IT?
AREN'T YOU THE LEAST BIT INTERESTED IN WHY IT DOESN'T FEEL RIGHT?
NOPE.
IT'S THE SAME OLD CRAP WITH YOU EVERY TIME, FRANCINE. I DON'T NEED TO HEAR IT OVER AND OVER AGAIN.
IF YOU DON'T WANT TO GO TO NEW YORK WITH US, DON'T! JUST SPARE ME THE THERAPY SESSION, OKAY?
THIS IS WHY I'M NOT GOING — WHAT YOU'RE DOING RIGHT NOW!

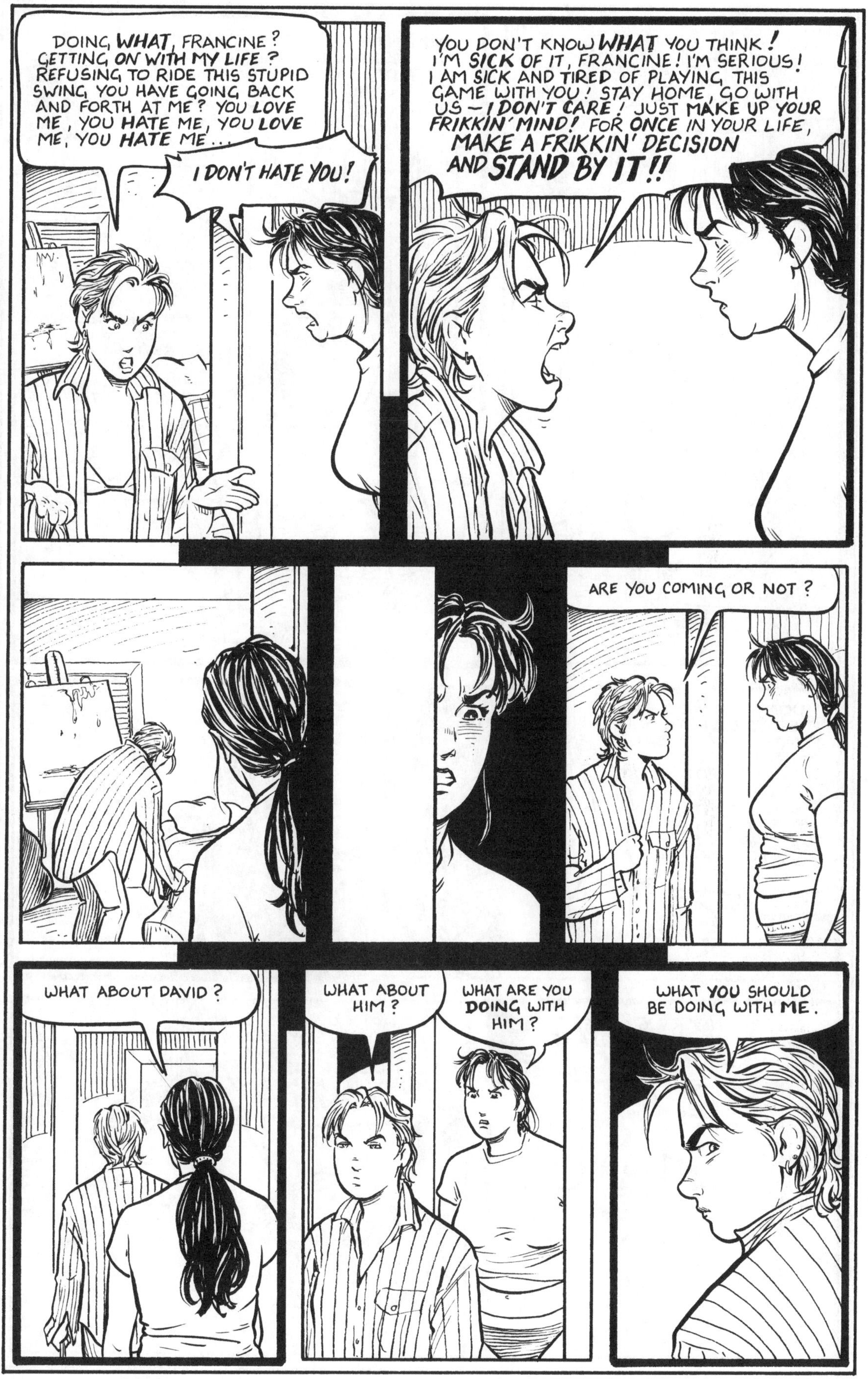

DOING WHAT, FRANCINE? GETTING ON WITH MY LIFE? REFUSING TO RIDE THIS STUPID SWING YOU HAVE GOING BACK AND FORTH AT ME? YOU LOVE ME, YOU HATE ME, YOU LOVE ME, YOU HATE ME...
I DON'T HATE YOU!
YOU DON'T KNOW WHAT YOU THINK! I'M SICK OF IT, FRANCINE! I'M SERIOUS! I AM SICK AND TIRED OF PLAYING THIS GAME WITH YOU! STAY HOME, GO WITH US — I DON'T CARE! JUST MAKE UP YOUR FRIKKIN' MIND! FOR ONCE IN YOUR LIFE, MAKE A FRIKKIN' DECISION AND STAND BY IT!!
ARE YOU COMING OR NOT?
WHAT ABOUT DAVID?
WHAT ABOUT HIM?
WHAT ARE YOU DOING WITH HIM?
WHAT YOU SHOULD BE DOING WITH ME.

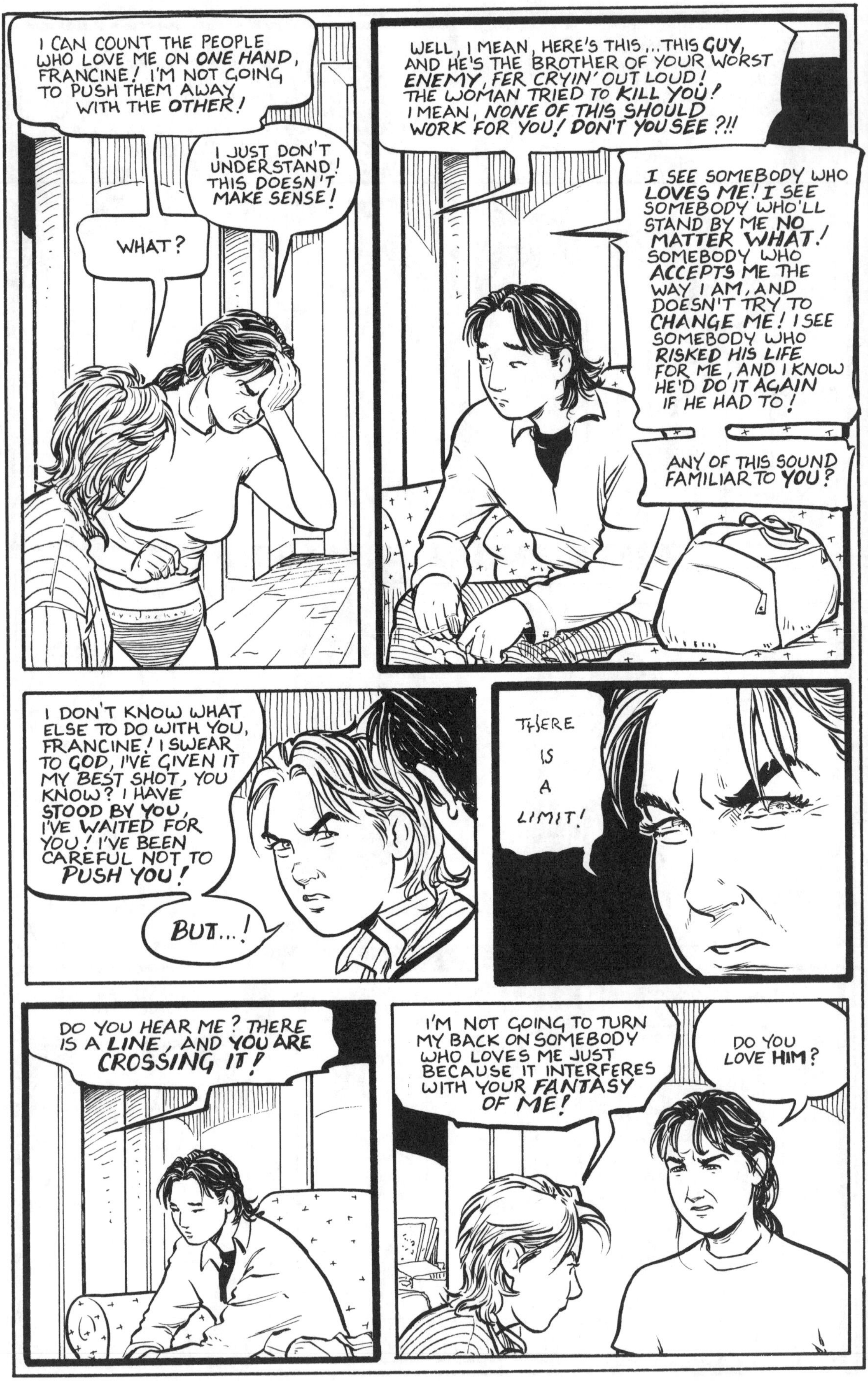
I CAN COUNT THE PEOPLE WHO LOVE ME ON ONE HAND, FRANCINE! I'M NOT GOING TO PUSH THEM AWAY WITH THE OTHER!
I JUST DON'T UNDERSTAND! THIS DOESN'T MAKE SENSE!
WHAT?
WELL, I MEAN, HERE'S THIS... THIS GUY, AND HE'S THE BROTHER OF YOUR WORST ENEMY, FER CRYIN' OUT LOUD! THE WOMAN TRIED TO KILL YOU! I MEAN, NONE OF THIS SHOULD WORK FOR YOU! DON'T YOU SEE?!!
I SEE SOMEBODY WHO LOVES ME! I SEE SOMEBODY WHO'LL STAND BY ME NO MATTER WHAT! SOMEBODY WHO ACCEPTS ME THE WAY I AM, AND DOESN'T TRY TO CHANGE ME! I SEE SOMEBODY WHO RISKED HIS LIFE FOR ME, AND I KNOW HE'D DO IT AGAIN IF HE HAD TO!
ANY OF THIS SOUND FAMILIAR TO YOU?
I DON'T KNOW WHAT ELSE TO DO WITH YOU, FRANCINE! I SWEAR TO GOD, I'VE GIVEN IT MY BEST SHOT, YOU KNOW? I HAVE STOOD BY YOU, I'VE WAITED FOR YOU! I'VE BEEN CAREFUL NOT TO PUSH YOU!
BUT...!
THERE IS A LIMIT!
DO YOU HEAR ME? THERE IS A LINE, AND YOU ARE CROSSING IT!
I'M NOT GOING TO TURN MY BACK ON SOMEBODY WHO LOVES ME JUST BECAUSE IT INTERFERES WITH YOUR FANTASY OF ME!
DO YOU LOVE HIM?

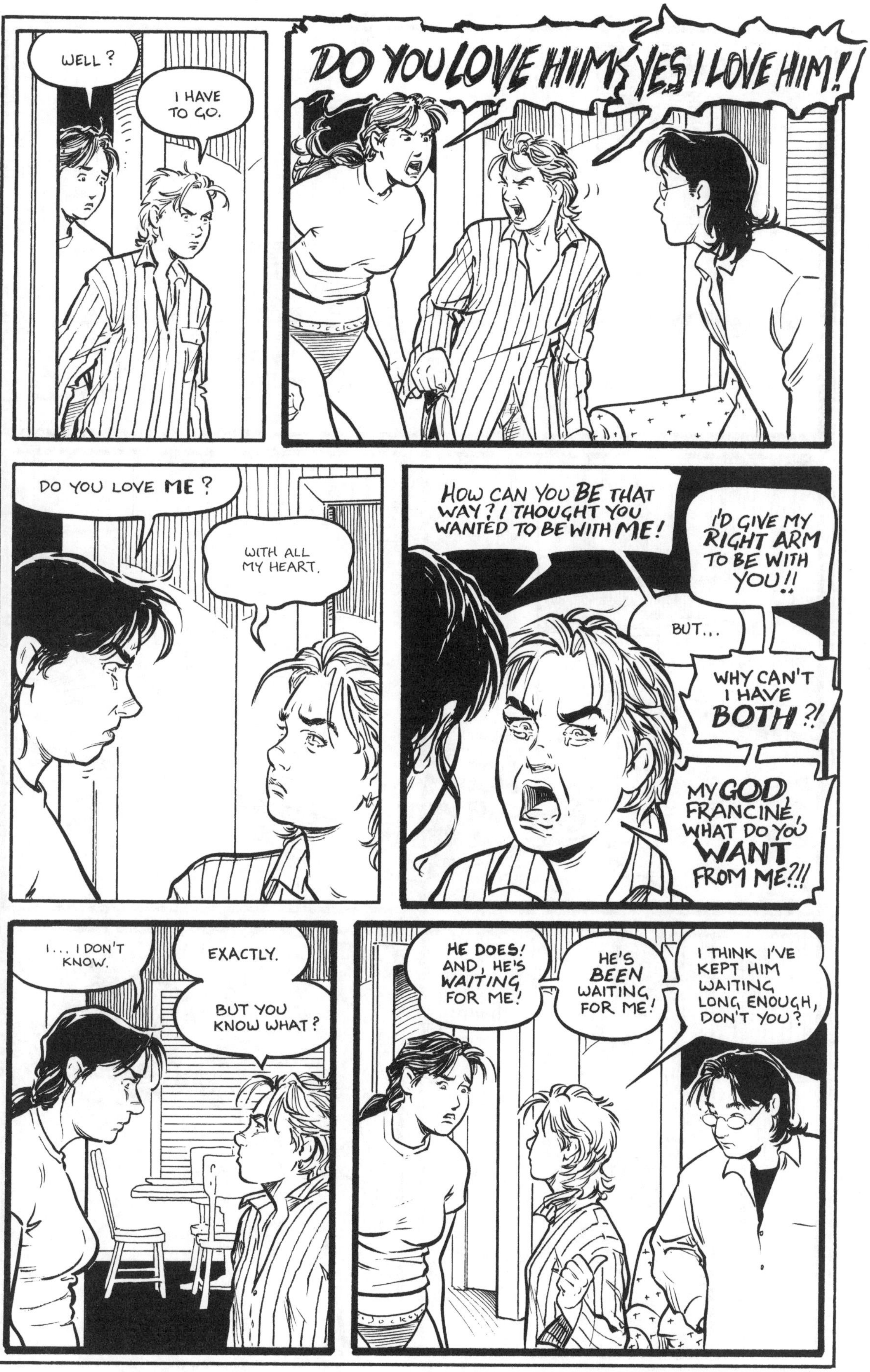
WELL ?
I HAVE TO GO.
DO YOU LOVE HIM?
YES I LOVE HIM!!
DO YOU LOVE ME ?
WITH ALL MY HEART.
HOW CAN YOU BE THAT WAY? I THOUGHT YOU WANTED TO BE WITH ME!
I'D GIVE MY RIGHT ARM TO BE WITH YOU!!
BUT...
WHY CAN'T I HAVE BOTH ?!
MY GOD, FRANCINE, WHAT DO YOU WANT FROM ME?!!
I... I DON'T KNOW.
EXACTLY.
BUT YOU KNOW WHAT ?
HE DOES! AND, HE'S WAITING FOR ME!
HE'S BEEN WAITING FOR ME!
I THINK I'VE KEPT HIM WAITING LONG ENOUGH, DON'T YOU ?

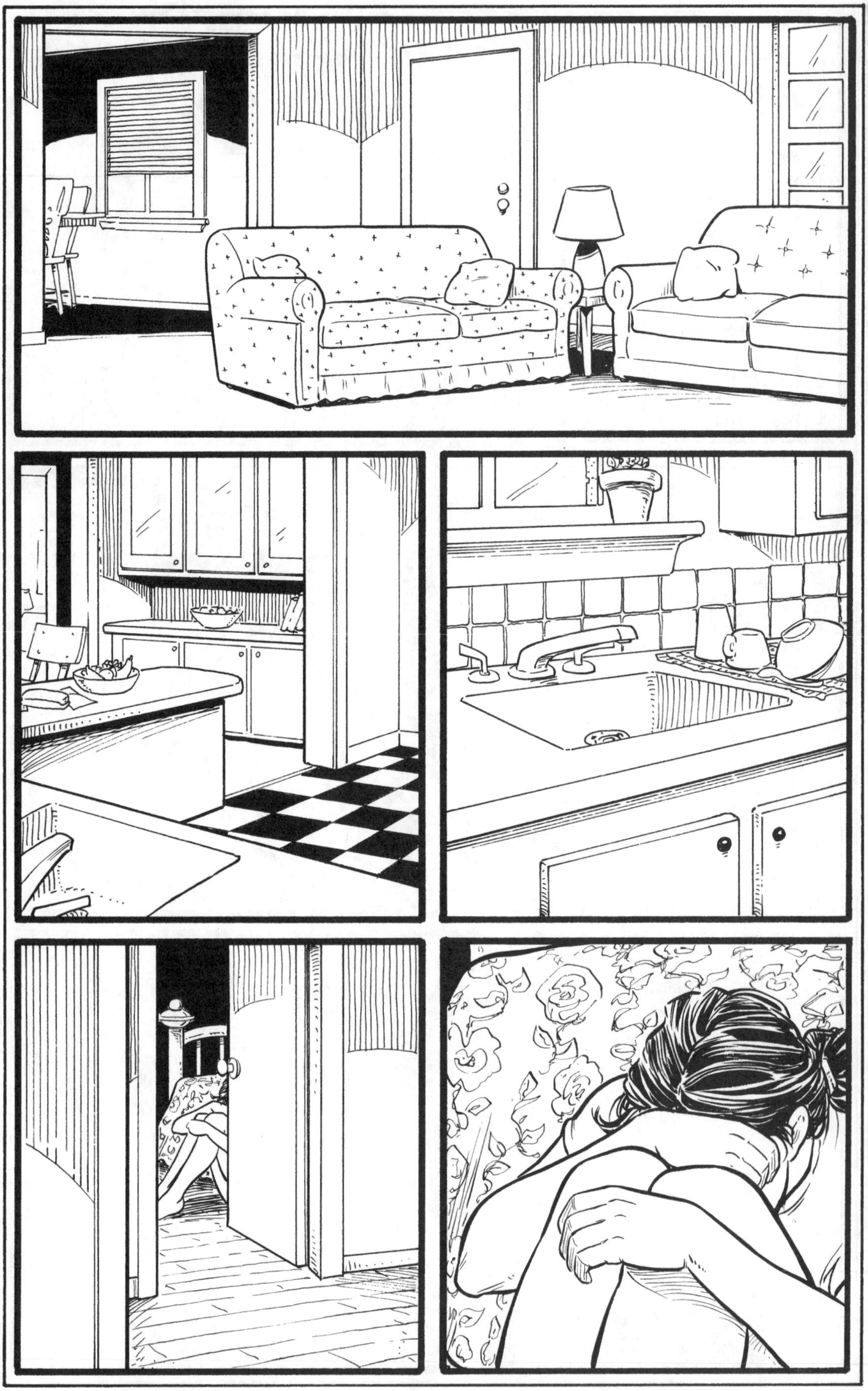

RING!

HELLO? KATCHOO?!

OH. CASEY. HI.

WHAT'S THE MATTER, WHY ARE YOU CRYING?

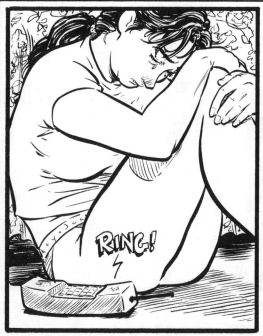

HE LEFT YOU? WHEN?

I'M SORRY.

I KNOW, BELIEVE ME, I know...

UH... ⸝SNIFF⸝ I'M KIND OF EXPECTING A CALL RIGHT NOW.

I HAVEN'T TAKEN A SHOWER YET OR ANYTHING.

⸝SNIFF⸝

OKAY, OKAY...

I'M ON MY WAY.

SIGH...

⸝SNIFF⸝

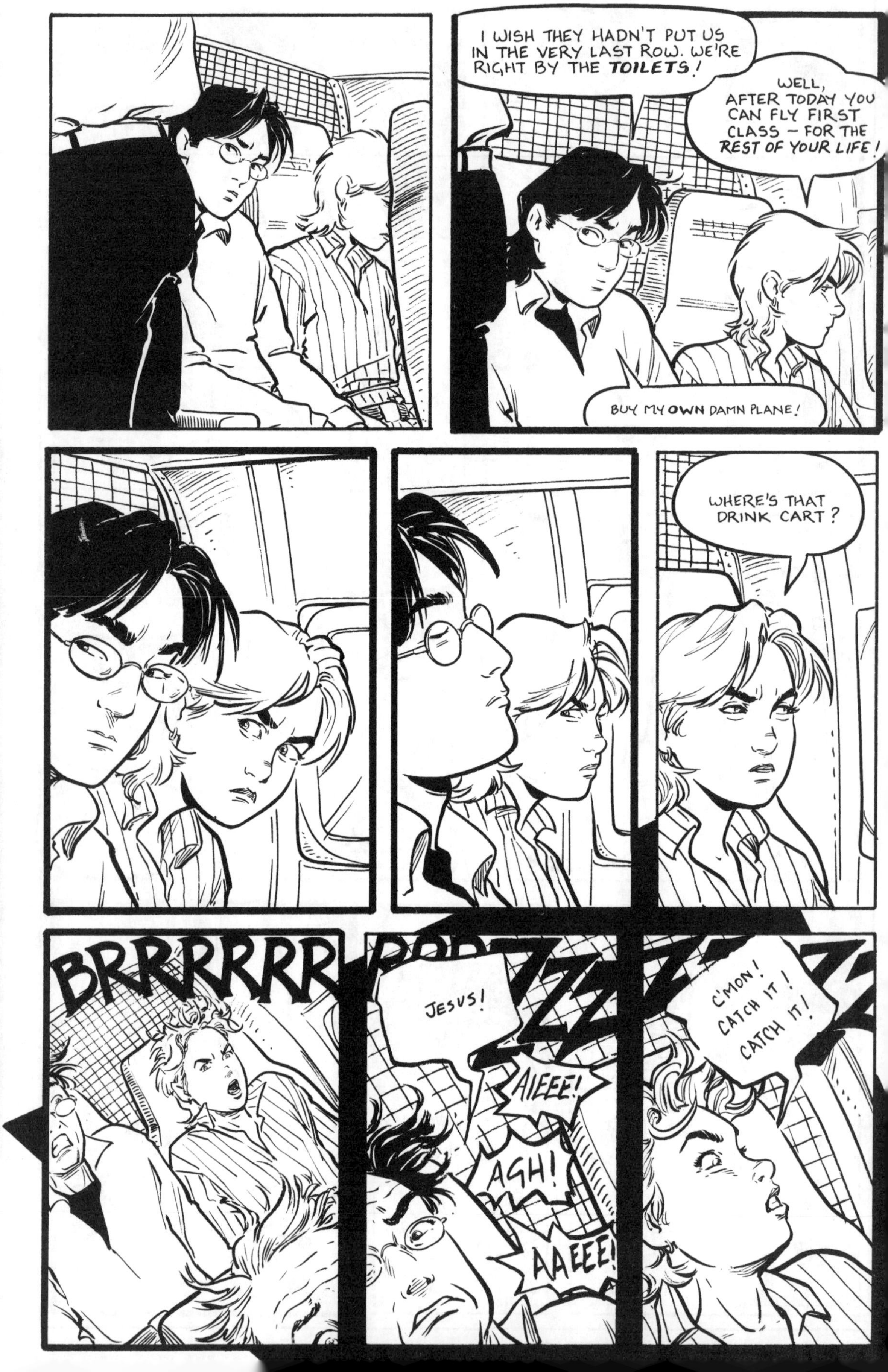
I WISH THEY HADN'T PUT US IN THE VERY LAST ROW. WE'RE RIGHT BY THE TOILETS!
WELL, AFTER TODAY YOU CAN FLY FIRST CLASS – FOR THE REST OF YOUR LIFE!
BUY MY OWN DAMN PLANE!
WHERE'S THAT DRINK CART?
BRRRRRRR
JESUS!
AIEEE!
AGH!
AAEEE!
C'MON! CATCH IT! CATCH IT!

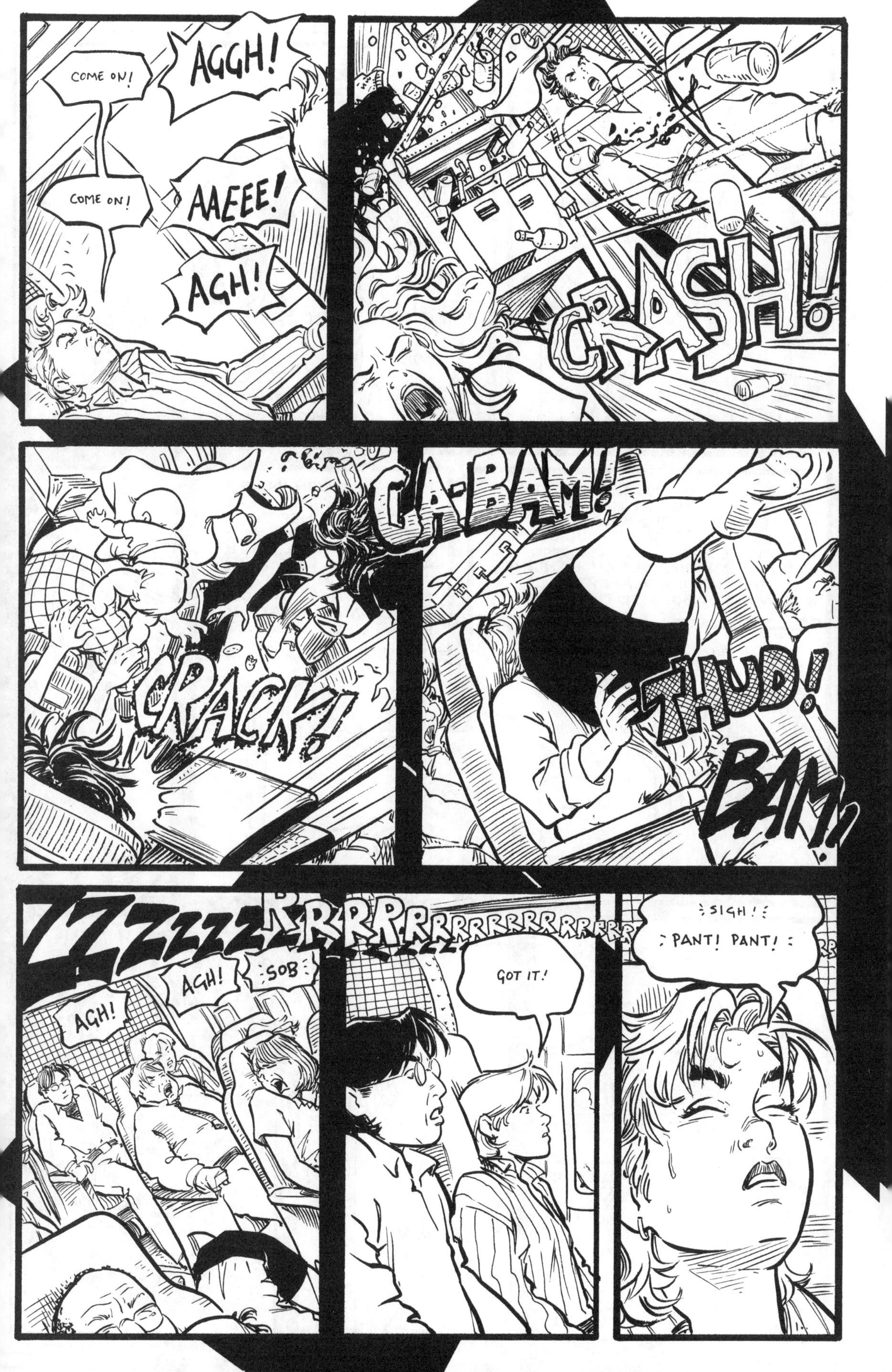

COME ON!
AGGH!
COME ON!
AAEEE!
AGH!
CRASH!
CA-BAM!
CRACK!
THUD!
BAM!
ZZZZZZRRRRRRRRRRRRRRRR
AGH!
AGH!
SOB
GOT IT!
SIGH!
PANT! PANT!

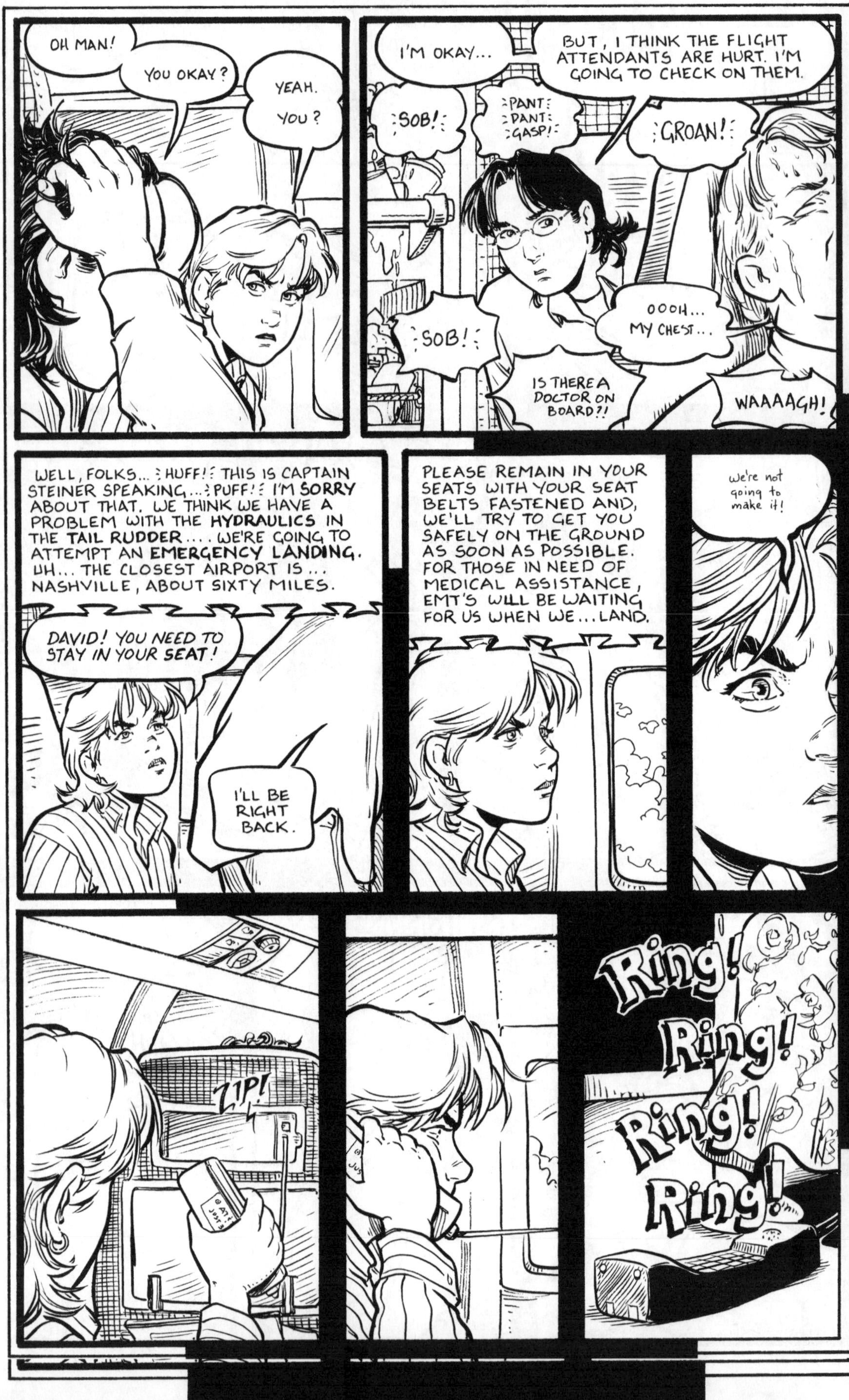
OH MAN!
YOU OKAY?
YEAH. YOU?
I'M OKAY...
BUT, I THINK THE FLIGHT ATTENDANTS ARE HURT. I'M GOING TO CHECK ON THEM.
SOB!
PANT PANT GASP!
GROAN!
SOB!
OOOH... MY CHEST...
IS THERE A DOCTOR ON BOARD?!
WAAAAGH!
WELL, FOLKS... HUFF! THIS IS CAPTAIN STEINER SPEAKING... PUFF! I'M SORRY ABOUT THAT. WE THINK WE HAVE A PROBLEM WITH THE HYDRAULICS IN THE TAIL RUDDER.... WE'RE GOING TO ATTEMPT AN EMERGENCY LANDING. UH... THE CLOSEST AIRPORT IS... NASHVILLE, ABOUT SIXTY MILES.
DAVID! YOU NEED TO STAY IN YOUR SEAT!
I'LL BE RIGHT BACK.
PLEASE REMAIN IN YOUR SEATS WITH YOUR SEAT BELTS FASTENED AND, WE'LL TRY TO GET YOU SAFELY ON THE GROUND AS SOON AS POSSIBLE. FOR THOSE IN NEED OF MEDICAL ASSISTANCE, EMT'S WILL BE WAITING FOR US WHEN WE... LAND.
we're not going to make it!
ZIP!
Ring! Ring! Ring! Ring!

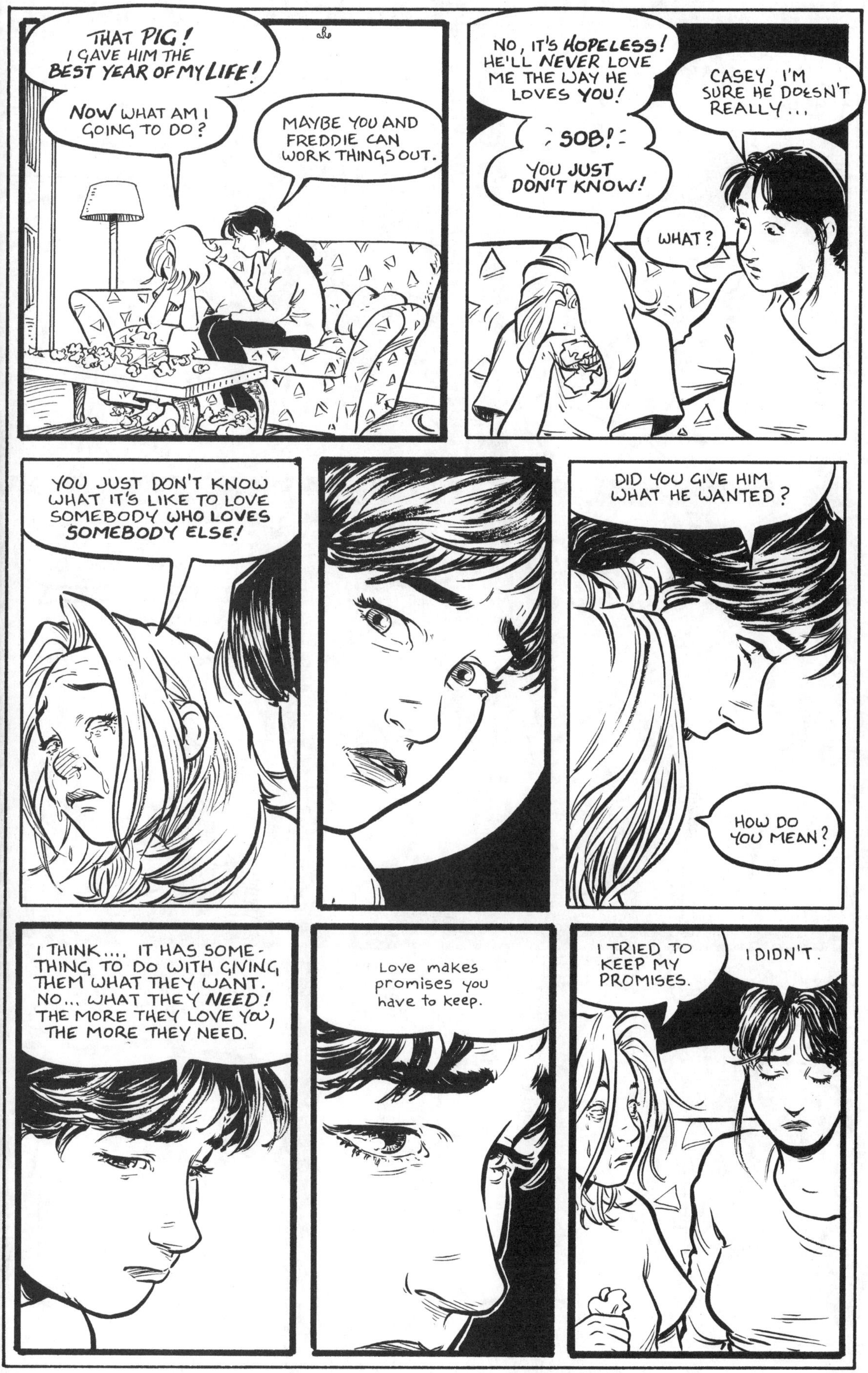
THAT PIG! I GAVE HIM THE BEST YEAR OF MY LIFE!
NOW WHAT AM I GOING TO DO?
MAYBE YOU AND FREDDIE CAN WORK THINGS OUT.
NO, IT'S HOPELESS! HE'LL NEVER LOVE ME THE WAY HE LOVES YOU!
SOB!
YOU JUST DON'T KNOW!
CASEY, I'M SURE HE DOESN'T REALLY...
WHAT?
YOU JUST DON'T KNOW WHAT IT'S LIKE TO LOVE SOMEBODY WHO LOVES SOMEBODY ELSE!
DID YOU GIVE HIM WHAT HE WANTED?
HOW DO YOU MEAN?
I THINK.... IT HAS SOMETHING TO DO WITH GIVING THEM WHAT THEY WANT. NO... WHAT THEY NEED! THE MORE THEY LOVE YOU, THE MORE THEY NEED.
Love makes promises you have to keep.
I TRIED TO KEEP MY PROMISES.
I DIDN'T.

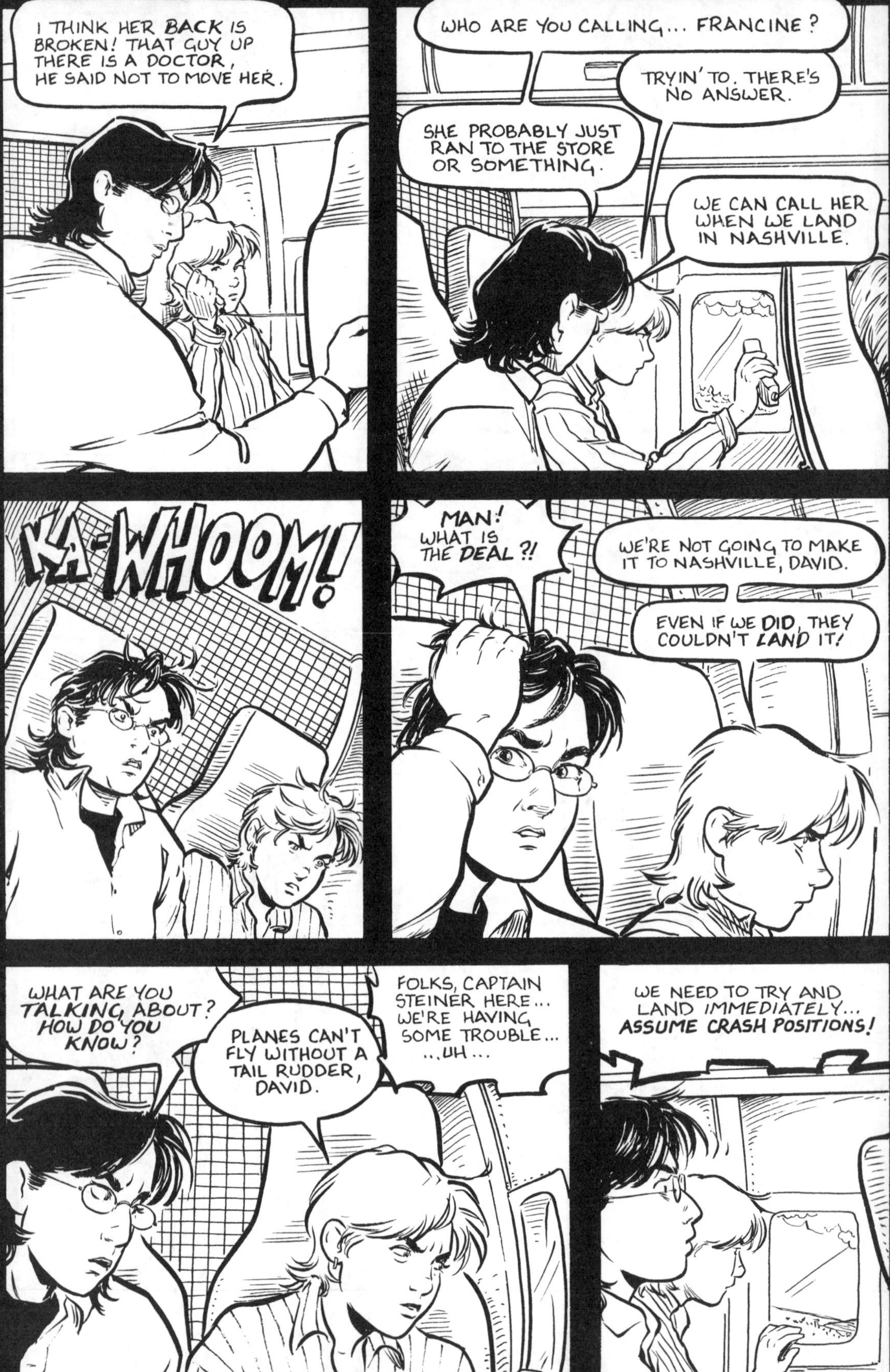
I THINK HER BACK IS BROKEN! THAT GUY UP THERE IS A DOCTOR, HE SAID NOT TO MOVE HER.
WHO ARE YOU CALLING... FRANCINE?
TRYIN' TO. THERE'S NO ANSWER.
SHE PROBABLY JUST RAN TO THE STORE OR SOMETHING.
WE CAN CALL HER WHEN WE LAND IN NASHVILLE.
KA-WHOOM!
MAN! WHAT IS THE DEAL?!
WE'RE NOT GOING TO MAKE IT TO NASHVILLE, DAVID.
EVEN IF WE DID, THEY COULDN'T LAND IT!
WHAT ARE YOU TALKING ABOUT? HOW DO YOU KNOW?
PLANES CAN'T FLY WITHOUT A TAIL RUDDER, DAVID.
FOLKS, CAPTAIN STEINER HERE... WE'RE HAVING SOME TROUBLE... ...UH...
WE NEED TO TRY AND LAND IMMEDIATELY... ASSUME CRASH POSITIONS!

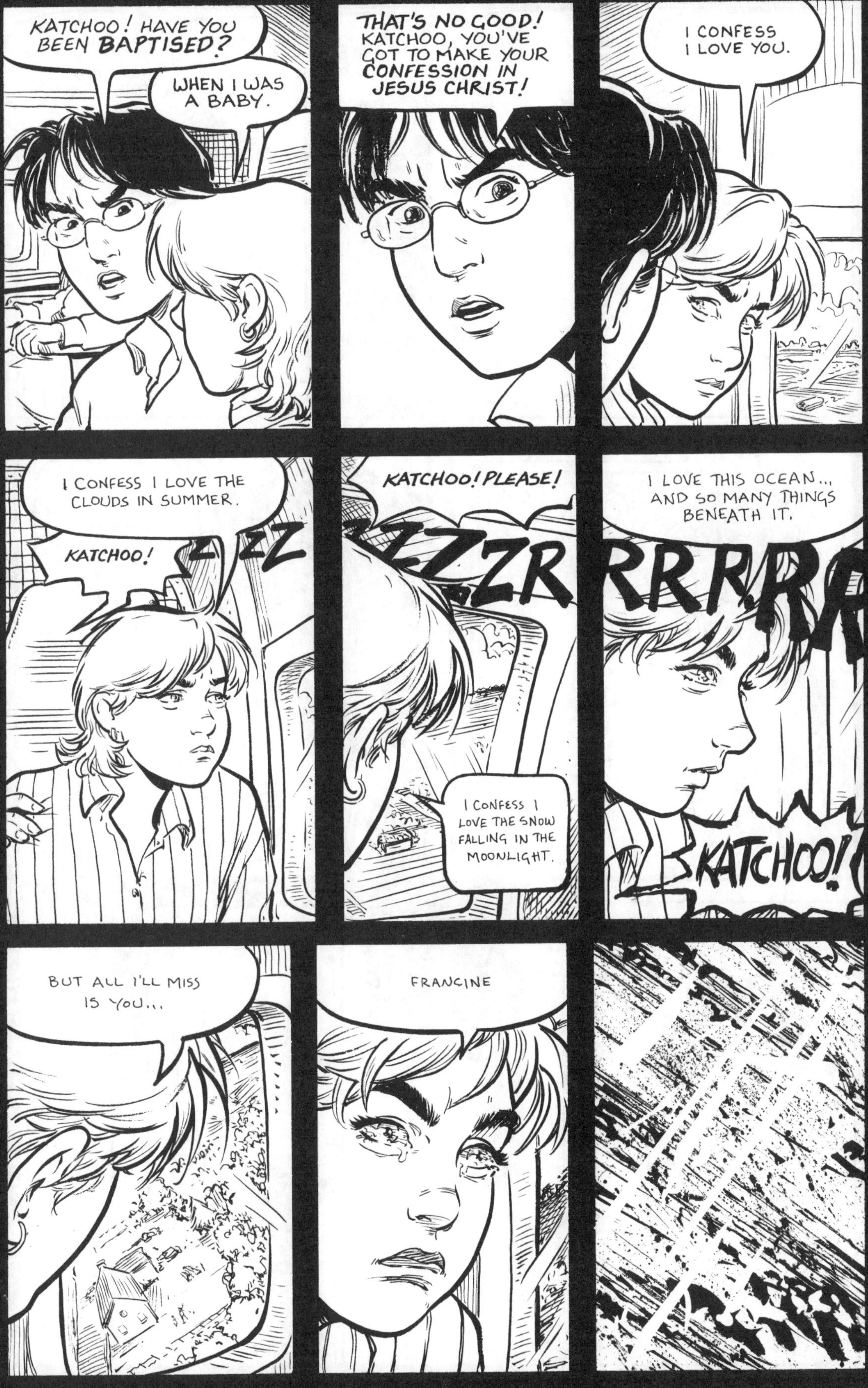
KATCHOO! HAVE YOU BEEN BAPTISED?
WHEN I WAS A BABY.
THAT'S NO GOOD! KATCHOO, YOU'VE GOT TO MAKE YOUR CONFESSION IN JESUS CHRIST!
I CONFESS I LOVE YOU.
I CONFESS I LOVE THE CLOUDS IN SUMMER.
KATCHOO!
ZZZZZZZRRRRRR
KATCHOO! PLEASE!
I CONFESS I LOVE THE SNOW FALLING IN THE MOONLIGHT.
I LOVE THIS OCEAN... AND SO MANY THINGS BENEATH IT.
KATCHOO!
BUT ALL I'LL MISS IS YOU...
FRANCINE

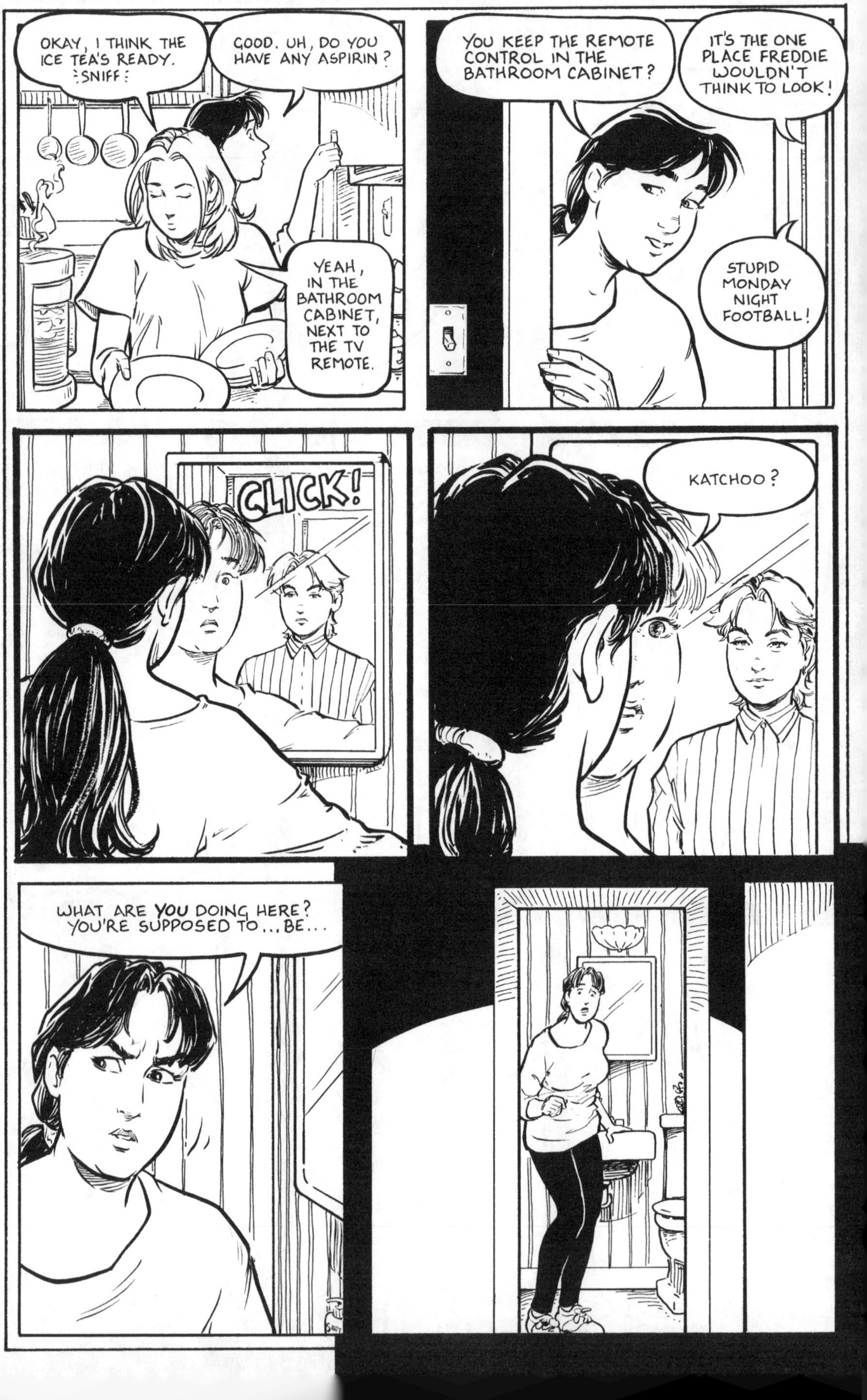
OKAY, I THINK THE ICE TEA'S READY. :SNIFF:
GOOD. UH, DO YOU HAVE ANY ASPIRIN?
YEAH, IN THE BATHROOM CABINET, NEXT TO THE TV REMOTE.
YOU KEEP THE REMOTE CONTROL IN THE BATHROOM CABINET?
IT'S THE ONE PLACE FREDDIE WOULDN'T THINK TO LOOK!
STUPID MONDAY NIGHT FOOTBALL!
CLICK!
KATCHOO?
WHAT ARE YOU DOING HERE? YOU'RE SUPPOSED TO... BE...

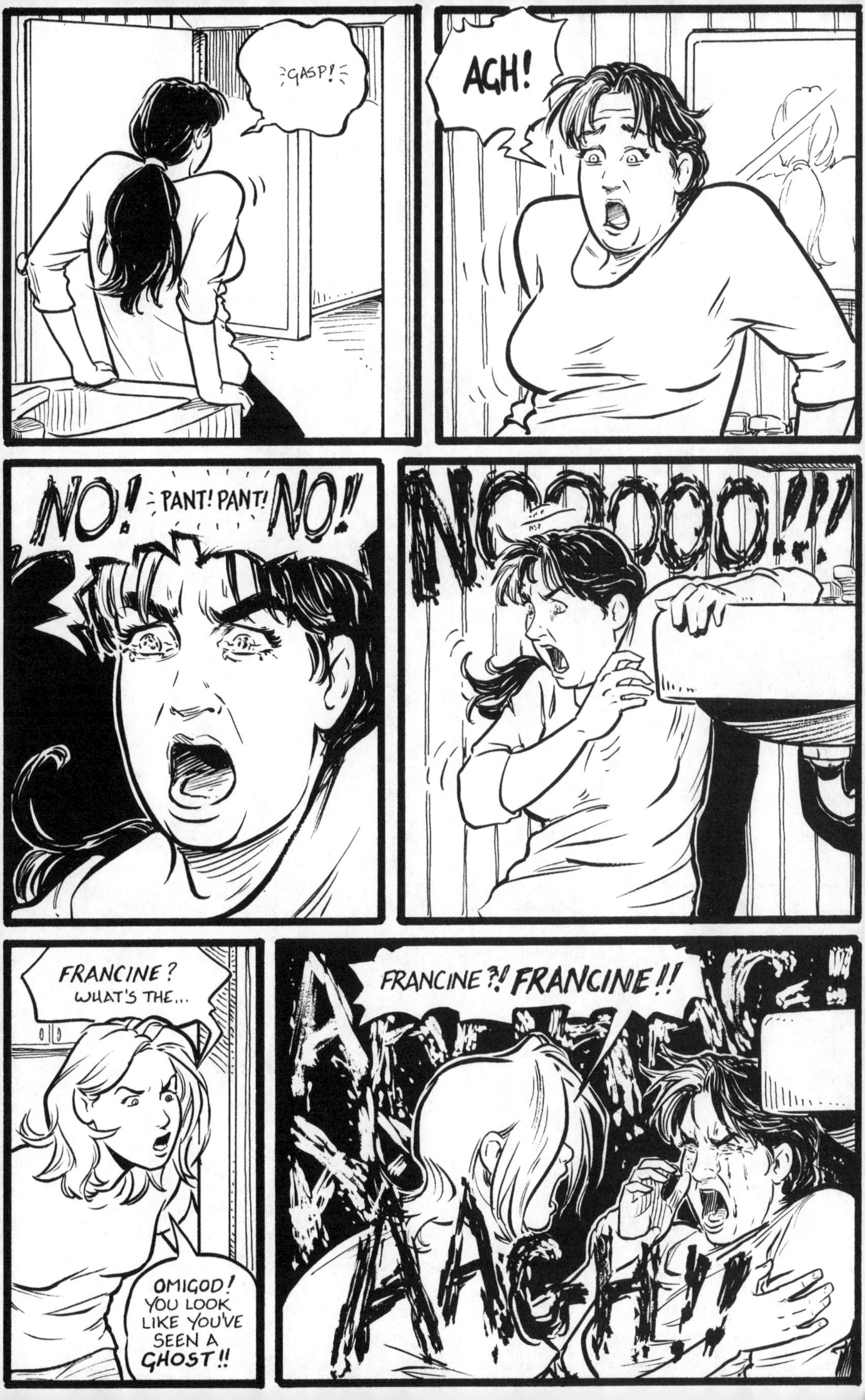
GASP!
AGH!
NO! PANT! PANT! NO!!
NOOOOOO!!!
FRANCINE? WHAT'S THE...
OMIGOD! YOU LOOK LIKE YOU'VE SEEN A GHOST!!
FRANCINE?! FRANCINE!!
AAAGH!!

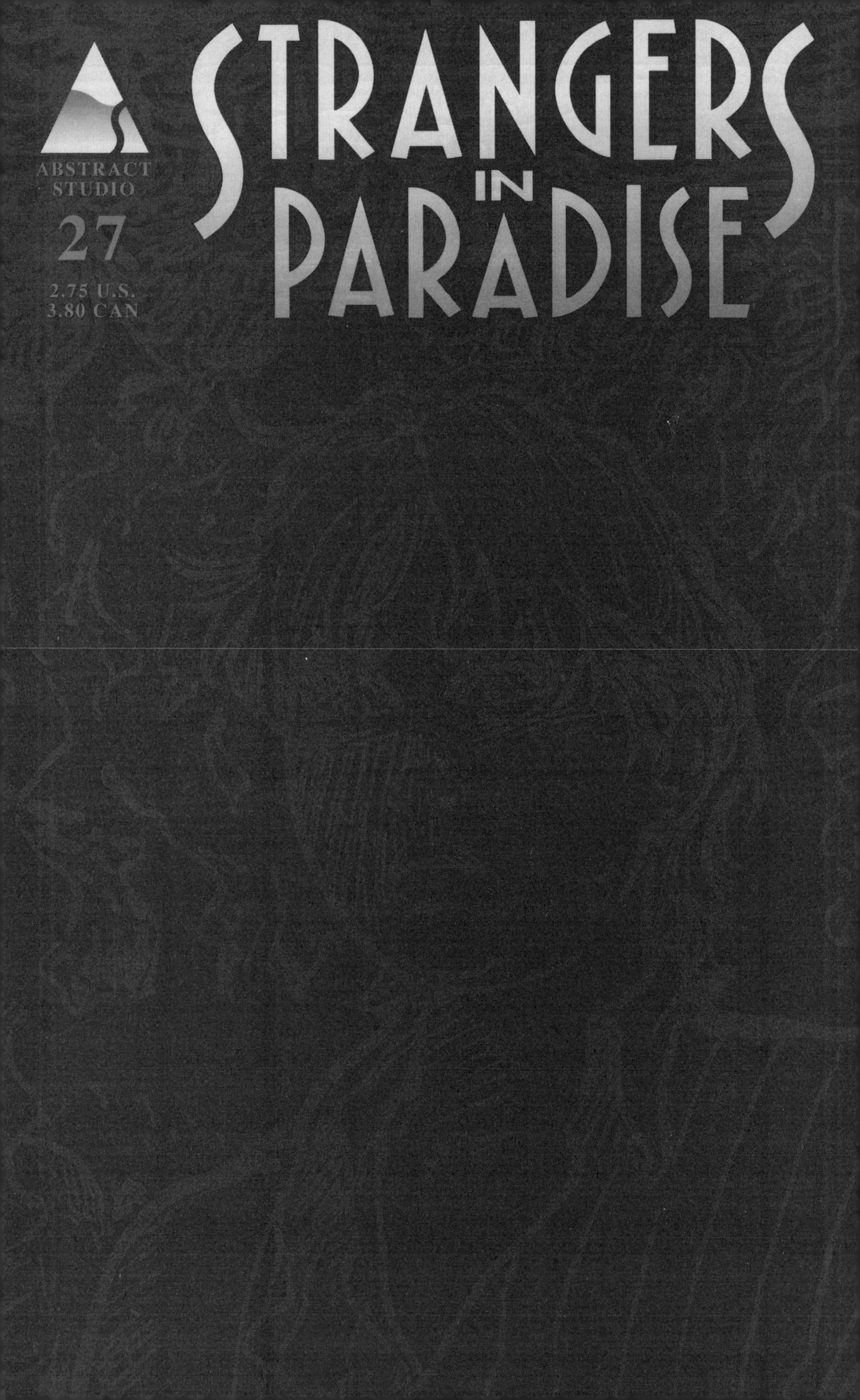
ABSTRACT
STUDIO
27
2.75 U.S.
3.80 CAN
STRANGERS
IN
PARADISE

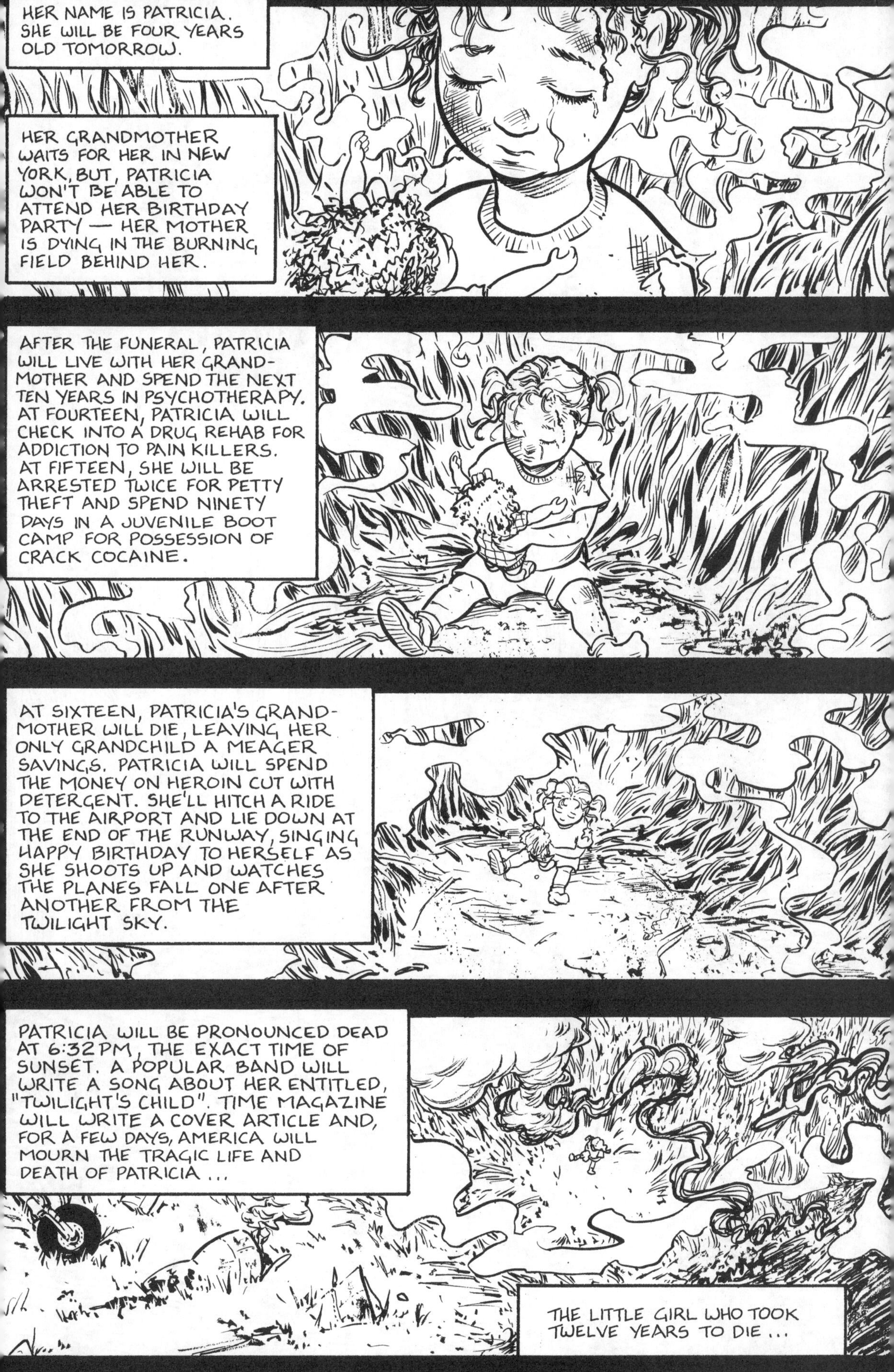
HER NAME IS PATRICIA. SHE WILL BE FOUR YEARS OLD TOMORROW.
HER GRANDMOTHER WAITS FOR HER IN NEW YORK, BUT, PATRICIA WON'T BE ABLE TO ATTEND HER BIRTHDAY PARTY — HER MOTHER IS DYING IN THE BURNING FIELD BEHIND HER.
AFTER THE FUNERAL, PATRICIA WILL LIVE WITH HER GRANDMOTHER AND SPEND THE NEXT TEN YEARS IN PSYCHOTHERAPY. AT FOURTEEN, PATRICIA WILL CHECK INTO A DRUG REHAB FOR ADDICTION TO PAIN KILLERS. AT FIFTEEN, SHE WILL BE ARRESTED TWICE FOR PETTY THEFT AND SPEND NINETY DAYS IN A JUVENILE BOOT CAMP FOR POSSESSION OF CRACK COCAINE.
AT SIXTEEN, PATRICIA'S GRANDMOTHER WILL DIE, LEAVING HER ONLY GRANDCHILD A MEAGER SAVINGS. PATRICIA WILL SPEND THE MONEY ON HEROIN CUT WITH DETERGENT. SHE'LL HITCH A RIDE TO THE AIRPORT AND LIE DOWN AT THE END OF THE RUNWAY, SINGING HAPPY BIRTHDAY TO HERSELF AS SHE SHOOTS UP AND WATCHES THE PLANES FALL ONE AFTER ANOTHER FROM THE TWILIGHT SKY.
PATRICIA WILL BE PRONOUNCED DEAD AT 6:32PM, THE EXACT TIME OF SUNSET. A POPULAR BAND WILL WRITE A SONG ABOUT HER ENTITLED, "TWILIGHT'S CHILD". TIME MAGAZINE WILL WRITE A COVER ARTICLE AND, FOR A FEW DAYS, AMERICA WILL MOURN THE TRAGIC LIFE AND DEATH OF PATRICIA ...
THE LITTLE GIRL WHO TOOK TWELVE YEARS TO DIE ...

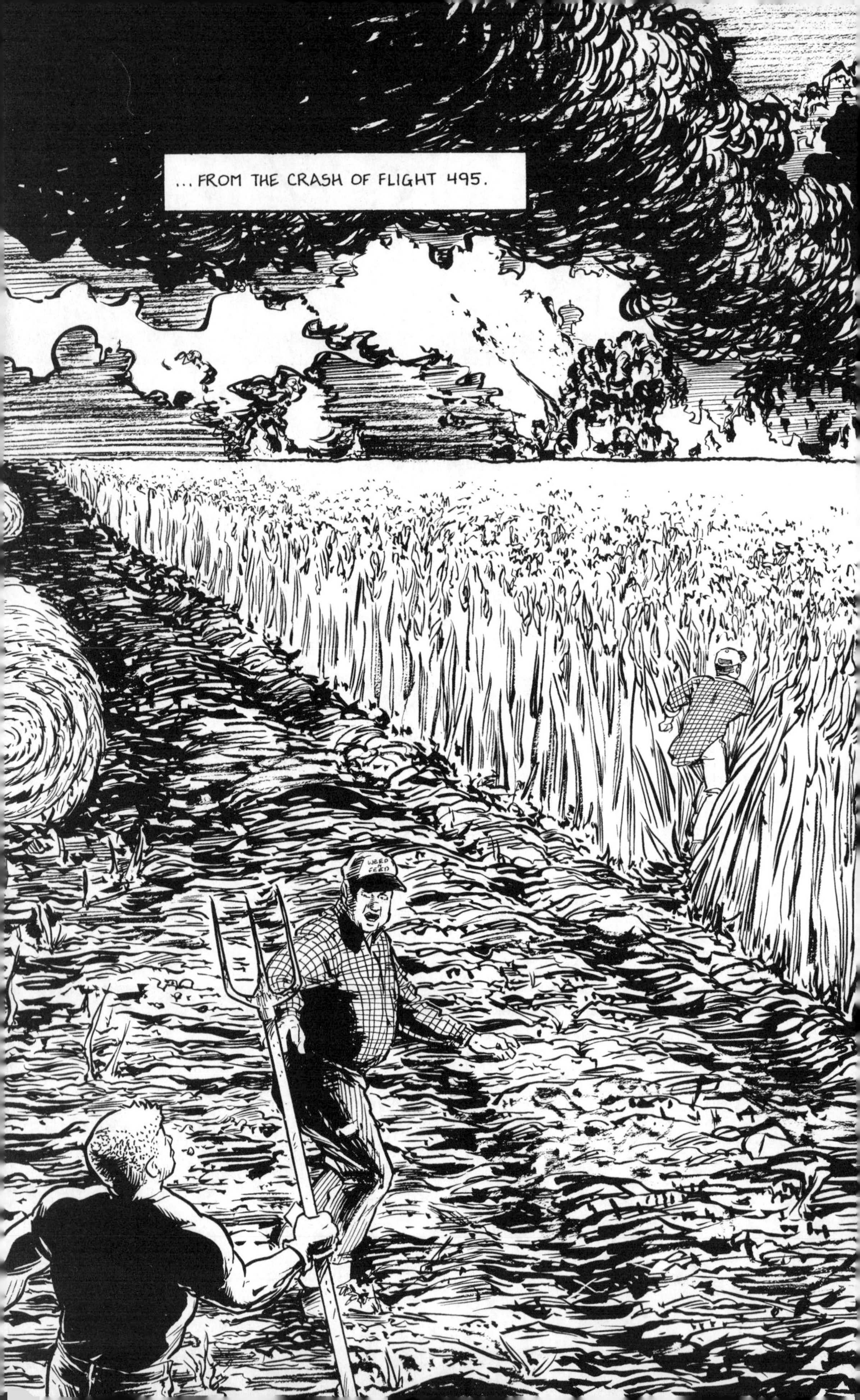
...FROM THE CRASH OF FLIGHT 495.
WEED N FEED

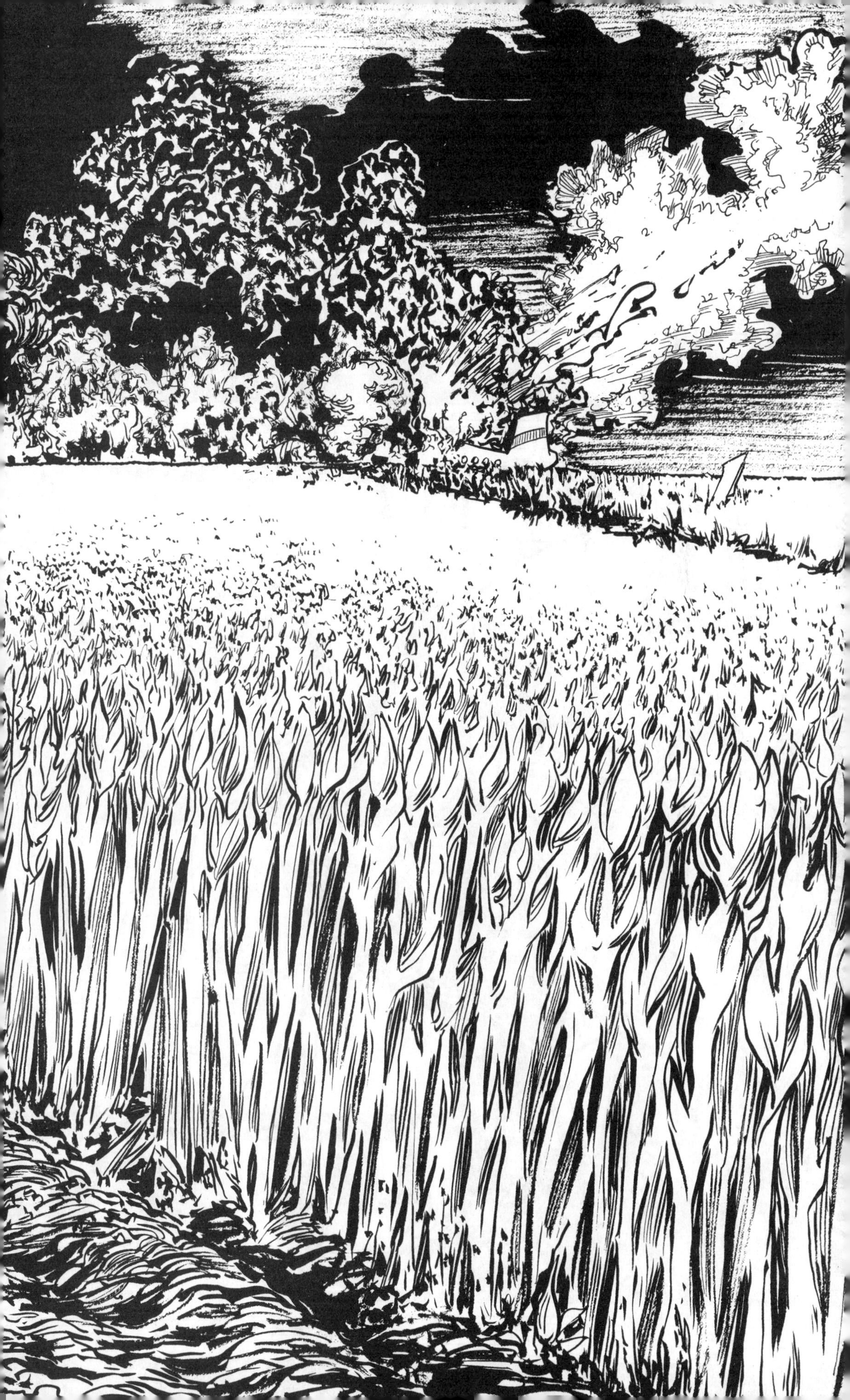

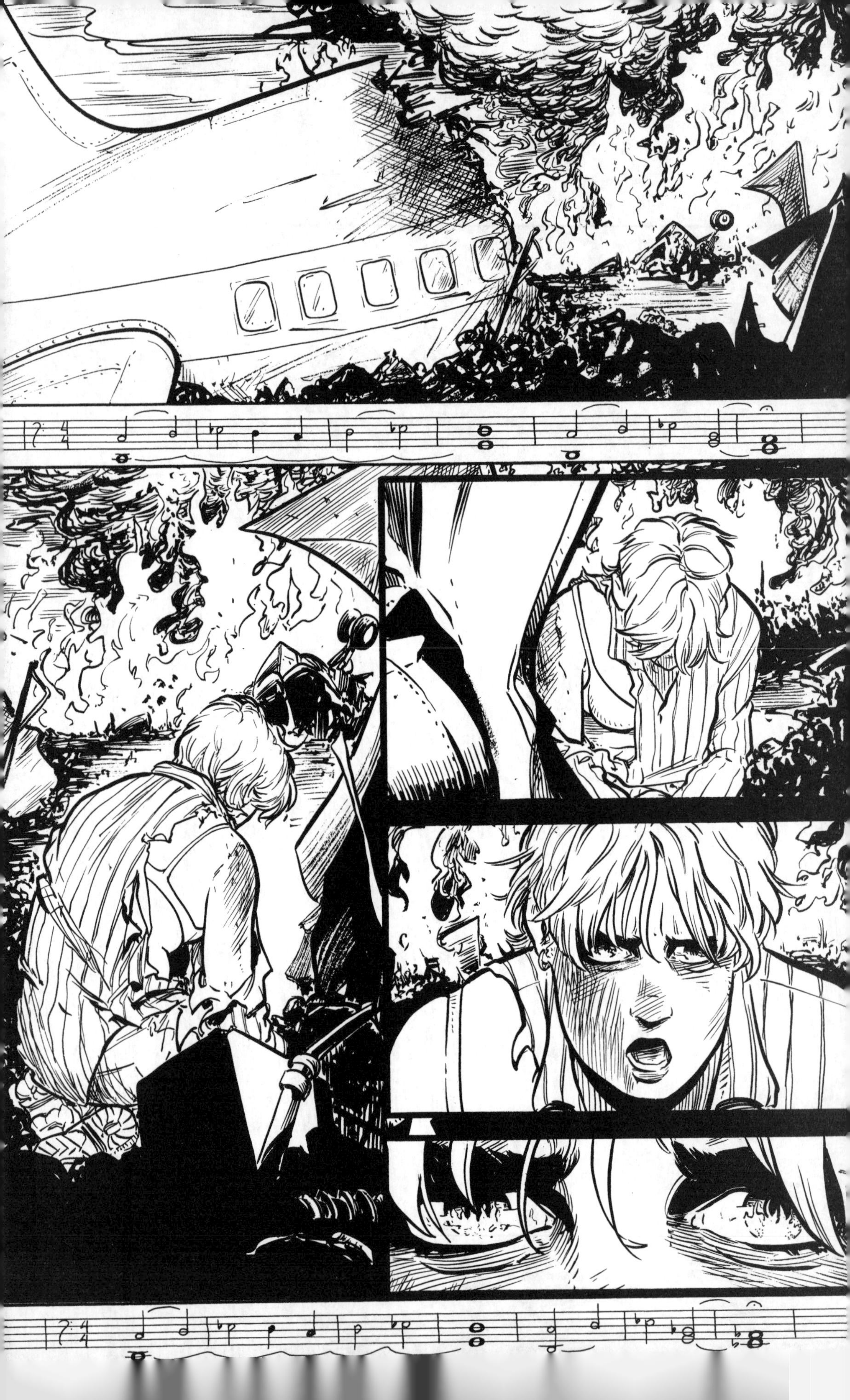

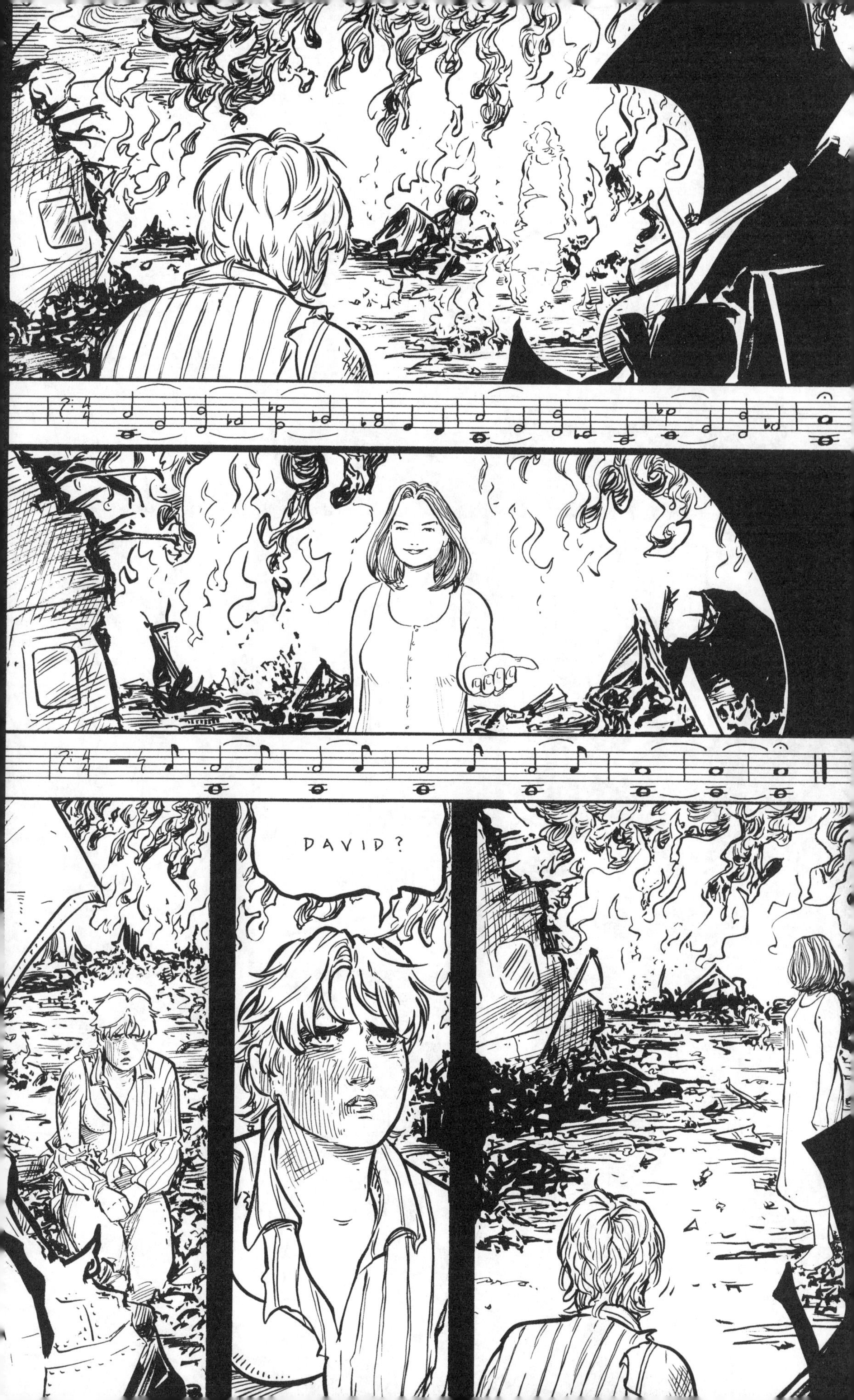
DAVID?

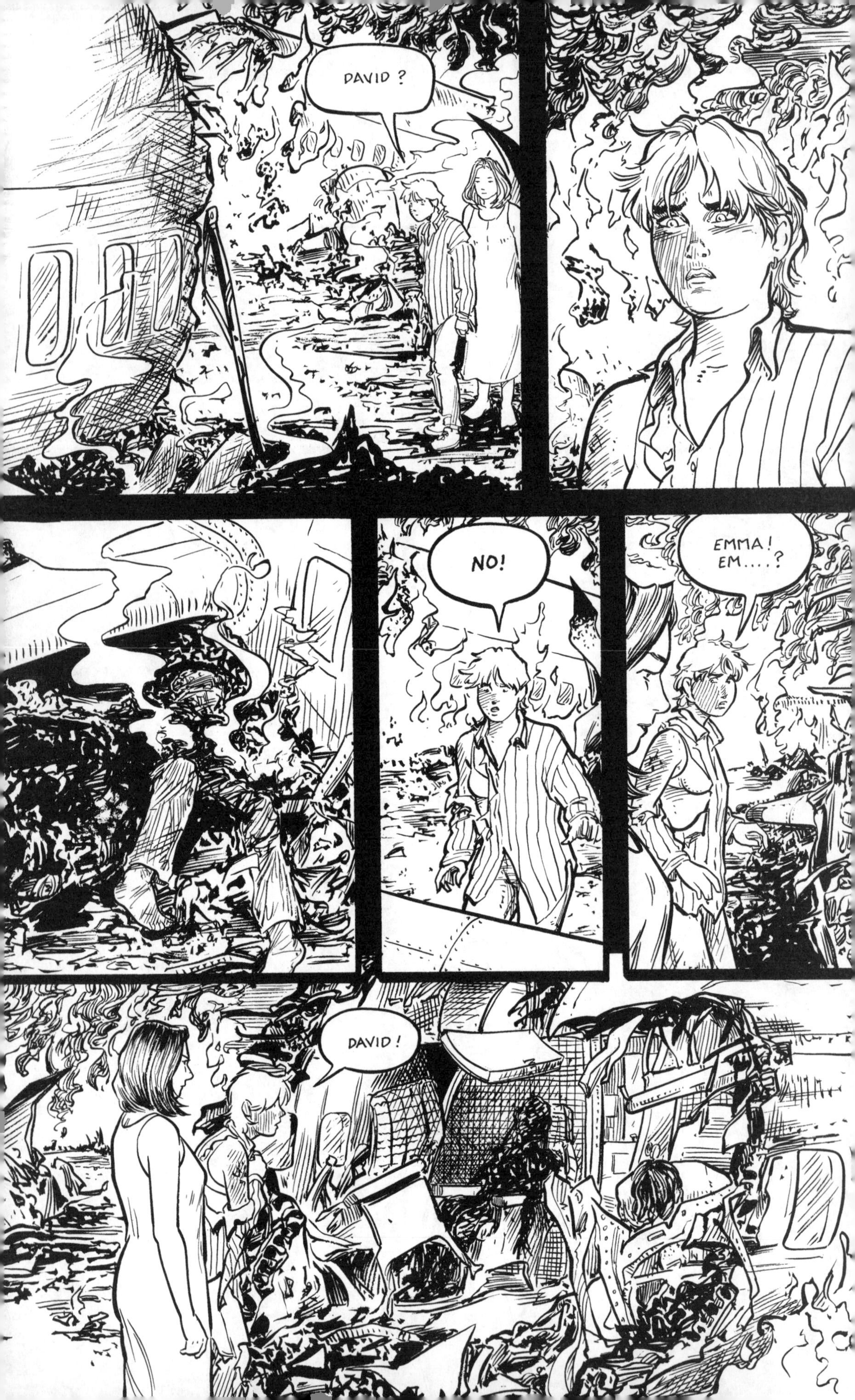
DAVID ?
NO!
EMMA!
EM....?
DAVID!

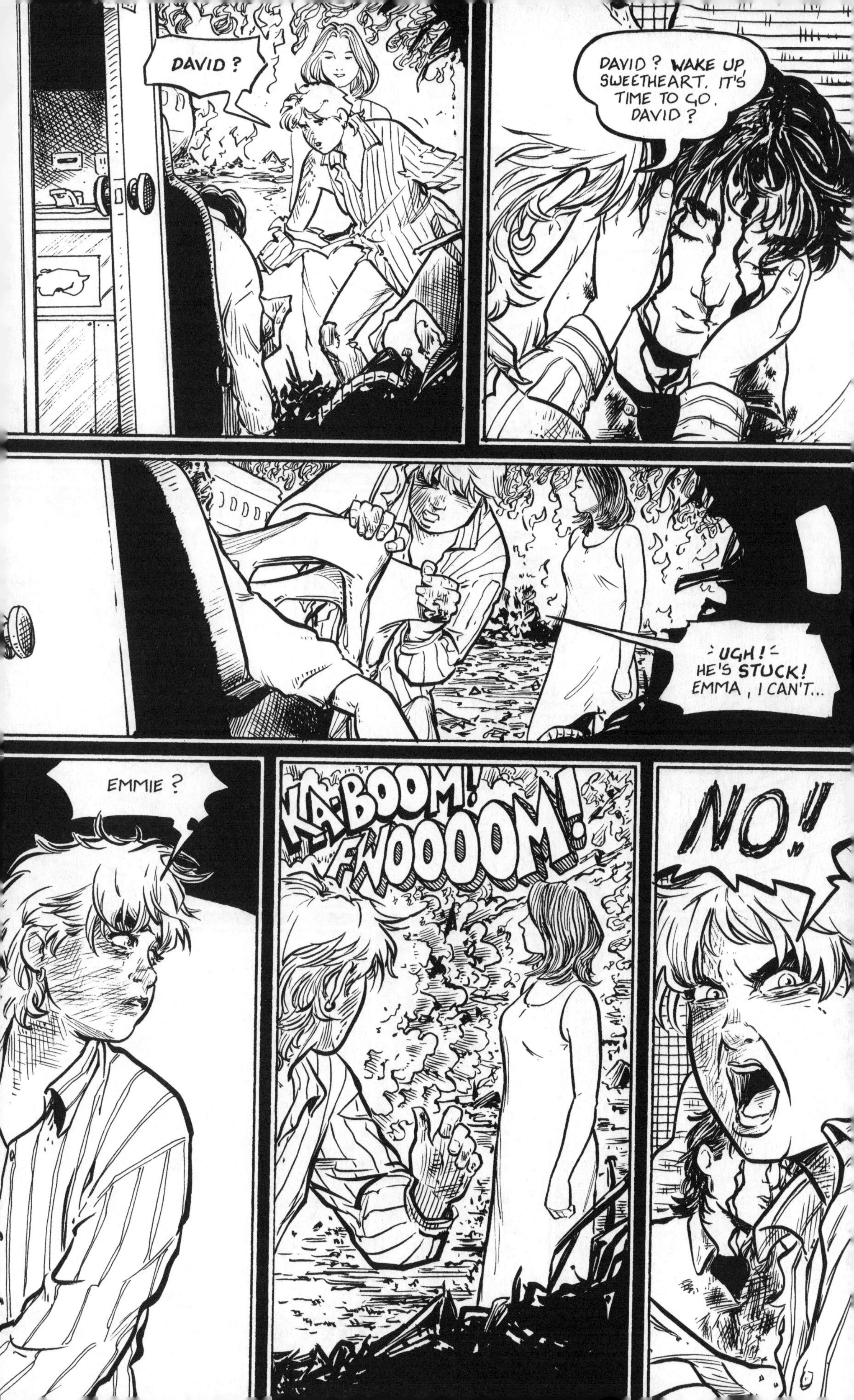
DAVID ?
DAVID ? WAKE UP, SWEETHEART. IT'S TIME TO GO. DAVID ?
UGH! HE'S STUCK! EMMA, I CAN'T...
EMMIE ?
KA-BOOM! FWOOOOM!
NO!!

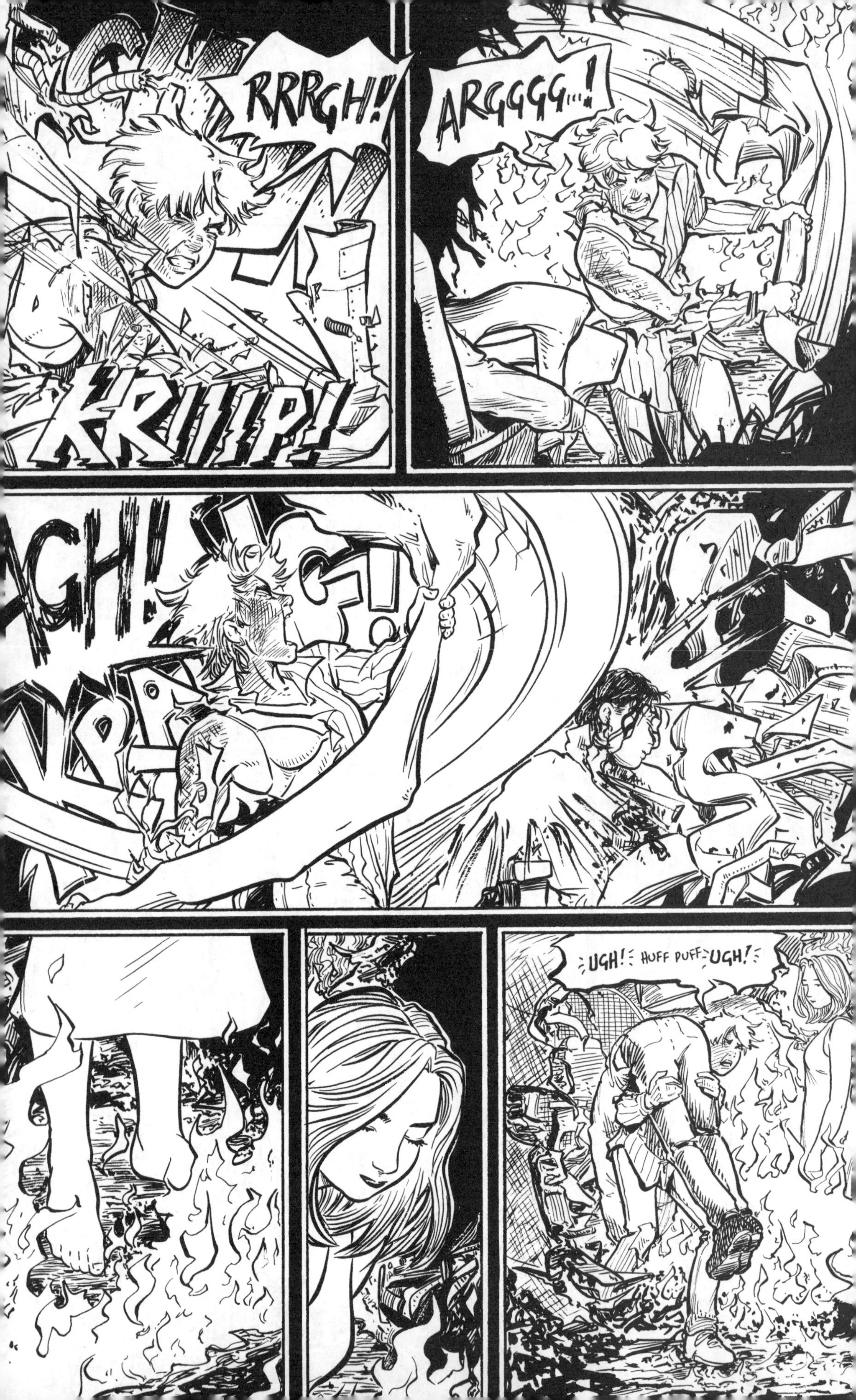
RRRGH!!
ARGGGG...!
KRIIIP!
UGH! HUFF PUFF UGH!

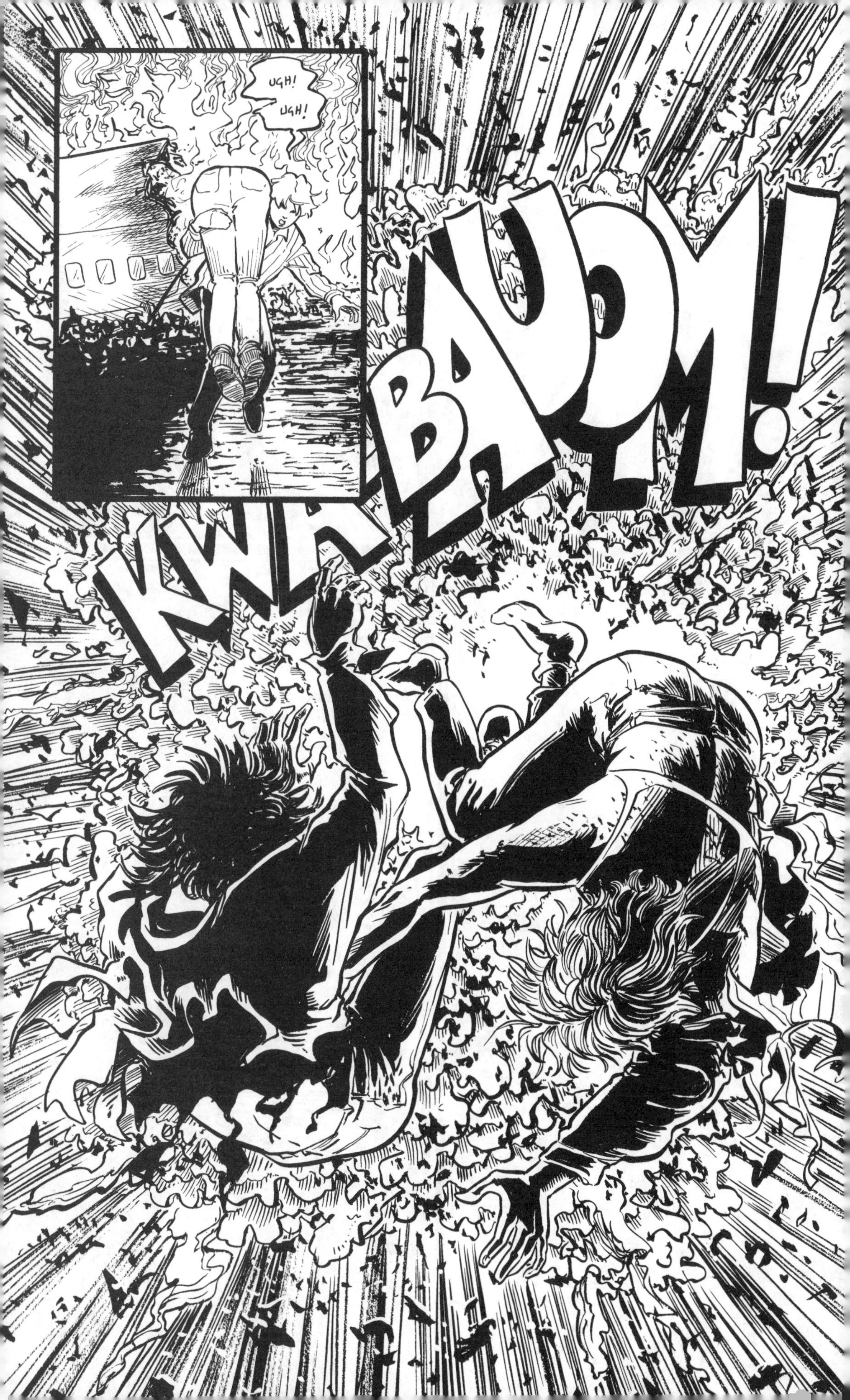
UGH!
UGH!
KWA-BAAOOM!

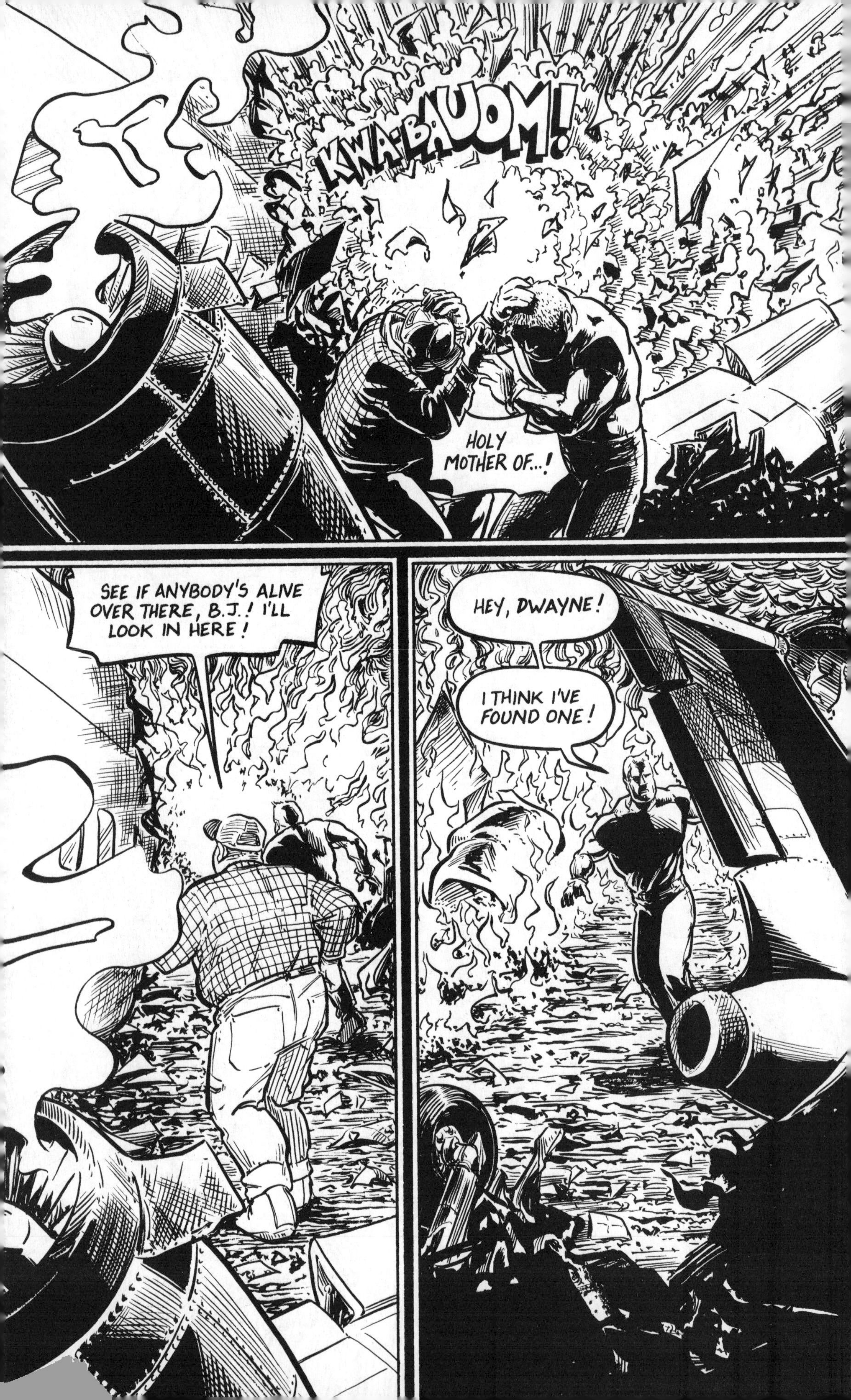
KWA-BAUOM!
HOLY MOTHER OF...!
SEE IF ANYBODY'S ALIVE OVER THERE, B.J.! I'LL LOOK IN HERE!
HEY, DWAYNE!
I THINK I'VE FOUND ONE!

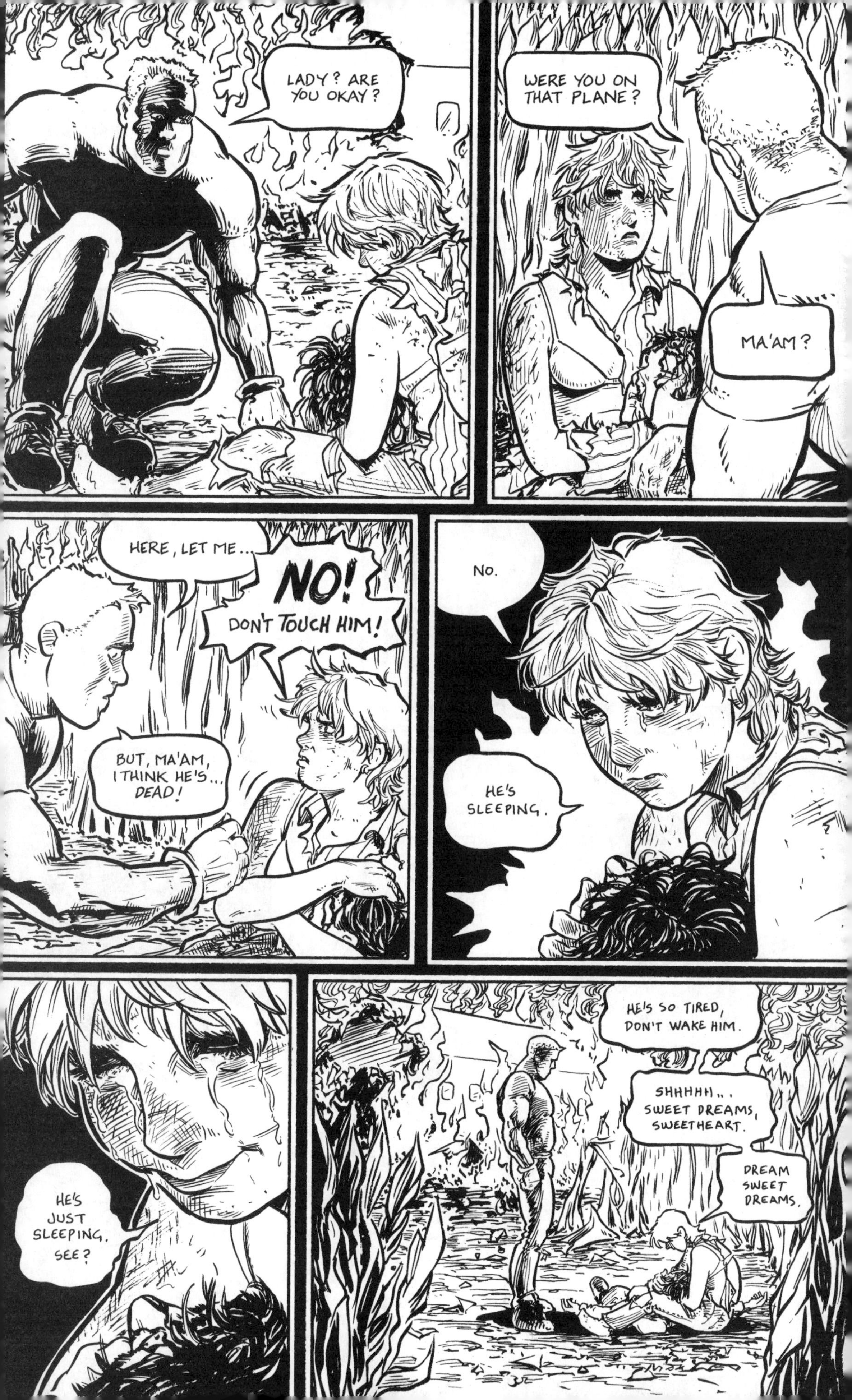
LADY? ARE YOU OKAY?
WERE YOU ON THAT PLANE?
MA'AM?
HERE, LET ME...
NO! DON'T TOUCH HIM!
BUT, MA'AM, I THINK HE'S... DEAD!
NO.
HE'S SLEEPING.
HE'S JUST SLEEPING. SEE?
HE'S SO TIRED, DON'T WAKE HIM.
SHHHHH.. SWEET DREAMS, SWEETHEART.
DREAM SWEET DREAMS.

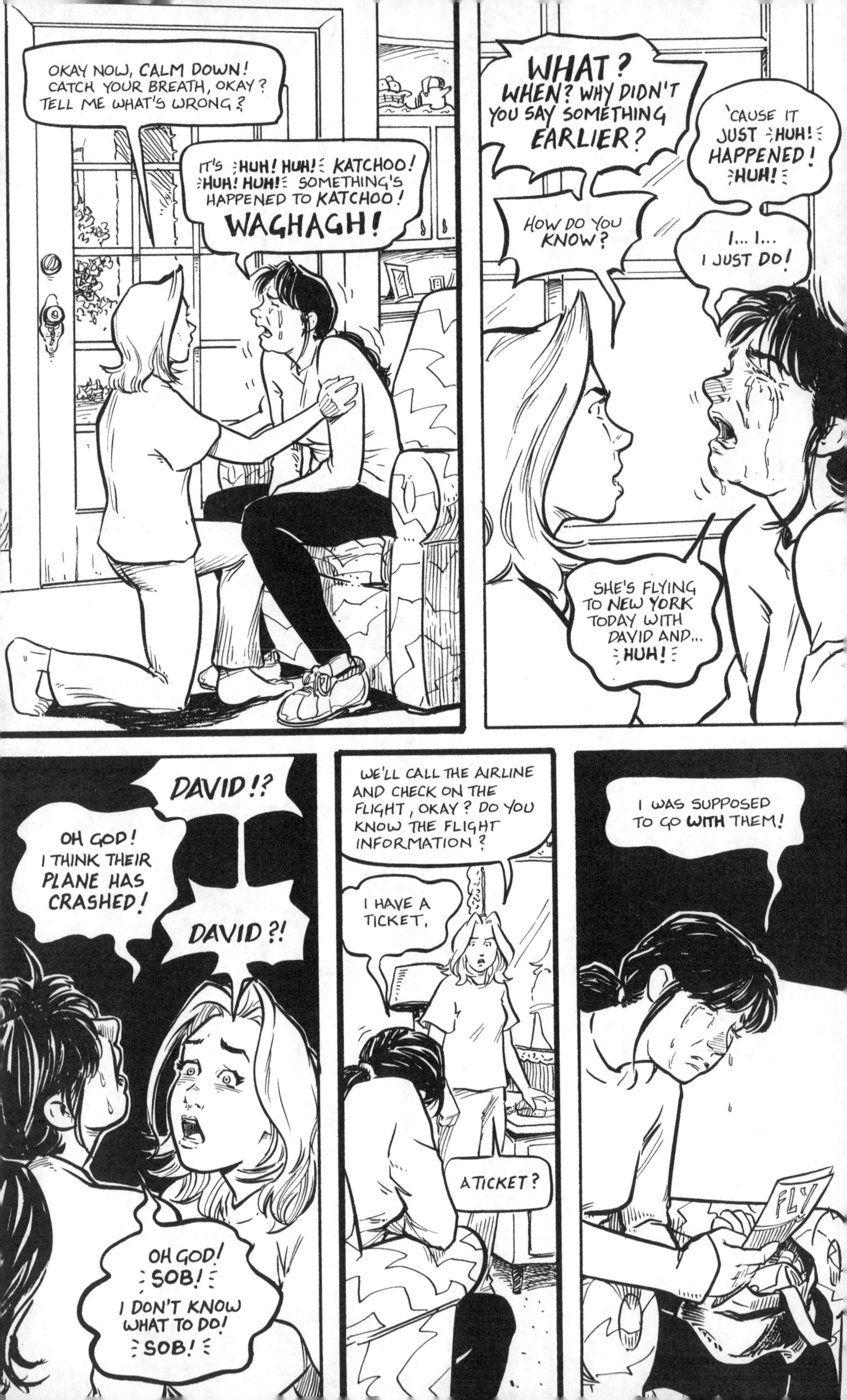
OKAY NOW, CALM DOWN! CATCH YOUR BREATH, OKAY? TELL ME WHAT'S WRONG?
IT'S HUH! HUH! KATCHOO! HUH! HUH! SOMETHING'S HAPPENED TO KATCHOO! WAGHAGH!
WHAT? WHEN? WHY DIDN'T YOU SAY SOMETHING EARLIER?
'CAUSE IT JUST HUH! HAPPENED! HUH!
HOW DO YOU KNOW?
I... I... I JUST DO!
SHE'S FLYING TO NEW YORK TODAY WITH DAVID AND... HUH!
OH GOD! I THINK THEIR PLANE HAS CRASHED!
DAVID!?
DAVID?!
OH GOD! SOB! I DON'T KNOW WHAT TO DO! SOB!
WE'LL CALL THE AIRLINE AND CHECK ON THE FLIGHT, OKAY? DO YOU KNOW THE FLIGHT INFORMATION?
I HAVE A TICKET.
A TICKET?
I WAS SUPPOSED TO GO WITH THEM!
FLY

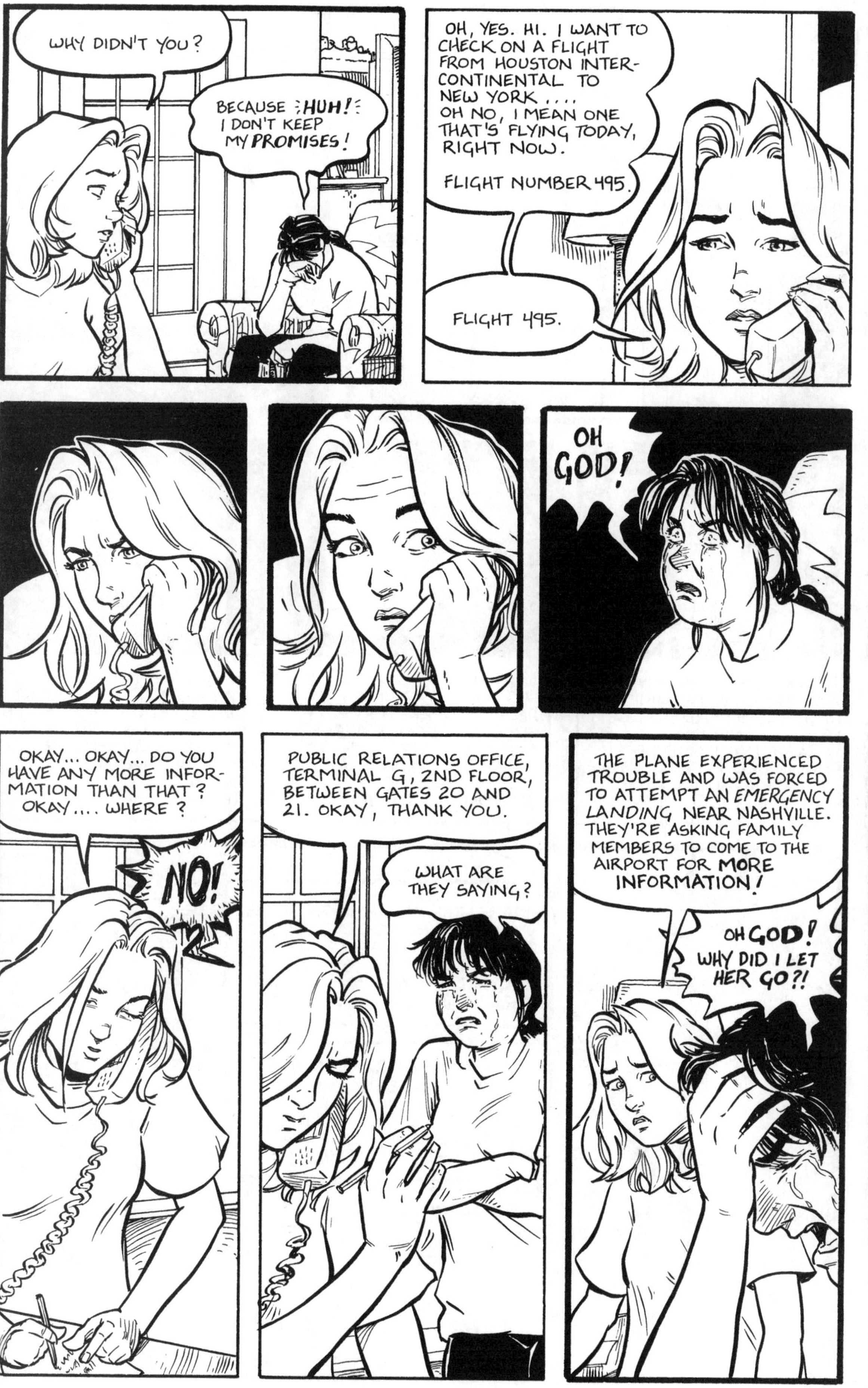
WHY DIDN'T YOU?
BECAUSE HUH! I DON'T KEEP MY PROMISES!
OH, YES. HI. I WANT TO CHECK ON A FLIGHT FROM HOUSTON INTER-CONTINENTAL TO NEW YORK....
OH NO, I MEAN ONE THAT'S FLYING TODAY, RIGHT NOW.
FLIGHT NUMBER 495.
FLIGHT 495.
OH GOD!
OKAY... OKAY... DO YOU HAVE ANY MORE INFOR-MATION THAN THAT? OKAY.... WHERE?
NO!
PUBLIC RELATIONS OFFICE, TERMINAL G, 2ND FLOOR, BETWEEN GATES 20 AND 21. OKAY, THANK YOU.
WHAT ARE THEY SAYING?
THE PLANE EXPERIENCED TROUBLE AND WAS FORCED TO ATTEMPT AN EMERGENCY LANDING NEAR NASHVILLE. THEY'RE ASKING FAMILY MEMBERS TO COME TO THE AIRPORT FOR MORE INFORMATION!
OH GOD! WHY DID I LET HER GO?!

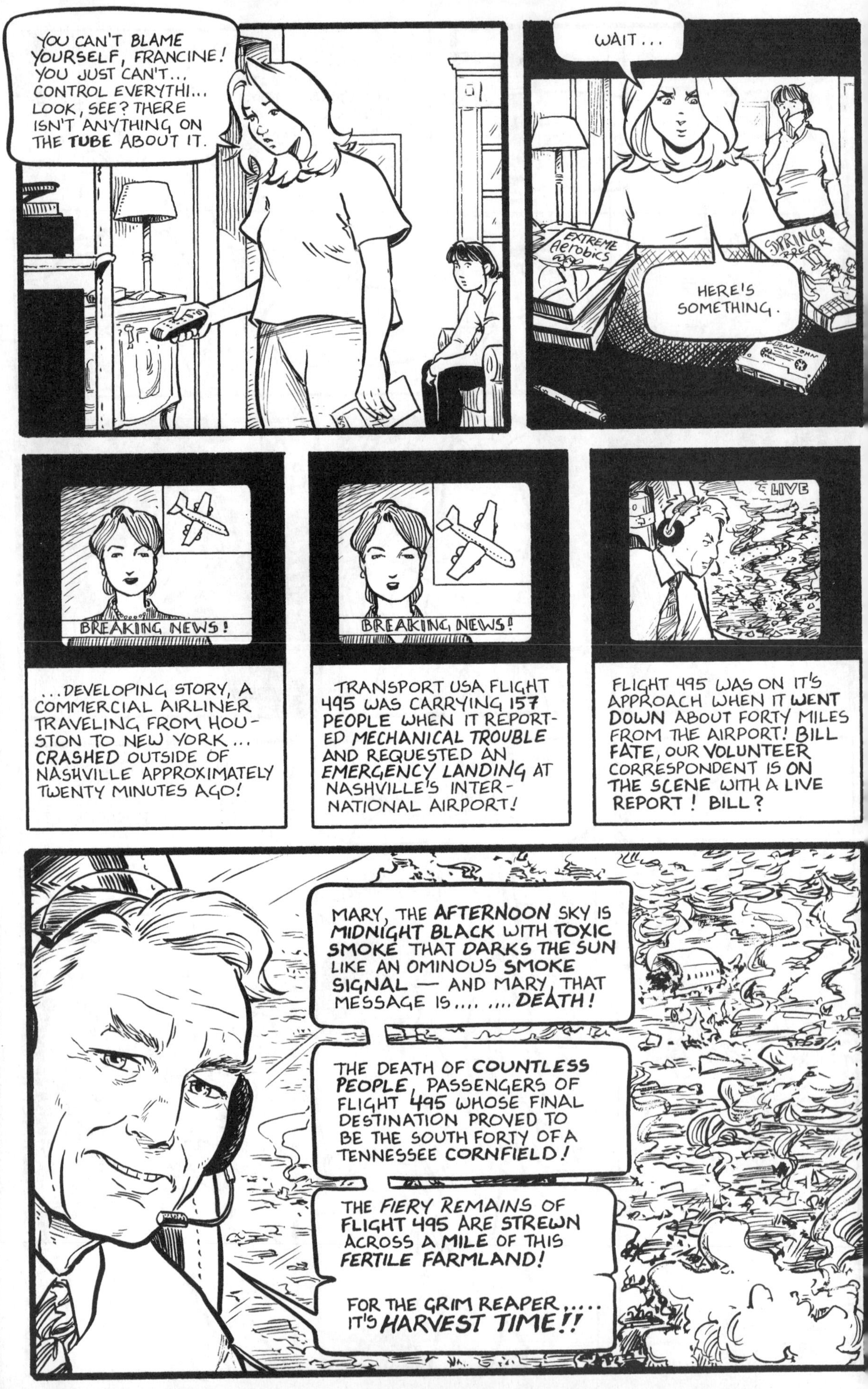
YOU CAN'T BLAME YOURSELF, FRANCINE! YOU JUST CAN'T... CONTROL EVERYTHI... LOOK, SEE? THERE ISN'T ANYTHING ON THE TUBE ABOUT IT.
WAIT...
EXTREME Aerobics
SPRING BREAK II
HERE'S SOMETHING.
BREAKING NEWS!
...DEVELOPING STORY, A COMMERCIAL AIRLINER TRAVELING FROM HOUSTON TO NEW YORK... CRASHED OUTSIDE OF NASHVILLE APPROXIMATELY TWENTY MINUTES AGO!
BREAKING NEWS!
TRANSPORT USA FLIGHT 495 WAS CARRYING 157 PEOPLE WHEN IT REPORTED MECHANICAL TROUBLE AND REQUESTED AN EMERGENCY LANDING AT NASHVILLE'S INTERNATIONAL AIRPORT!
LIVE
FLIGHT 495 WAS ON IT'S APPROACH WHEN IT WENT DOWN ABOUT FORTY MILES FROM THE AIRPORT! BILL FATE, OUR VOLUNTEER CORRESPONDENT IS ON THE SCENE WITH A LIVE REPORT! BILL?
MARY, THE AFTERNOON SKY IS MIDNIGHT BLACK WITH TOXIC SMOKE THAT DARKS THE SUN LIKE AN OMINOUS SMOKE SIGNAL — AND MARY, THAT MESSAGE IS.... ....DEATH!
THE DEATH OF COUNTLESS PEOPLE, PASSENGERS OF FLIGHT 495 WHOSE FINAL DESTINATION PROVED TO BE THE SOUTH FORTY OF A TENNESSEE CORNFIELD!
THE FIERY REMAINS OF FLIGHT 495 ARE STREWN ACROSS A MILE OF THIS FERTILE FARMLAND!
FOR THE GRIM REAPER..... IT'S HARVEST TIME!!

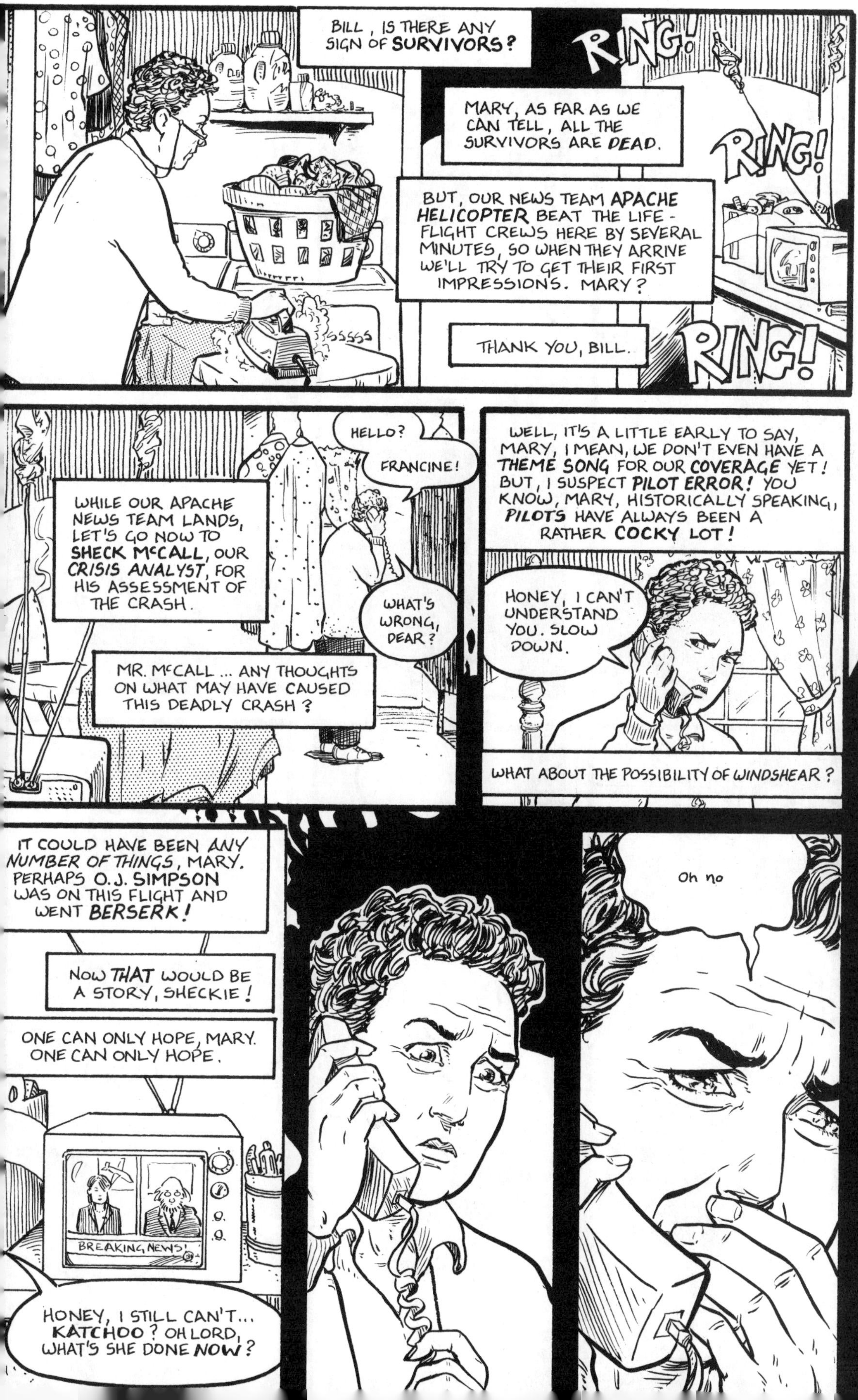
BILL, IS THERE ANY SIGN OF SURVIVORS?
RING!
MARY, AS FAR AS WE CAN TELL, ALL THE SURVIVORS ARE DEAD.
RING!
BUT, OUR NEWS TEAM APACHE HELICOPTER BEAT THE LIFE-FLIGHT CREWS HERE BY SEVERAL MINUTES, SO WHEN THEY ARRIVE WE'LL TRY TO GET THEIR FIRST IMPRESSIONS. MARY?
SSSSS
THANK YOU, BILL.
RING!
HELLO?
FRANCINE!
WHILE OUR APACHE NEWS TEAM LANDS, LET'S GO NOW TO SHECK McCALL, OUR CRISIS ANALYST, FOR HIS ASSESSMENT OF THE CRASH.
WHAT'S WRONG, DEAR?
MR. McCALL ... ANY THOUGHTS ON WHAT MAY HAVE CAUSED THIS DEADLY CRASH?
WELL, IT'S A LITTLE EARLY TO SAY, MARY, I MEAN, WE DON'T EVEN HAVE A THEME SONG FOR OUR COVERAGE YET! BUT, I SUSPECT PILOT ERROR! YOU KNOW, MARY, HISTORICALLY SPEAKING, PILOTS HAVE ALWAYS BEEN A RATHER COCKY LOT!
HONEY, I CAN'T UNDERSTAND YOU. SLOW DOWN.
WHAT ABOUT THE POSSIBILITY OF WINDSHEAR?
IT COULD HAVE BEEN ANY NUMBER OF THINGS, MARY. PERHAPS O.J. SIMPSON WAS ON THIS FLIGHT AND WENT BERSERK!
NOW THAT WOULD BE A STORY, SHECKIE!
ONE CAN ONLY HOPE, MARY. ONE CAN ONLY HOPE.
BREAKING NEWS!
HONEY, I STILL CAN'T... KATCHOO? OH LORD, WHAT'S SHE DONE NOW?
Oh no

RING!
RING!
RING!
YEAH.
WHAT?!

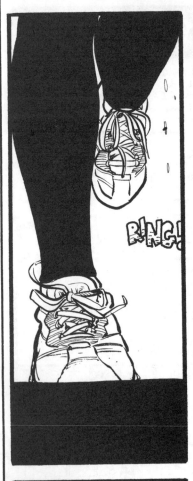

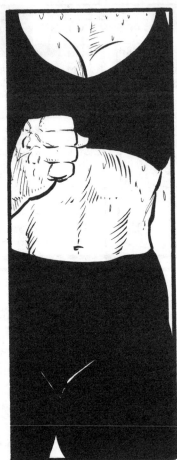

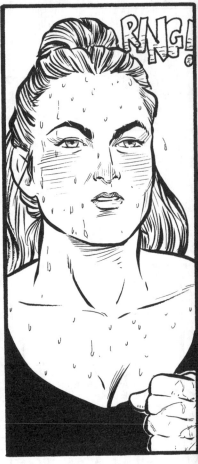

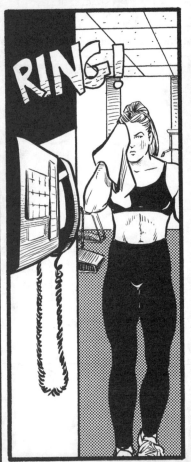

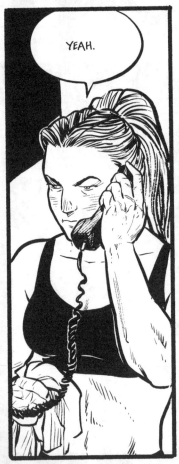

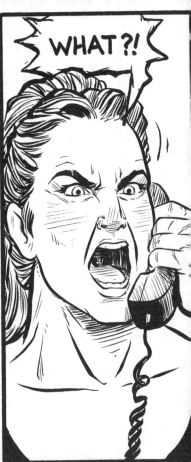

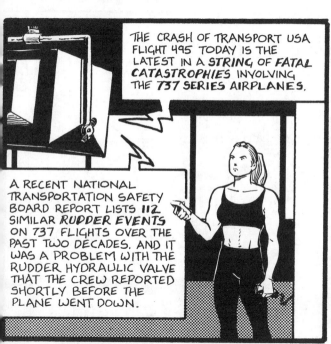

THE CRASH OF TRANSPORT USA FLIGHT 495 TODAY IS THE LATEST IN A **STRING OF FATAL CATASTROPHIES** INVOLVING THE **737 SERIES** AIRPLANES.

A RECENT NATIONAL TRANSPORTATION SAFETY BOARD REPORT LISTS 112 SIMILAR *RUDDER EVENTS* ON 737 FLIGHTS OVER THE PAST TWO DECADES. AND IT WAS A PROBLEM WITH THE RUDDER HYDRAULIC VALVE THAT THE CREW REPORTED SHORTLY BEFORE THE PLANE WENT DOWN.

TRANSPORT USA FLIGHT 495 WAS EN ROUTE FROM HOUSTON'S INTERCONTINENTAL AIRPORT TO **NEWARK** WHEN IT REQUESTED AN **EMERGENCY LANDING** IN NASHVILLE. TRAGICALLY, THE CRIPPLED PLANE CARRYING 157 PASSENGERS WENT DOWN SOME 40 MILES **WEST** OF NASHVILLE THIS AFTERNOON. EMERGENCY CREWS ON THE SCENE ARE LOOKING FOR ANY POSSIBLE SIGN OF **SURVIVORS.** BILL FATE, OUR MAN...

WHAT HAVE YOU DONE?

WHAT I HAVE DONE, DEAR *TAMBI*, IS ELIMINATE ALL OUR OBSTACLES IN ONE AFTERNOON. NICE, HUH?

I NEEDED THEM **ALIVE**! MR. **TUCCANNI** WAS SCHEDULED TO MEET WITH THEM TOMORROW AND MAKE THEM AN OFFER ON DARCY'S SHARE OF THE GROUP.

HA! TELL SAL HE CAN *KISS MY BUTT,* BLONDIE! I HAVE DARCY'S SHARE NOW!

I'M WARNING YOU, IF *CHOOVANSKI'S* DEAD...

SORRY, CAN'T CHAT NOW, I HAVE A LOT OF WORK TO CATCH UP ON. *BYE!*

≧CLICK!≦ BZZZZZZZ!

...YOU'RE DEAD.

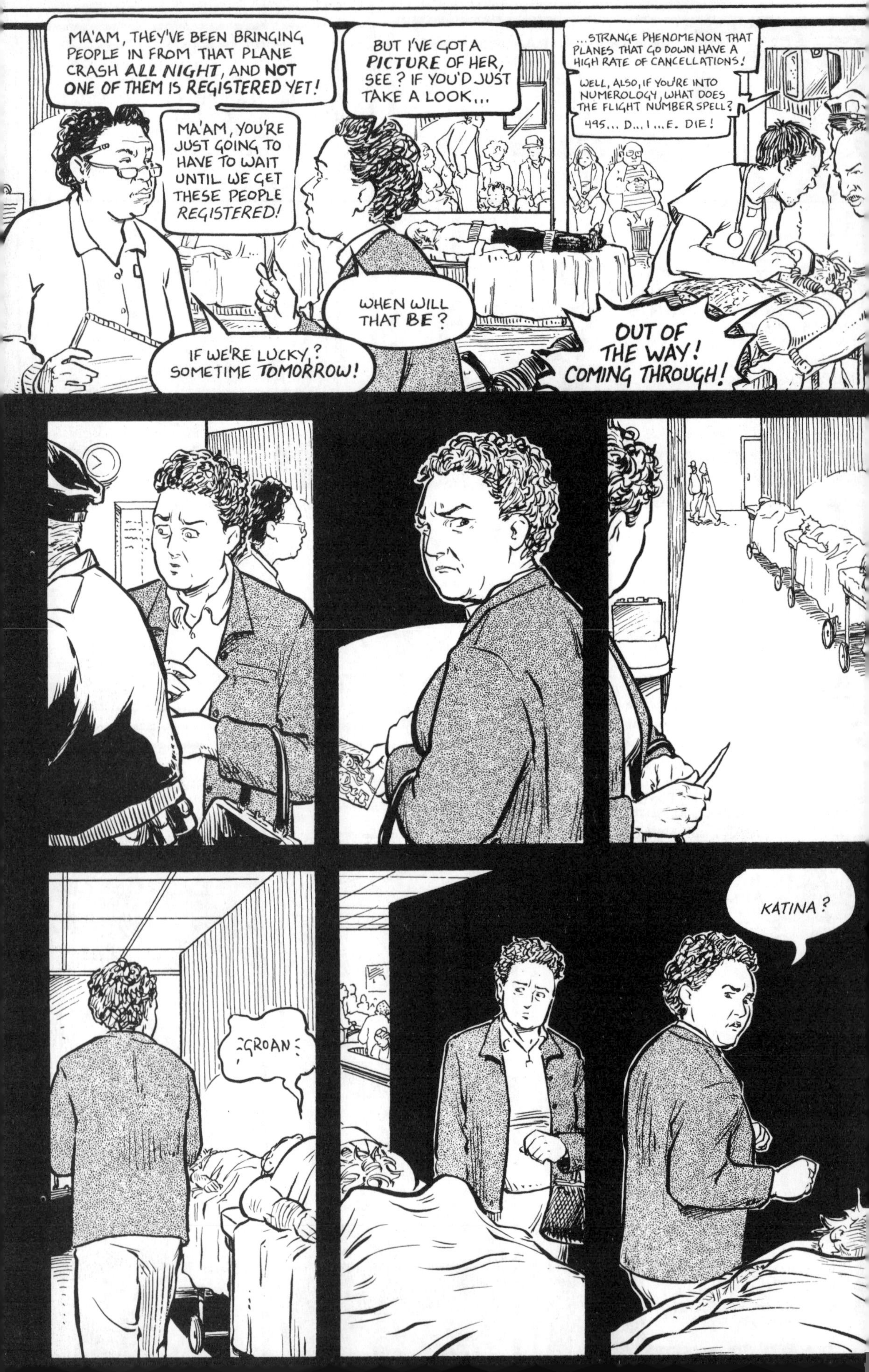
MA'AM, THEY'VE BEEN BRINGING PEOPLE IN FROM THAT PLANE CRASH ALL NIGHT, AND NOT ONE OF THEM IS REGISTERED YET!
MA'AM, YOU'RE JUST GOING TO HAVE TO WAIT UNTIL WE GET THESE PEOPLE REGISTERED!
BUT I'VE GOT A PICTURE OF HER, SEE? IF YOU'D JUST TAKE A LOOK...
...STRANGE PHENOMENON THAT PLANES THAT GO DOWN HAVE A HIGH RATE OF CANCELLATIONS!
WELL, ALSO, IF YOU'RE INTO NUMEROLOGY, WHAT DOES THE FLIGHT NUMBER SPELL?
495... D...I...E. DIE!
WHEN WILL THAT BE?
IF WE'RE LUCKY? SOMETIME TOMORROW!
OUT OF THE WAY! COMING THROUGH!
GROAN
KATINA?

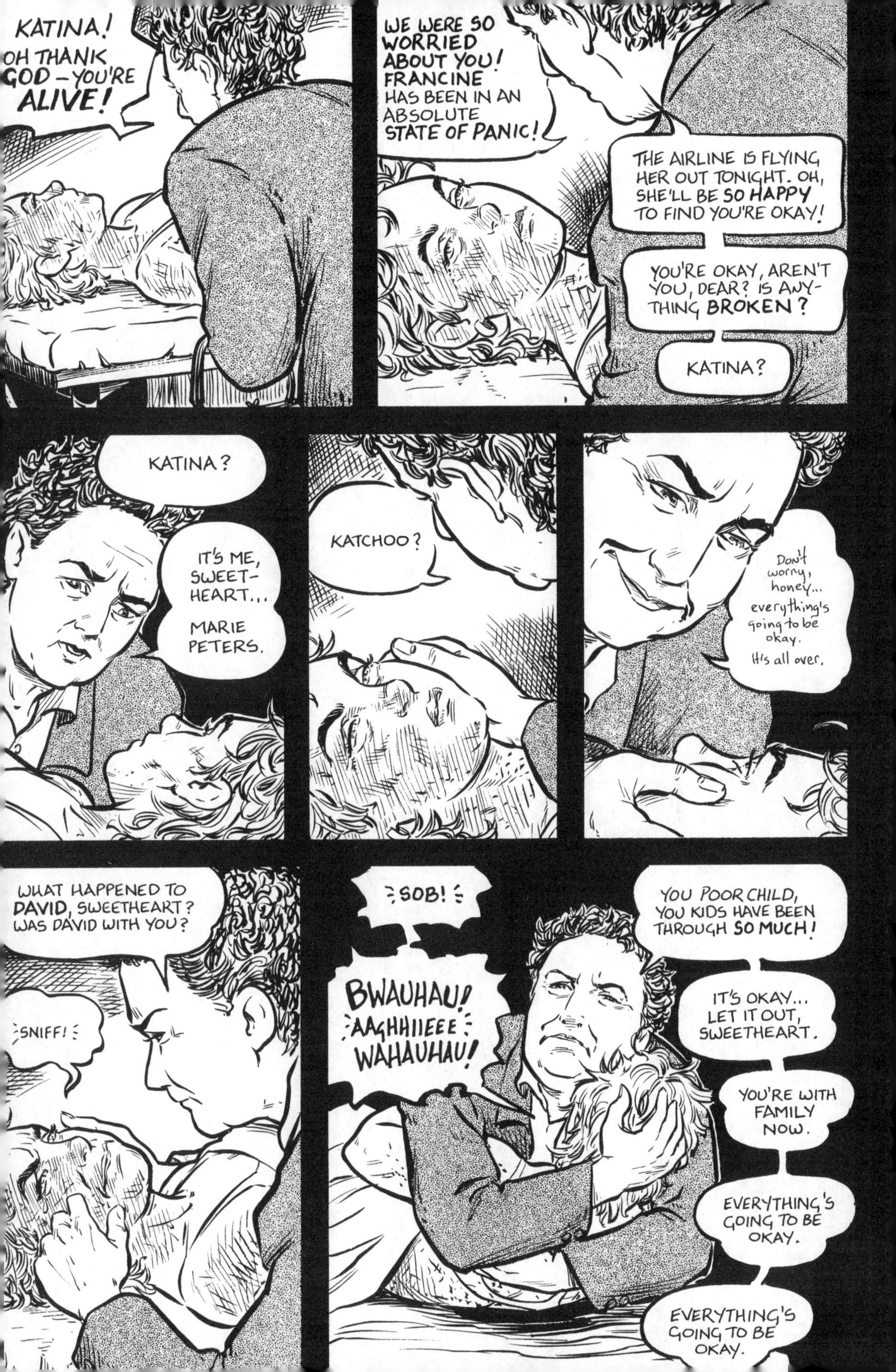
KATINA! OH THANK GOD — YOU'RE ALIVE!
WE WERE SO WORRIED ABOUT YOU! FRANCINE HAS BEEN IN AN ABSOLUTE STATE OF PANIC!
THE AIRLINE IS FLYING HER OUT TONIGHT. OH, SHE'LL BE SO HAPPY TO FIND YOU'RE OKAY!
YOU'RE OKAY, AREN'T YOU, DEAR? IS ANYTHING BROKEN?
KATINA?
KATINA?
IT'S ME, SWEETHEART... MARIE PETERS.
KATCHOO?
Don't worry, honey... everything's going to be okay. It's all over.
WHAT HAPPENED TO DAVID, SWEETHEART? WAS DAVID WITH YOU?
SNIFF!
SOB!
BWAUHAU! AAGHHIIEEE WAHAUHAU!
YOU POOR CHILD, YOU KIDS HAVE BEEN THROUGH SO MUCH!
IT'S OKAY... LET IT OUT, SWEETHEART.
YOU'RE WITH FAMILY NOW.
EVERYTHING'S GOING TO BE OKAY.
EVERYTHING'S GOING TO BE OKAY.

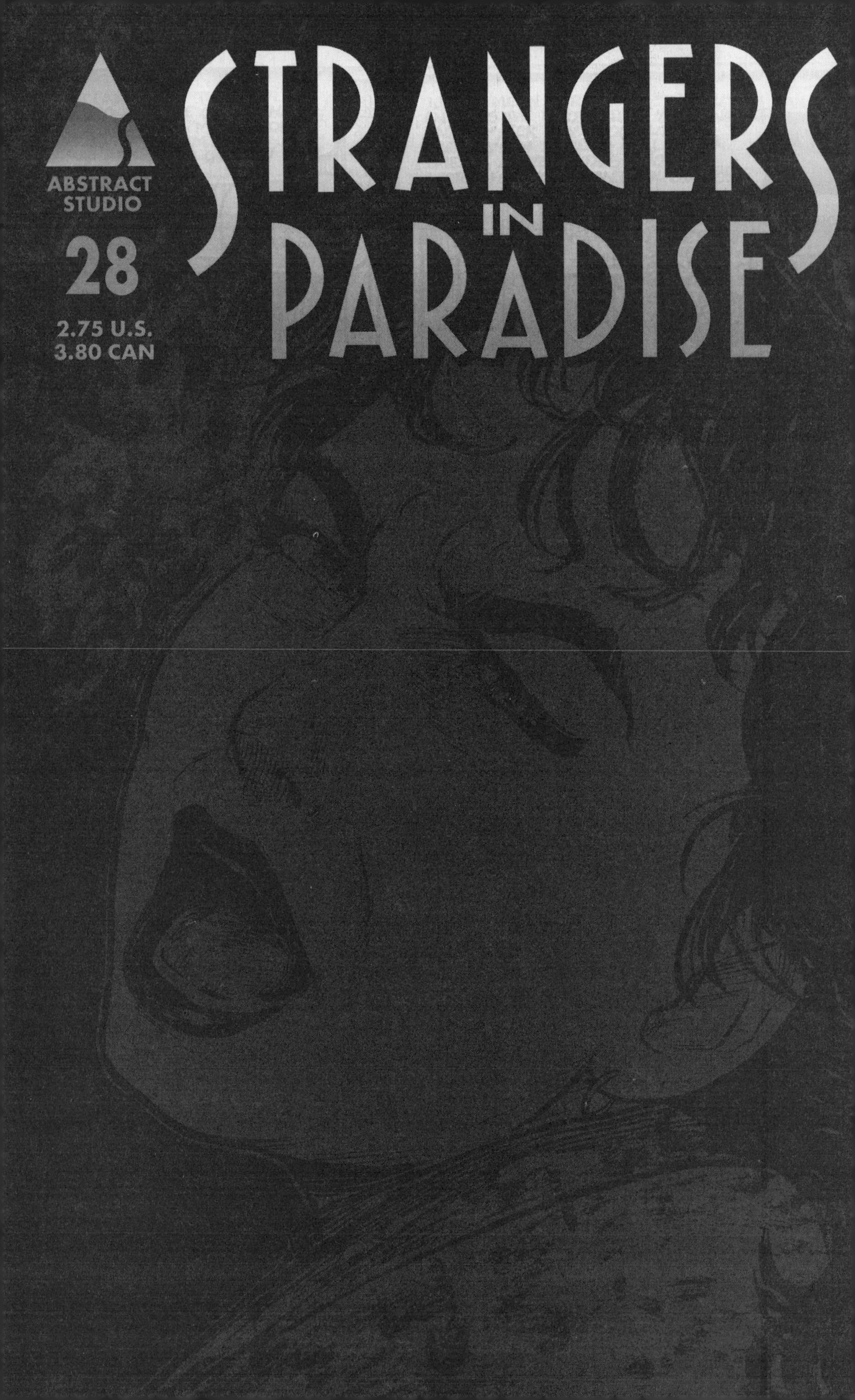
ABSTRACT
STUDIO
28
2.75 U.S.
3.80 CAN
STRANGERS
IN
PARADISE

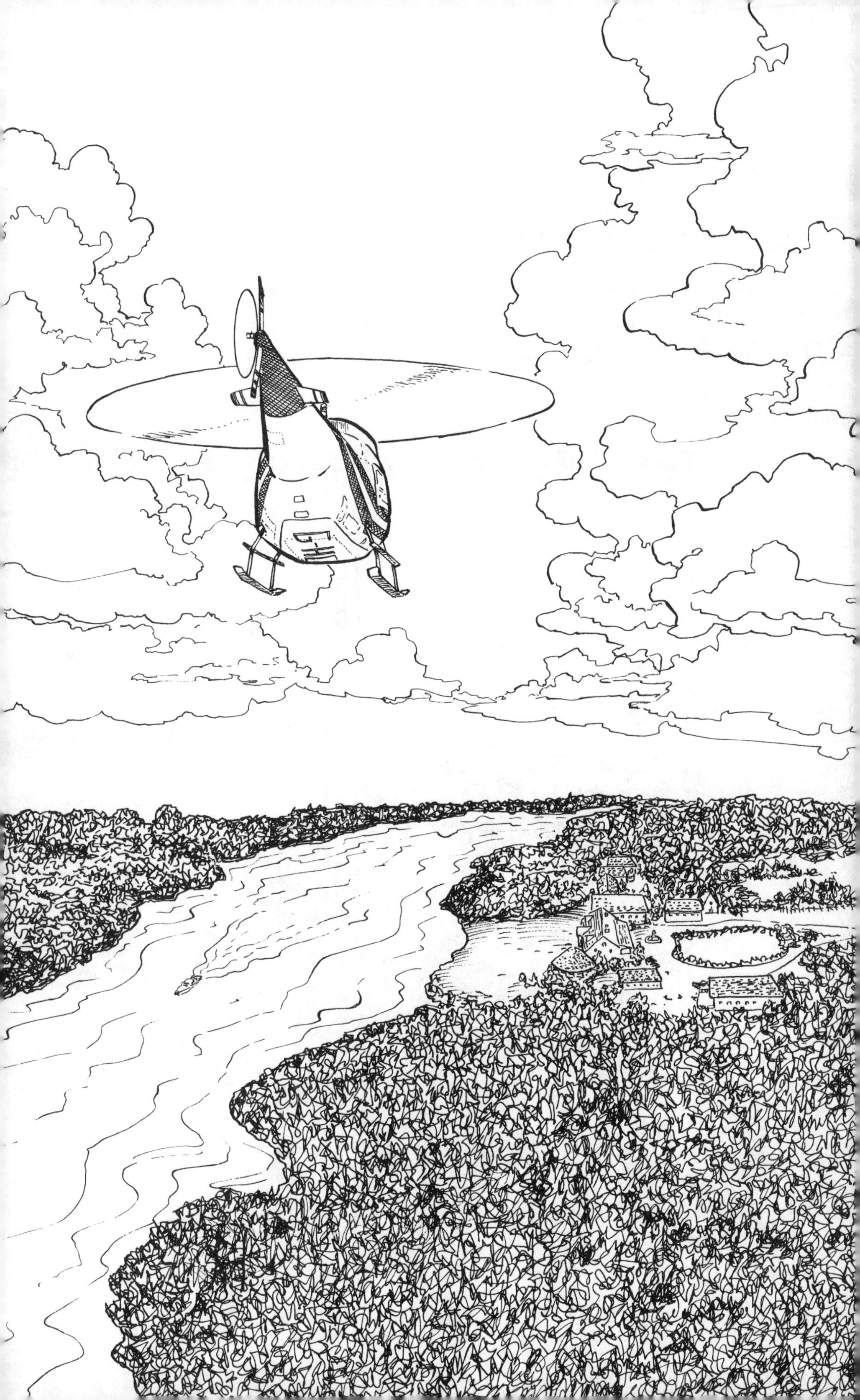

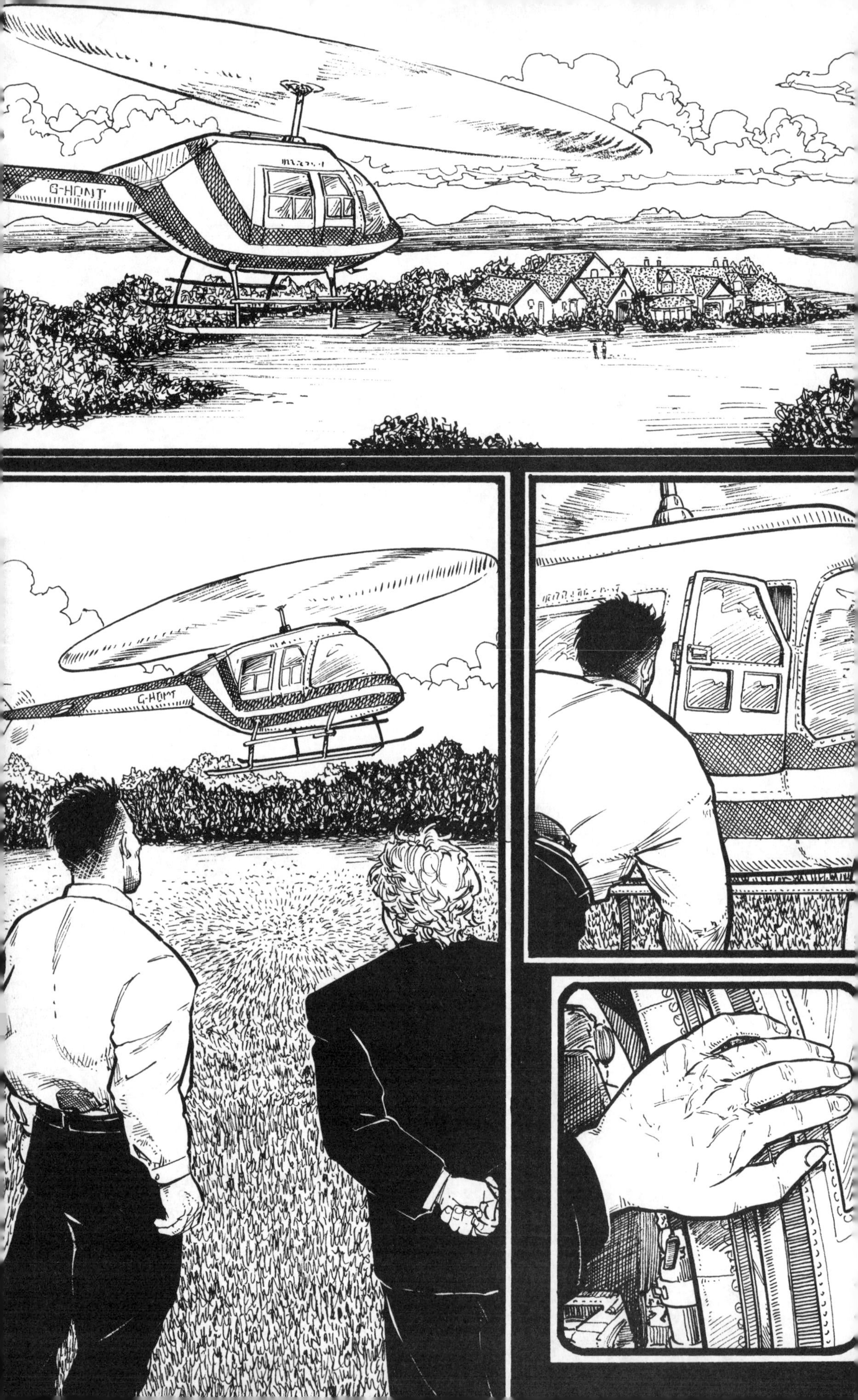
G-HONT

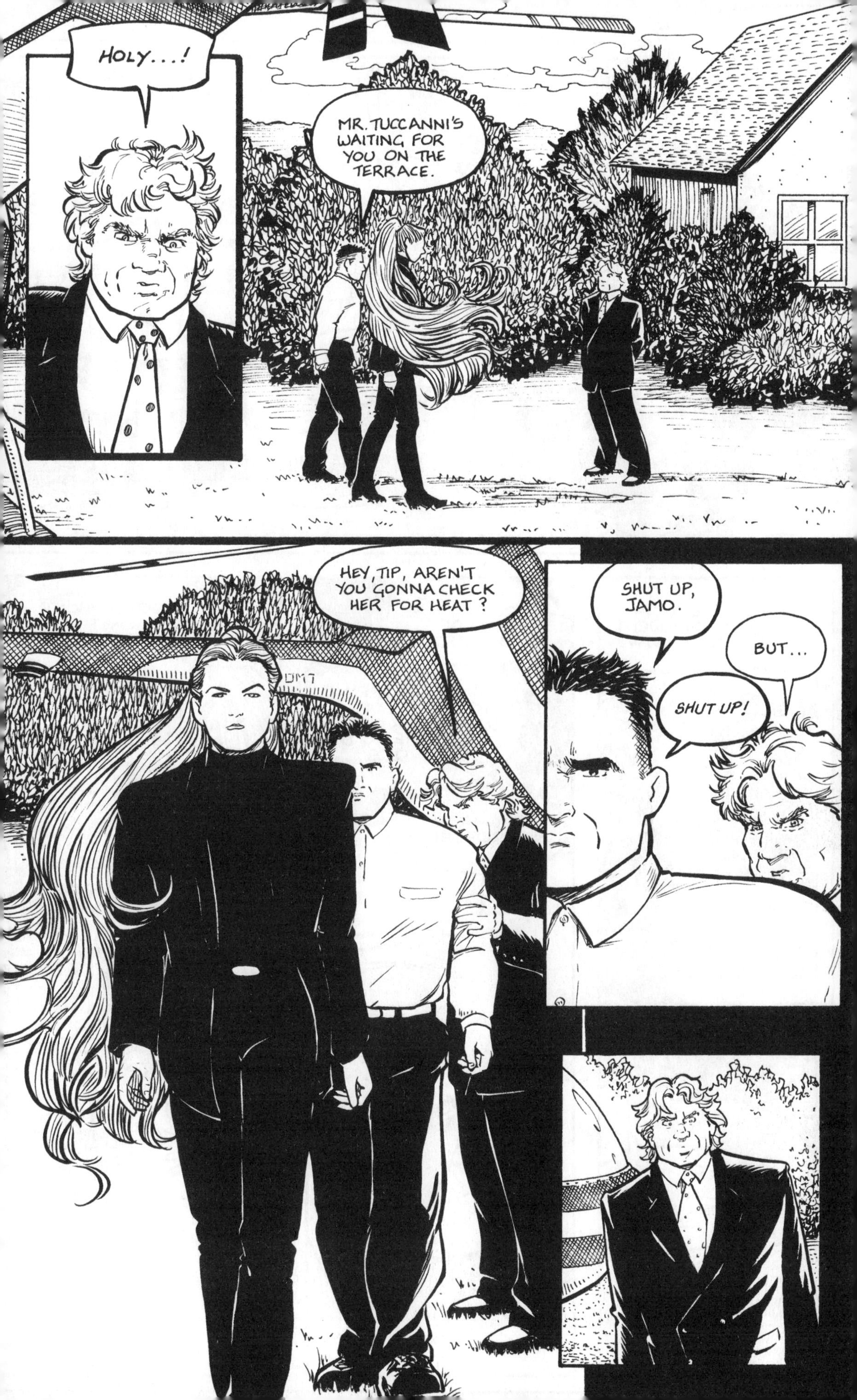
HOLY...!
MR. TUCCANNI'S WAITING FOR YOU ON THE TERRACE.
HEY, TIP, AREN'T YOU GONNA CHECK HER FOR HEAT?
SHUT UP, JAMO.
BUT...
SHUT UP!

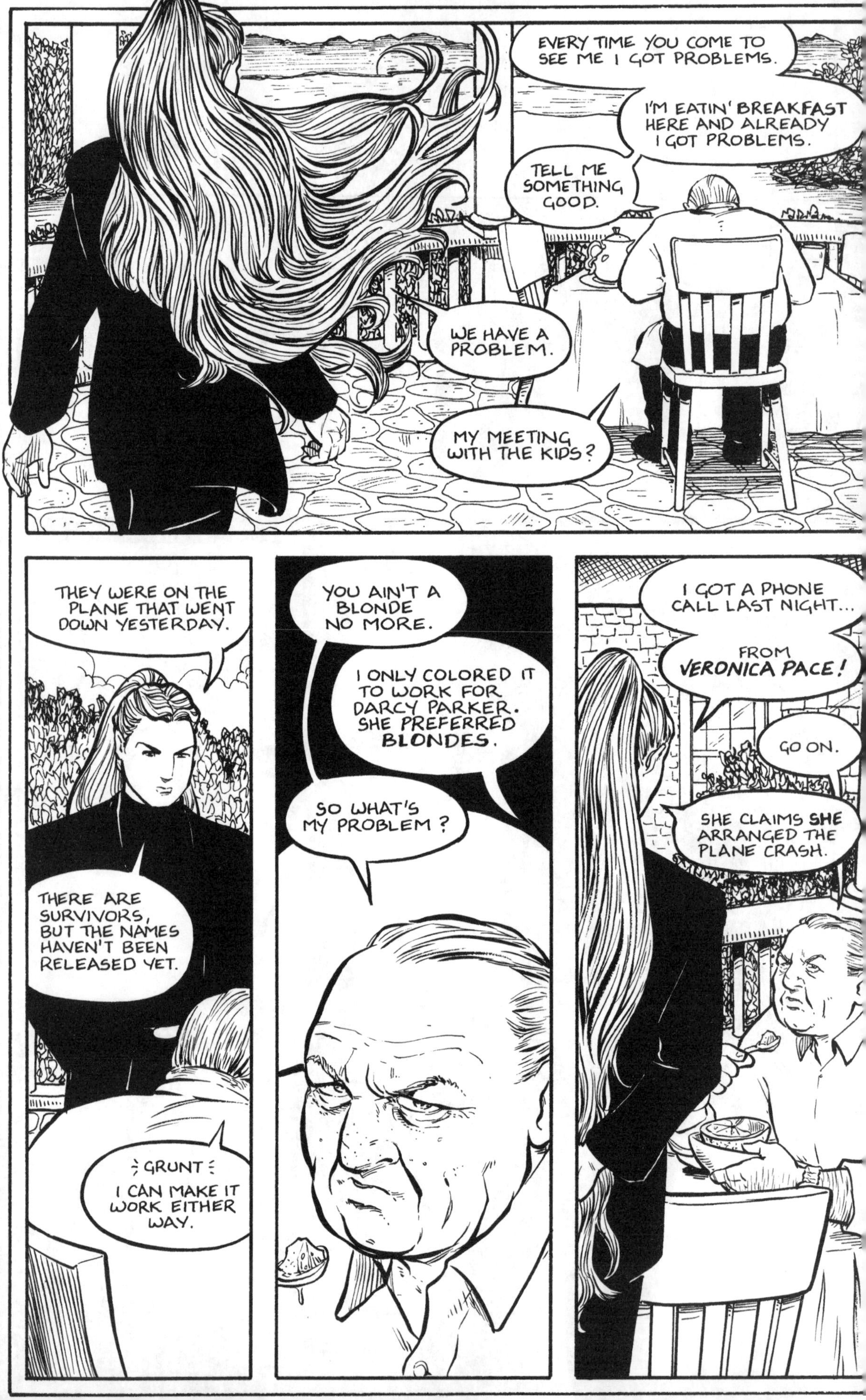
EVERY TIME YOU COME TO SEE ME I GOT PROBLEMS.
I'M EATIN' BREAKFAST HERE AND ALREADY I GOT PROBLEMS.
TELL ME SOMETHING GOOD.
WE HAVE A PROBLEM.
MY MEETING WITH THE KIDS?
THEY WERE ON THE PLANE THAT WENT DOWN YESTERDAY.
THERE ARE SURVIVORS, BUT THE NAMES HAVEN'T BEEN RELEASED YET.
GRUNT
I CAN MAKE IT WORK EITHER WAY.
YOU AIN'T A BLONDE NO MORE.
I ONLY COLORED IT TO WORK FOR DARCY PARKER. SHE PREFERRED BLONDES.
SO WHAT'S MY PROBLEM?
I GOT A PHONE CALL LAST NIGHT...
FROM VERONICA PACE!
GO ON.
SHE CLAIMS SHE ARRANGED THE PLANE CRASH.

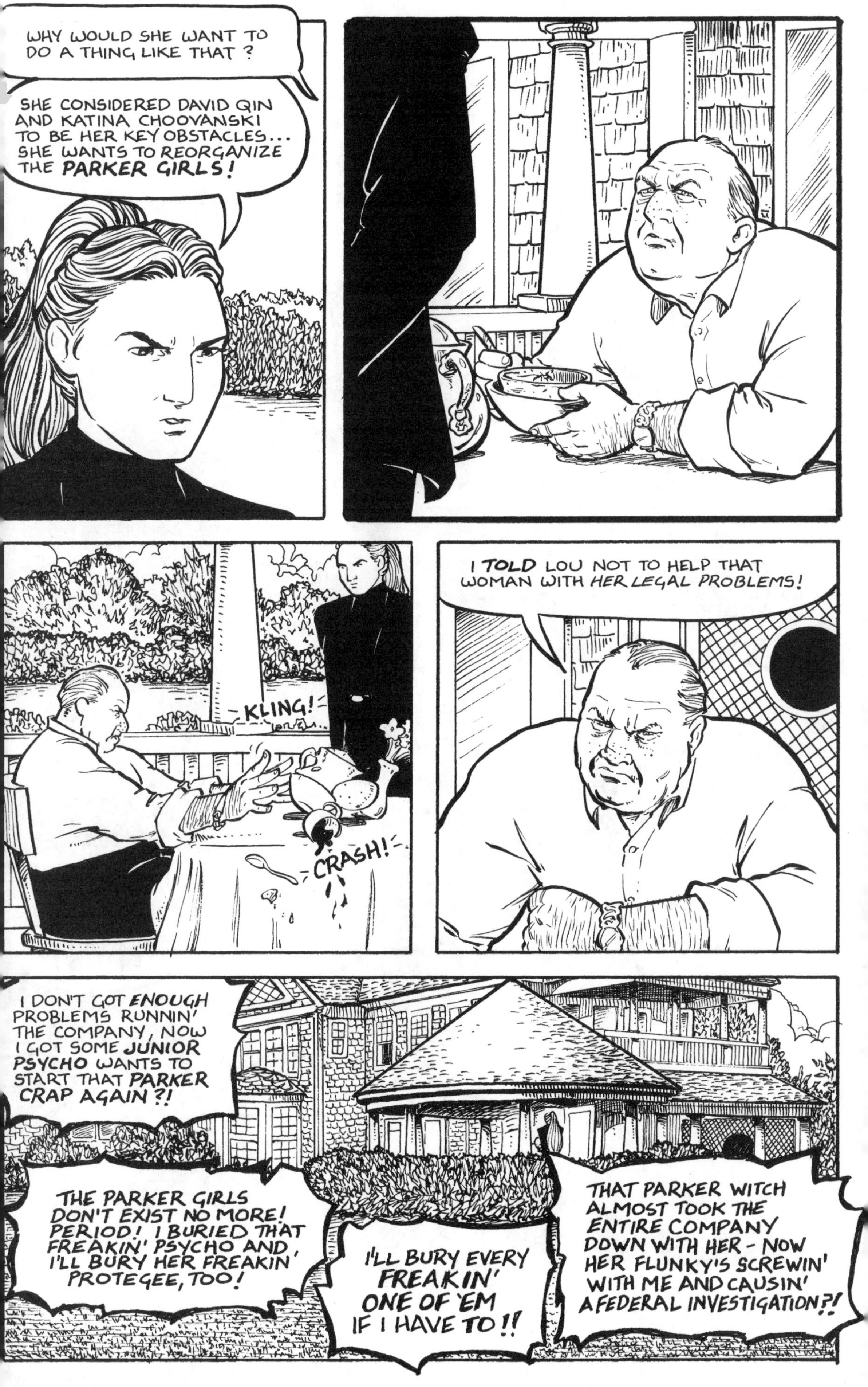

WHY WOULD SHE WANT TO DO A THING LIKE THAT ?
SHE CONSIDERED DAVID QIN AND KATINA CHOOVANSKI TO BE HER KEY OBSTACLES... SHE WANTS TO REORGANIZE THE PARKER GIRLS!
KLING!
CRASH!
I TOLD LOU NOT TO HELP THAT WOMAN WITH HER LEGAL PROBLEMS!
I DON'T GOT ENOUGH PROBLEMS RUNNIN' THE COMPANY, NOW I GOT SOME JUNIOR PSYCHO WANTS TO START THAT PARKER CRAP AGAIN ?!
THE PARKER GIRLS DON'T EXIST NO MORE! PERIOD! I BURIED THAT FREAKIN' PSYCHO AND, I'LL BURY HER FREAKIN' PROTEGEE, TOO!
I'LL BURY EVERY FREAKIN' ONE OF 'EM IF I HAVE TO!!
THAT PARKER WITCH ALMOST TOOK THE ENTIRE COMPANY DOWN WITH HER - NOW HER FLUNKY'S SCREWIN' WITH ME AND CAUSIN' A FEDERAL INVESTIGATION?!

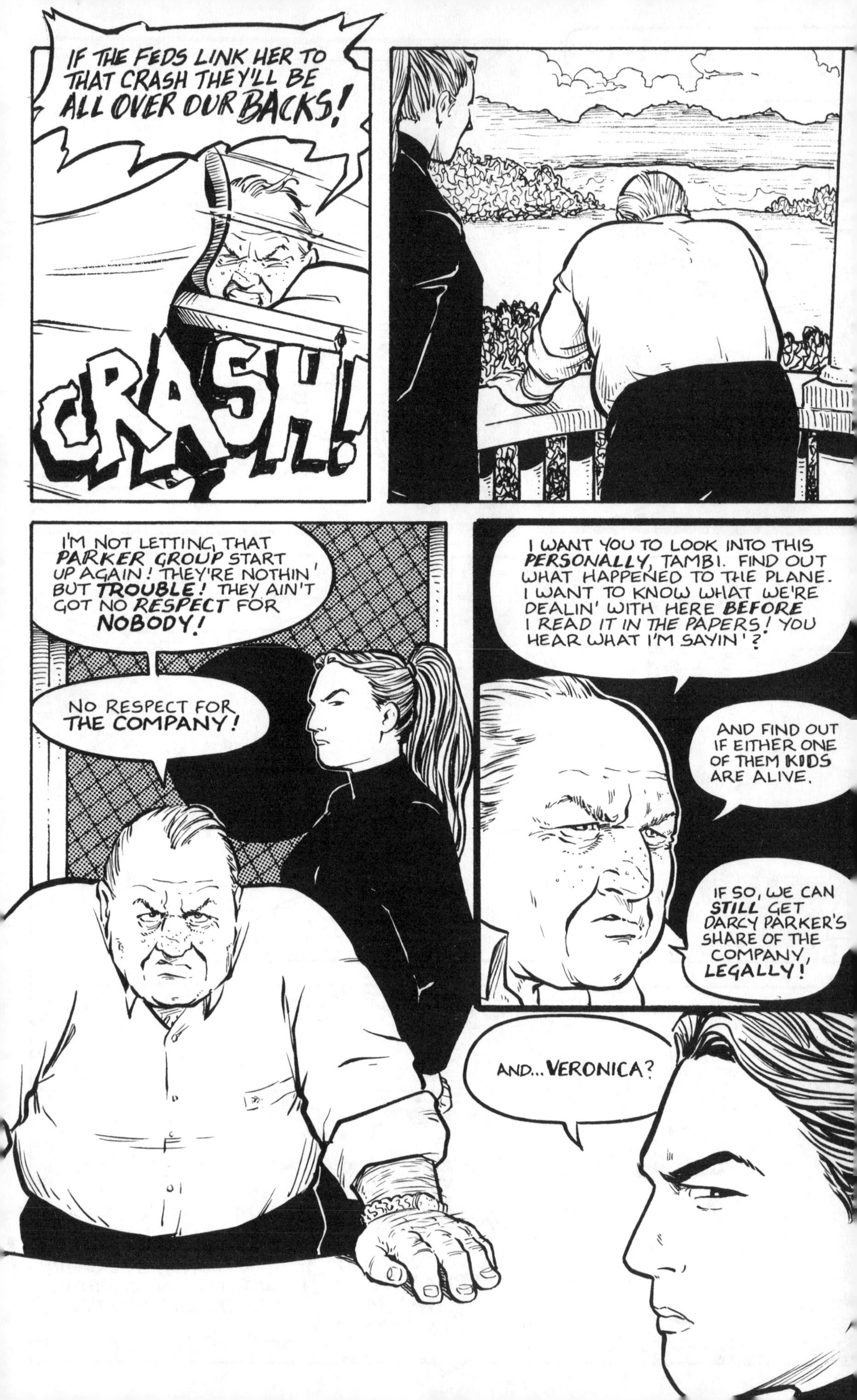
IF THE FEDS LINK HER TO THAT CRASH THEY'LL BE ALL OVER OUR BACKS!
CRASH!
I'M NOT LETTING THAT PARKER GROUP START UP AGAIN! THEY'RE NOTHIN' BUT TROUBLE! THEY AIN'T GOT NO RESPECT FOR NOBODY!
NO RESPECT FOR THE COMPANY!
I WANT YOU TO LOOK INTO THIS PERSONALLY, TAMBI. FIND OUT WHAT HAPPENED TO THE PLANE. I WANT TO KNOW WHAT WE'RE DEALIN' WITH HERE BEFORE I READ IT IN THE PAPERS! YOU HEAR WHAT I'M SAYIN'?
AND FIND OUT IF EITHER ONE OF THEM KIDS ARE ALIVE.
IF SO, WE CAN STILL GET DARCY PARKER'S SHARE OF THE COMPANY, LEGALLY!
AND... VERONICA?

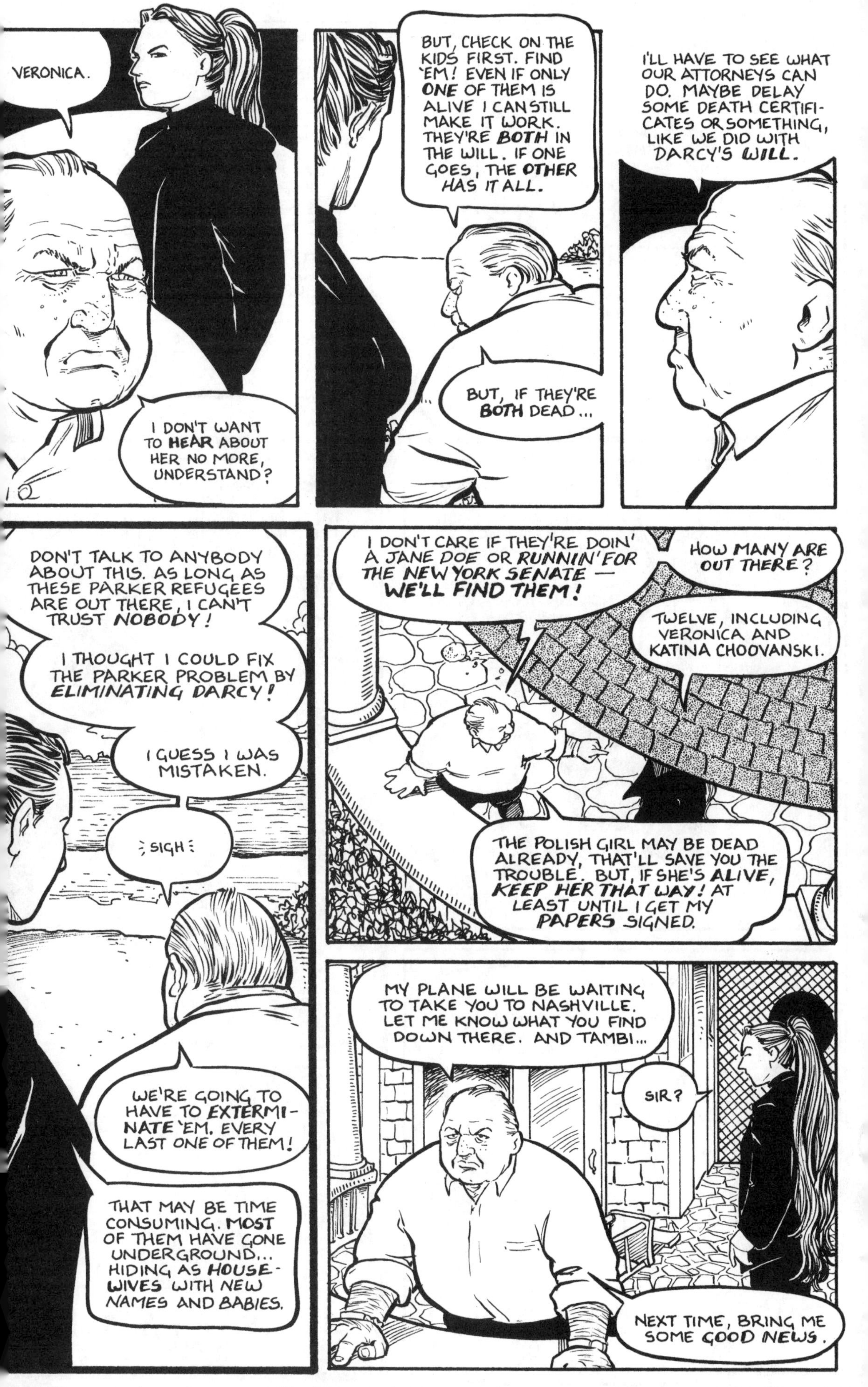

VERONICA.
I DON'T WANT TO HEAR ABOUT HER NO MORE, UNDERSTAND?
BUT, CHECK ON THE KIDS FIRST. FIND 'EM! EVEN IF ONLY ONE OF THEM IS ALIVE I CAN STILL MAKE IT WORK. THEY'RE BOTH IN THE WILL. IF ONE GOES, THE OTHER HAS IT ALL.
BUT, IF THEY'RE BOTH DEAD...
I'LL HAVE TO SEE WHAT OUR ATTORNEYS CAN DO. MAYBE DELAY SOME DEATH CERTIFICATES OR SOMETHING, LIKE WE DID WITH DARCY'S WILL.
DON'T TALK TO ANYBODY ABOUT THIS. AS LONG AS THESE PARKER REFUGEES ARE OUT THERE, I CAN'T TRUST NOBODY!
I THOUGHT I COULD FIX THE PARKER PROBLEM BY ELIMINATING DARCY!
I GUESS I WAS MISTAKEN.
SIGH
WE'RE GOING TO HAVE TO EXTERMINATE 'EM. EVERY LAST ONE OF THEM!
THAT MAY BE TIME CONSUMING. MOST OF THEM HAVE GONE UNDERGROUND... HIDING AS HOUSEWIVES WITH NEW NAMES AND BABIES.
I DON'T CARE IF THEY'RE DOIN' A JANE DOE OR RUNNIN' FOR THE NEW YORK SENATE — WE'LL FIND THEM!
HOW MANY ARE OUT THERE?
TWELVE, INCLUDING VERONICA AND KATINA CHOOVANSKI.
THE POLISH GIRL MAY BE DEAD ALREADY, THAT'LL SAVE YOU THE TROUBLE. BUT, IF SHE'S ALIVE, KEEP HER THAT WAY! AT LEAST UNTIL I GET MY PAPERS SIGNED.
MY PLANE WILL BE WAITING TO TAKE YOU TO NASHVILLE. LET ME KNOW WHAT YOU FIND DOWN THERE. AND TAMBI...
SIR?
NEXT TIME, BRING ME SOME GOOD NEWS.

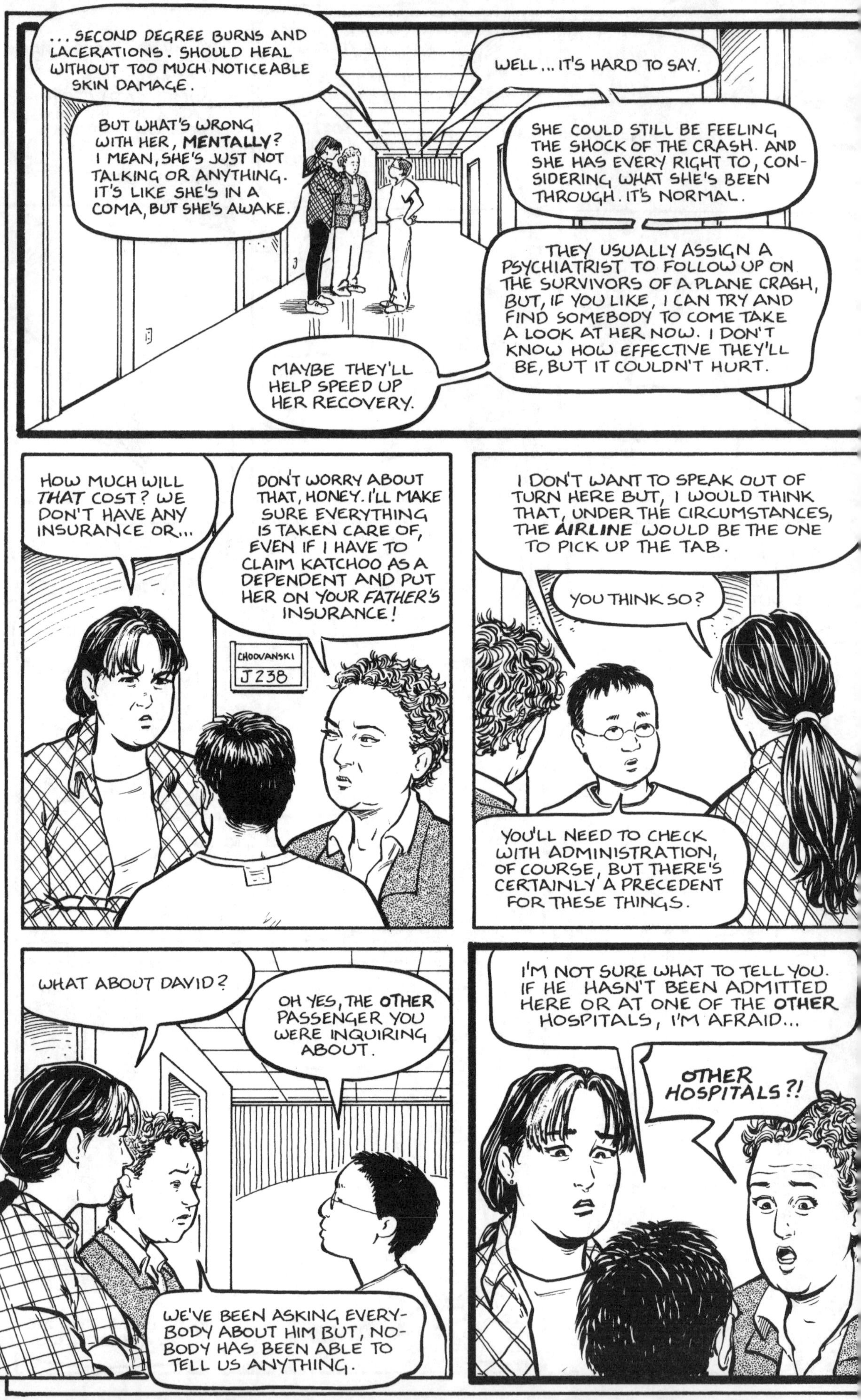

... SECOND DEGREE BURNS AND LACERATIONS. SHOULD HEAL WITHOUT TOO MUCH NOTICEABLE SKIN DAMAGE.
BUT WHAT'S WRONG WITH HER, MENTALLY? I MEAN, SHE'S JUST NOT TALKING OR ANYTHING. IT'S LIKE SHE'S IN A COMA, BUT SHE'S AWAKE.
WELL... IT'S HARD TO SAY.
SHE COULD STILL BE FEELING THE SHOCK OF THE CRASH. AND SHE HAS EVERY RIGHT TO, CONSIDERING WHAT SHE'S BEEN THROUGH. IT'S NORMAL.
THEY USUALLY ASSIGN A PSYCHIATRIST TO FOLLOW UP ON THE SURVIVORS OF A PLANE CRASH, BUT, IF YOU LIKE, I CAN TRY AND FIND SOMEBODY TO COME TAKE A LOOK AT HER NOW. I DON'T KNOW HOW EFFECTIVE THEY'LL BE, BUT IT COULDN'T HURT.
MAYBE THEY'LL HELP SPEED UP HER RECOVERY.
HOW MUCH WILL THAT COST? WE DON'T HAVE ANY INSURANCE OR...
DON'T WORRY ABOUT THAT, HONEY. I'LL MAKE SURE EVERYTHING IS TAKEN CARE OF, EVEN IF I HAVE TO CLAIM KATCHOO AS A DEPENDENT AND PUT HER ON YOUR FATHER'S INSURANCE!
CHOOVANSKI
J238
I DON'T WANT TO SPEAK OUT OF TURN HERE BUT, I WOULD THINK THAT, UNDER THE CIRCUMSTANCES, THE AIRLINE WOULD BE THE ONE TO PICK UP THE TAB.
YOU THINK SO?
YOU'LL NEED TO CHECK WITH ADMINISTRATION, OF COURSE, BUT THERE'S CERTAINLY A PRECEDENT FOR THESE THINGS.
WHAT ABOUT DAVID?
OH YES, THE OTHER PASSENGER YOU WERE INQUIRING ABOUT.
WE'VE BEEN ASKING EVERYBODY ABOUT HIM BUT, NOBODY HAS BEEN ABLE TO TELL US ANYTHING.
I'M NOT SURE WHAT TO TELL YOU. IF HE HASN'T BEEN ADMITTED HERE OR AT ONE OF THE OTHER HOSPITALS, I'M AFRAID...
OTHER HOSPITALS?!

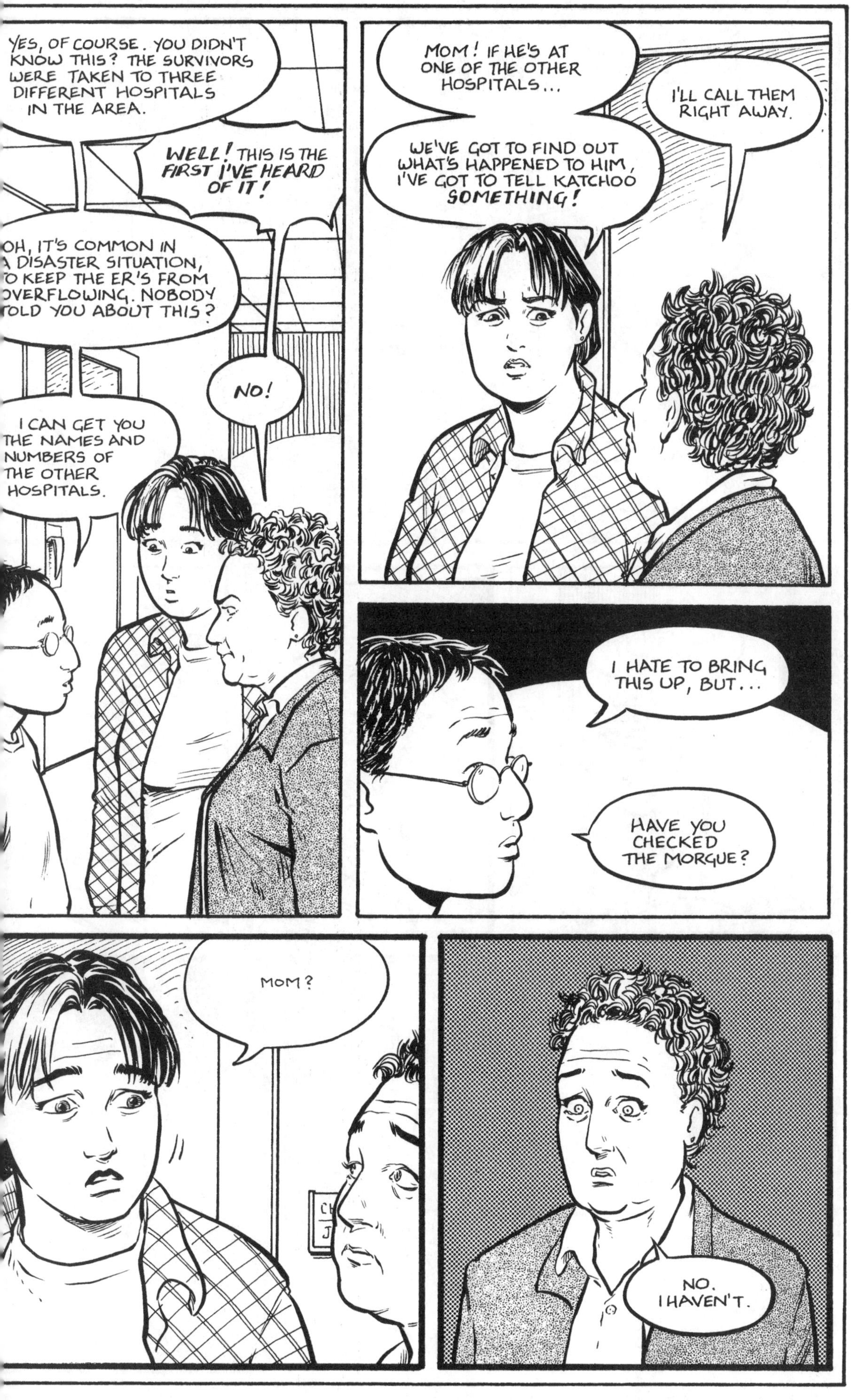
YES, OF COURSE. YOU DIDN'T KNOW THIS? THE SURVIVORS WERE TAKEN TO THREE DIFFERENT HOSPITALS IN THE AREA.
WELL! THIS IS THE FIRST I'VE HEARD OF IT!
OH, IT'S COMMON IN A DISASTER SITUATION, TO KEEP THE ER'S FROM OVERFLOWING. NOBODY TOLD YOU ABOUT THIS?
NO!
I CAN GET YOU THE NAMES AND NUMBERS OF THE OTHER HOSPITALS.
MOM! IF HE'S AT ONE OF THE OTHER HOSPITALS...
WE'VE GOT TO FIND OUT WHAT'S HAPPENED TO HIM, I'VE GOT TO TELL KATCHOO SOMETHING!
I'LL CALL THEM RIGHT AWAY.
I HATE TO BRING THIS UP, BUT...
HAVE YOU CHECKED THE MORGUE?
MOM?
NO. I HAVEN'T.

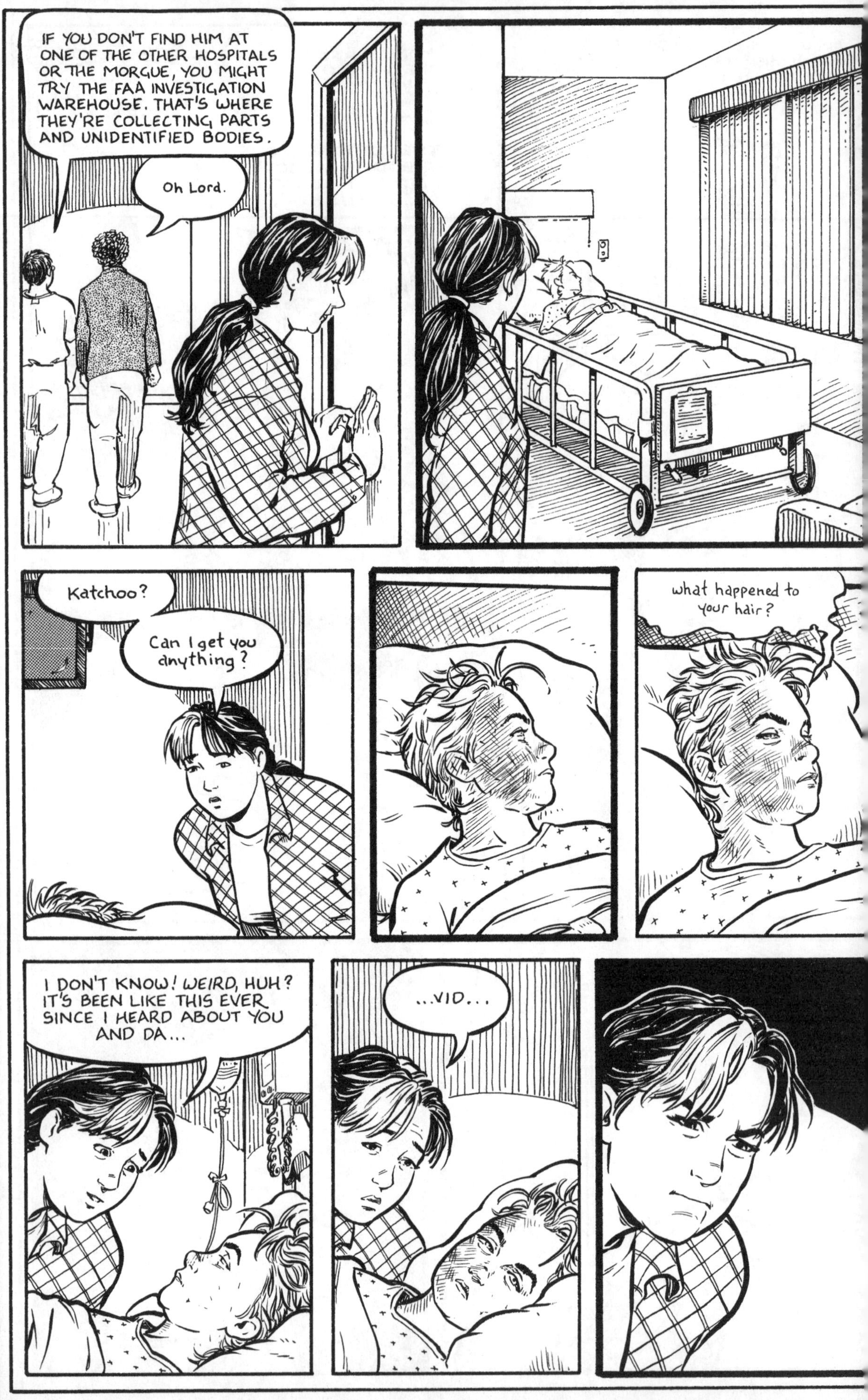
IF YOU DON'T FIND HIM AT ONE OF THE OTHER HOSPITALS OR THE MORGUE, YOU MIGHT TRY THE FAA INVESTIGATION WAREHOUSE. THAT'S WHERE THEY'RE COLLECTING PARTS AND UNIDENTIFIED BODIES.
Oh Lord.
Katchoo?
Can I get you anything?
...
what happened to your hair?
I DON'T KNOW! WEIRD, HUH? IT'S BEEN LIKE THIS EVER SINCE I HEARD ABOUT YOU AND DA...
...VID...

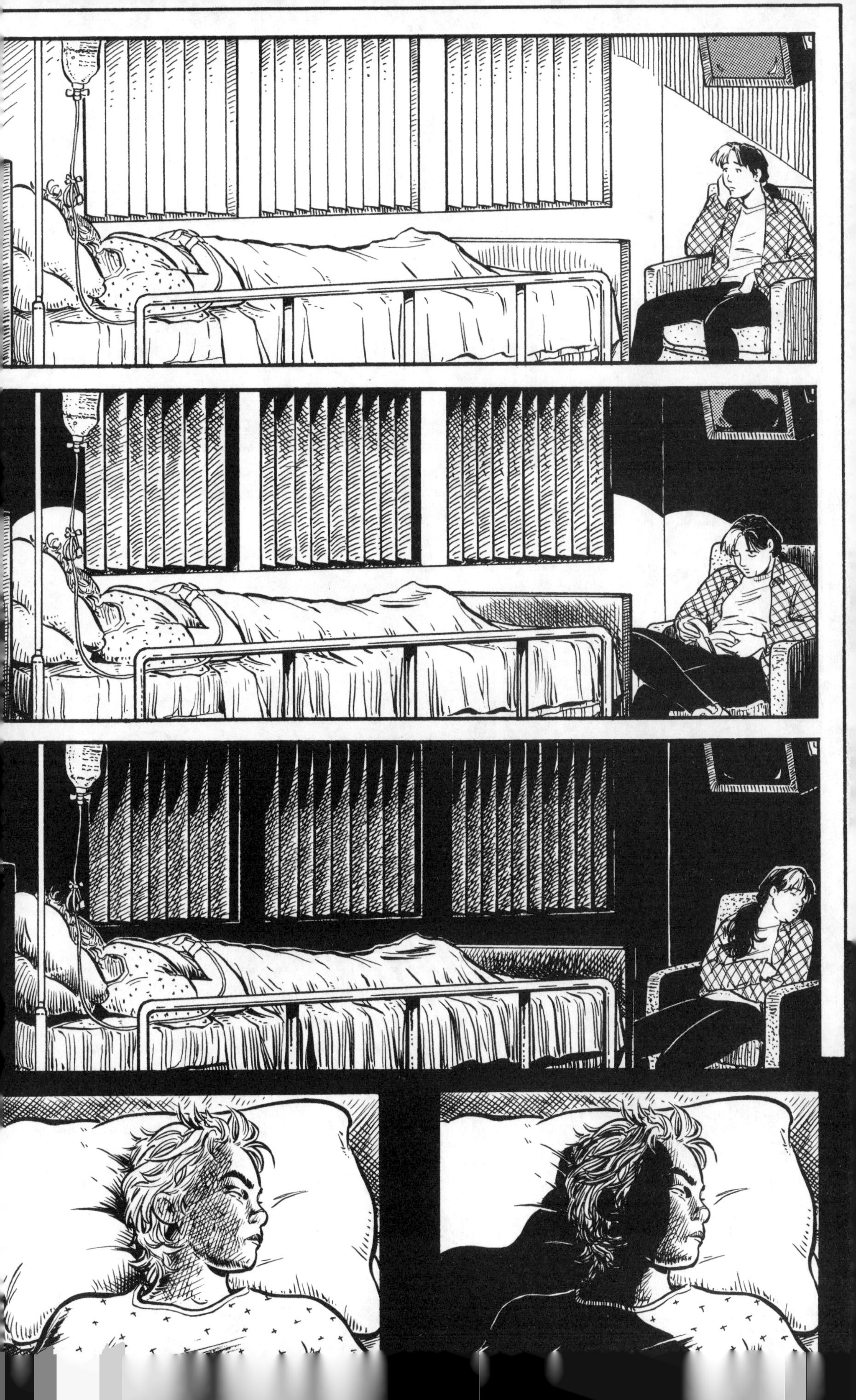

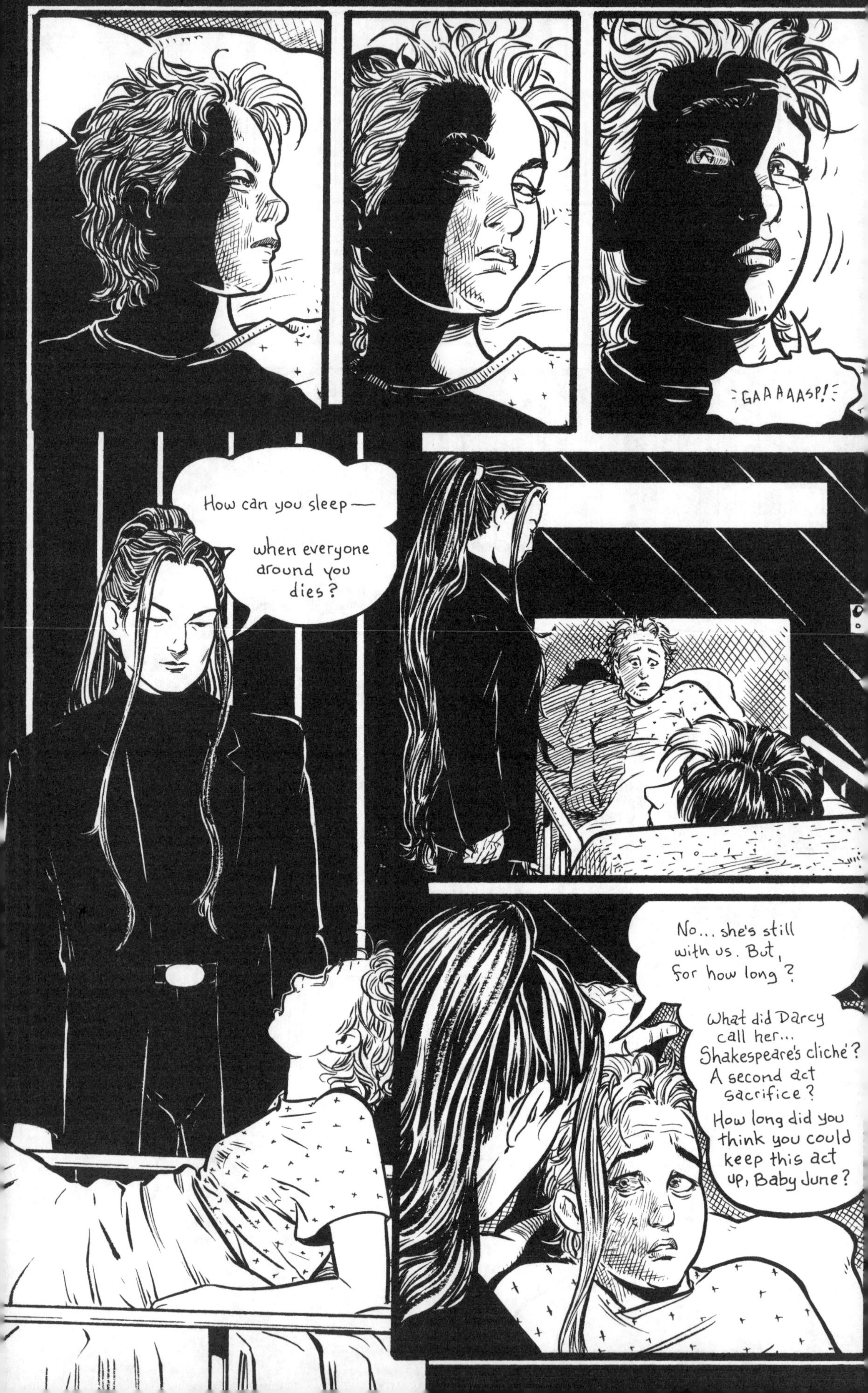
GAAAAASP!
How can you sleep—
when everyone around you dies?
No... she's still with us. But, for how long?
What did Darcy call her... Shakespeare's cliché? A second act sacrifice?
How long did you think you could keep this act up, Baby June?

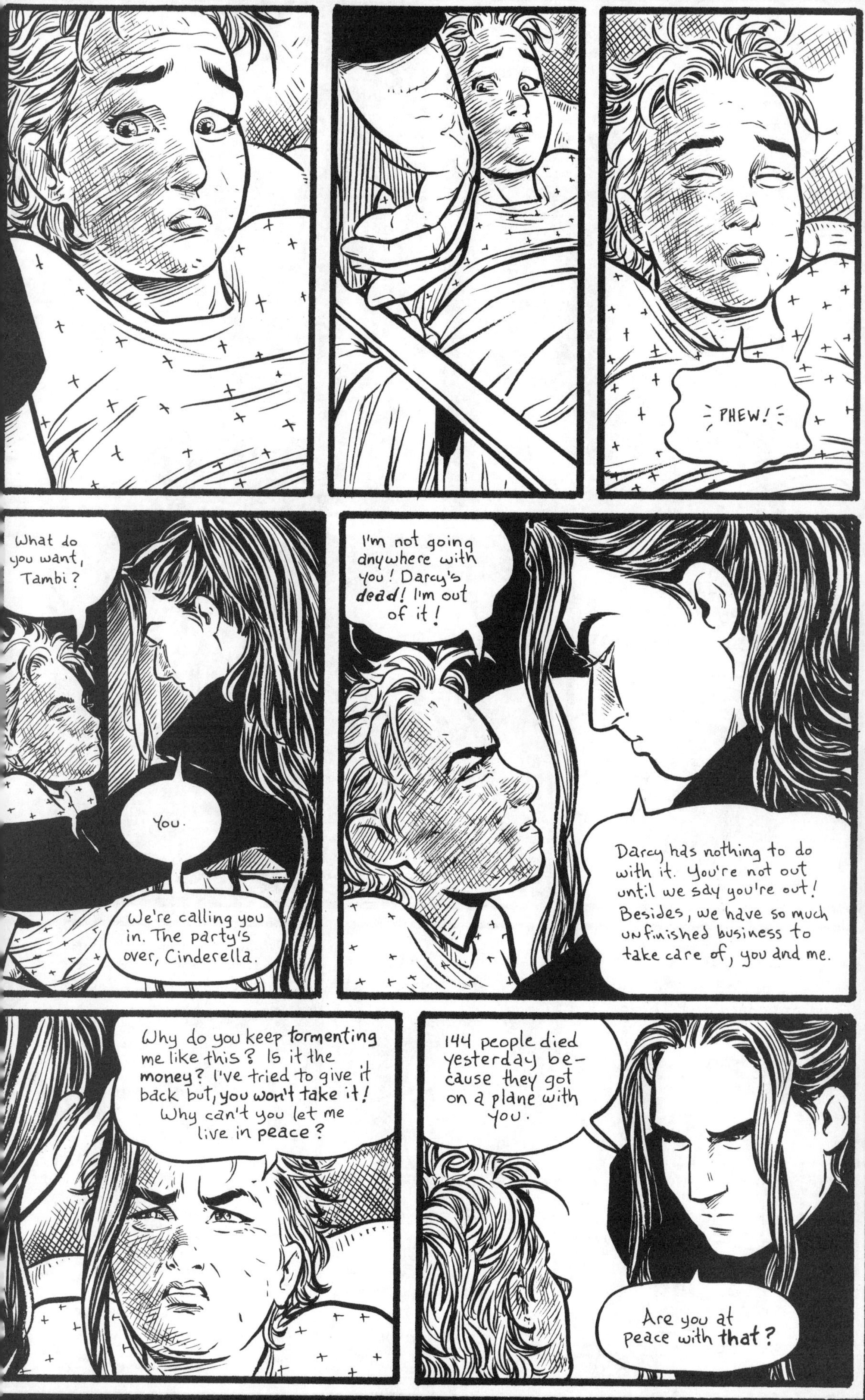
PHEW!
What do you want, Tambi?
You.
We're calling you in. The party's over, Cinderella.
I'm not going anywhere with you! Darcy's *dead*! I'm out of it!
Darcy has nothing to do with it. You're not out until we say you're out! Besides, we have so much unfinished business to take care of, you and me.
Why do you keep **tormenting** me like this? Is it the **money**? I've tried to give it back but, **you won't take it!** Why can't you let me live in **peace**?
144 people died yesterday because they got on a plane with you.
Are you at peace with **that**?

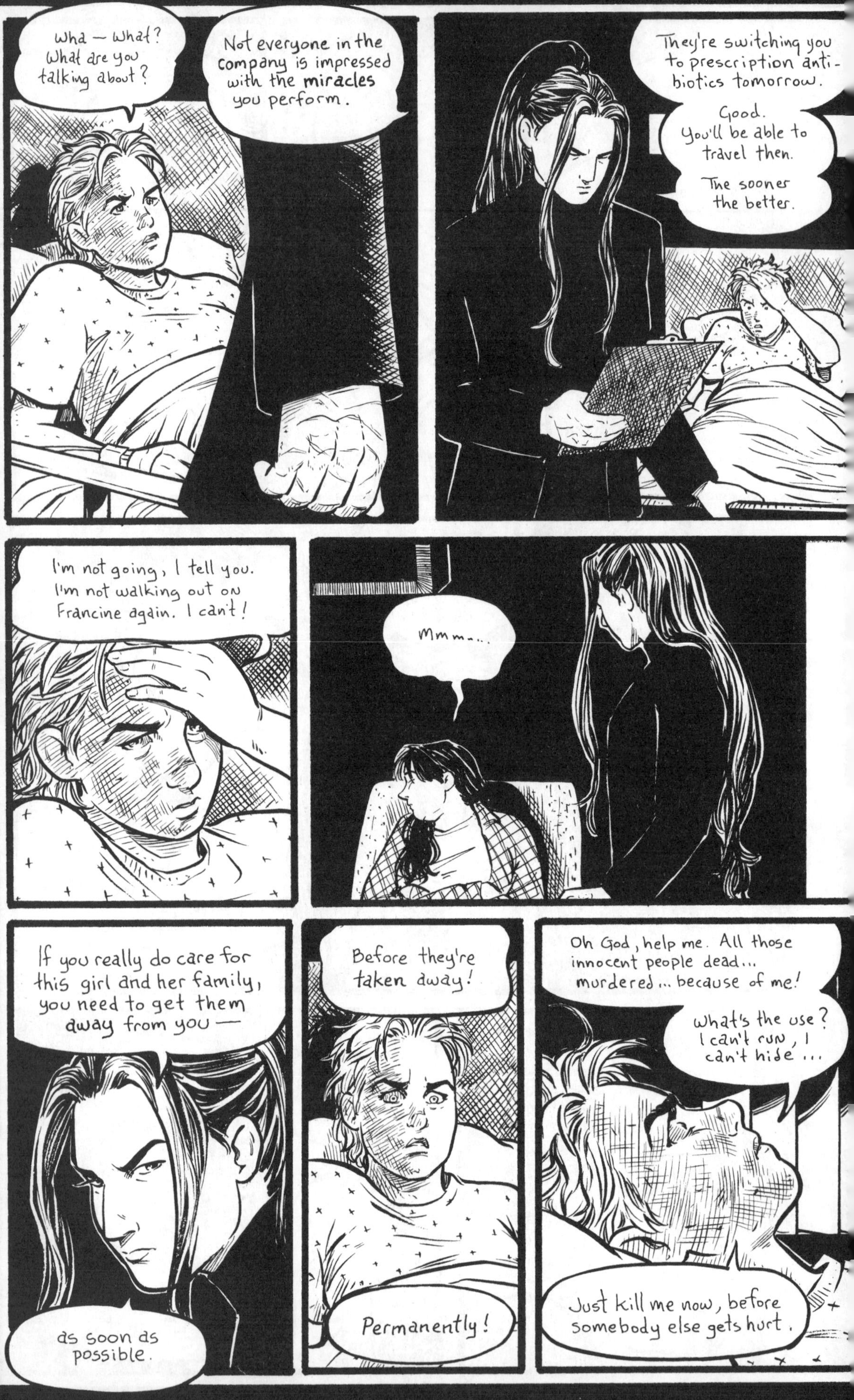
Wha — what? What are you talking about?
Not everyone in the company is impressed with the miracles you perform.
They're switching you to prescription antibiotics tomorrow.
Good. You'll be able to travel then.
The sooner the better.
I'm not going, I tell you. I'm not walking out on Francine again. I can't!
Mmm...
If you really do care for this girl and her family, you need to get them away from you —
as soon as possible.
Before they're taken away!
Permanently!
Oh God, help me. All those innocent people dead... murdered... because of me!
What's the use? I can't run, I can't hide...
Just kill me now, before somebody else gets hurt.

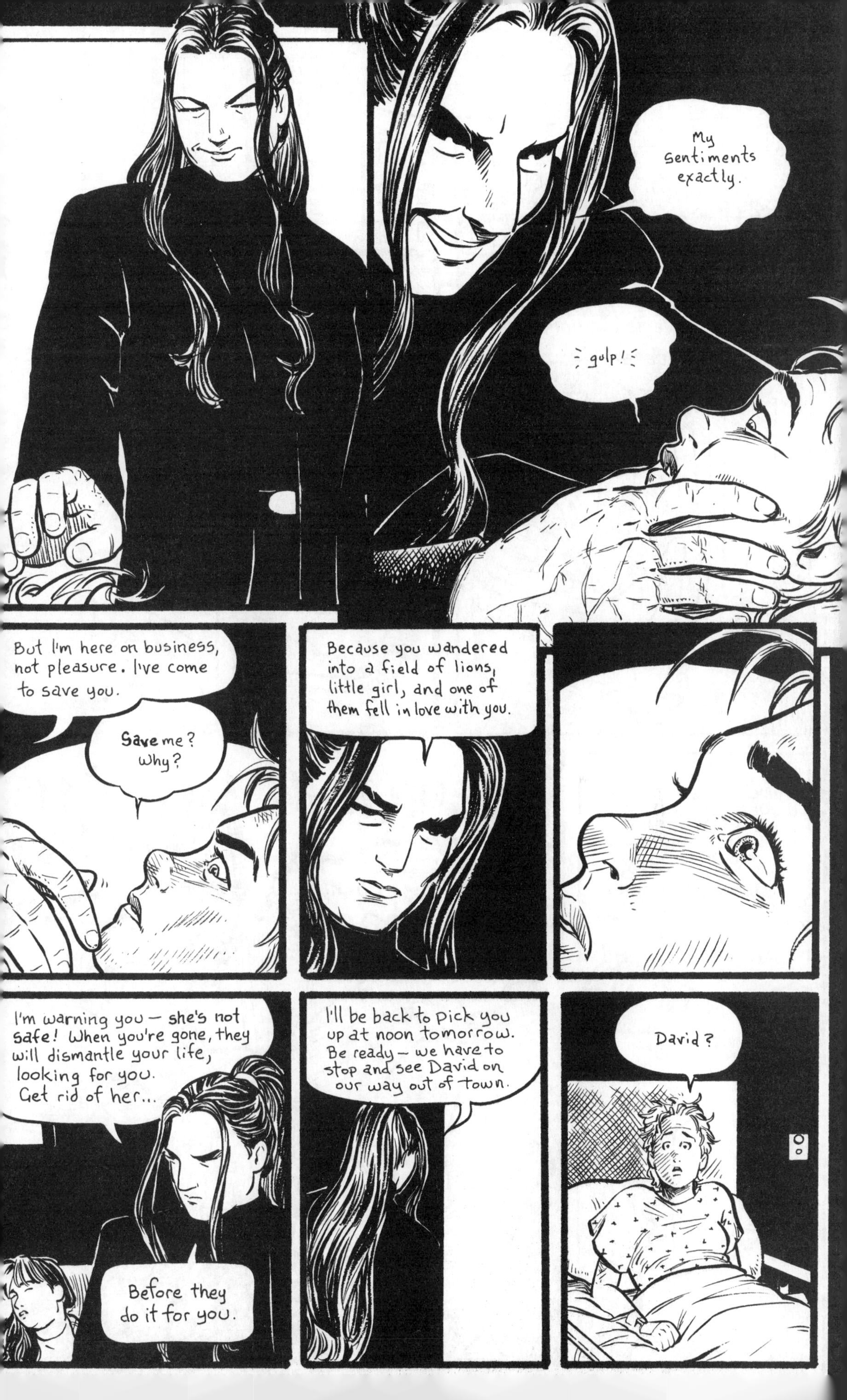
My sentiments exactly.
gulp!
But I'm here on business, not pleasure. I've come to save you.
Save me? Why?
Because you wandered into a field of lions, little girl, and one of them fell in love with you.
I'm warning you — she's not safe! When you're gone, they will dismantle your life, looking for you. Get rid of her...
Before they do it for you.
I'll be back to pick you up at noon tomorrow. Be ready — we have to stop and see David on our way out of town.
David?

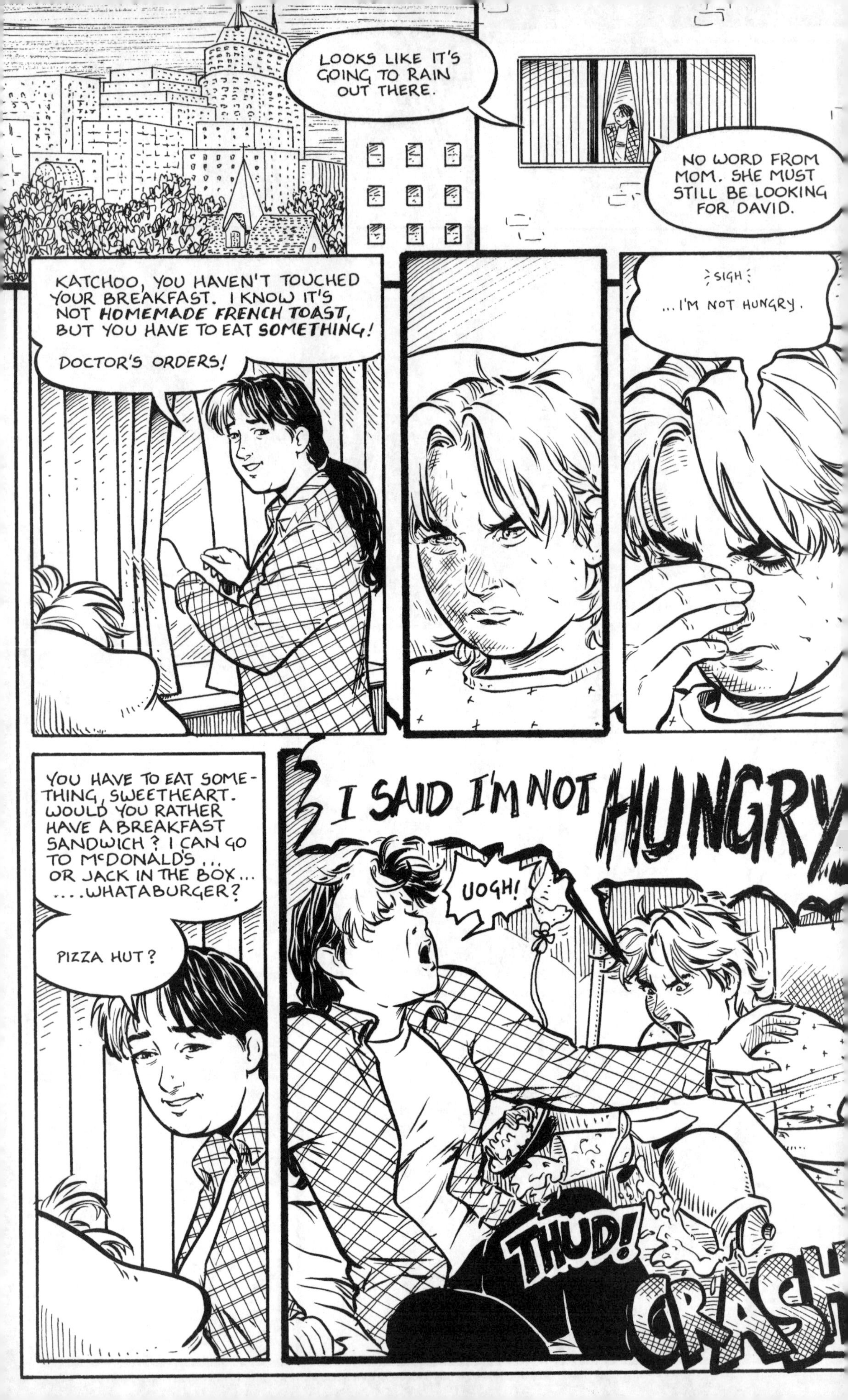
LOOKS LIKE IT'S GOING TO RAIN OUT THERE.
NO WORD FROM MOM. SHE MUST STILL BE LOOKING FOR DAVID.
KATCHOO, YOU HAVEN'T TOUCHED YOUR BREAKFAST. I KNOW IT'S NOT HOMEMADE FRENCH TOAST, BUT YOU HAVE TO EAT SOMETHING!
DOCTOR'S ORDERS!
SIGH
...I'M NOT HUNGRY.
YOU HAVE TO EAT SOMETHING, SWEETHEART. WOULD YOU RATHER HAVE A BREAKFAST SANDWICH? I CAN GO TO McDONALD'S... OR JACK IN THE BOX... ....WHATABURGER?
PIZZA HUT?
I SAID I'M NOT HUNGRY!
UOGH!
THUD!
CRASH

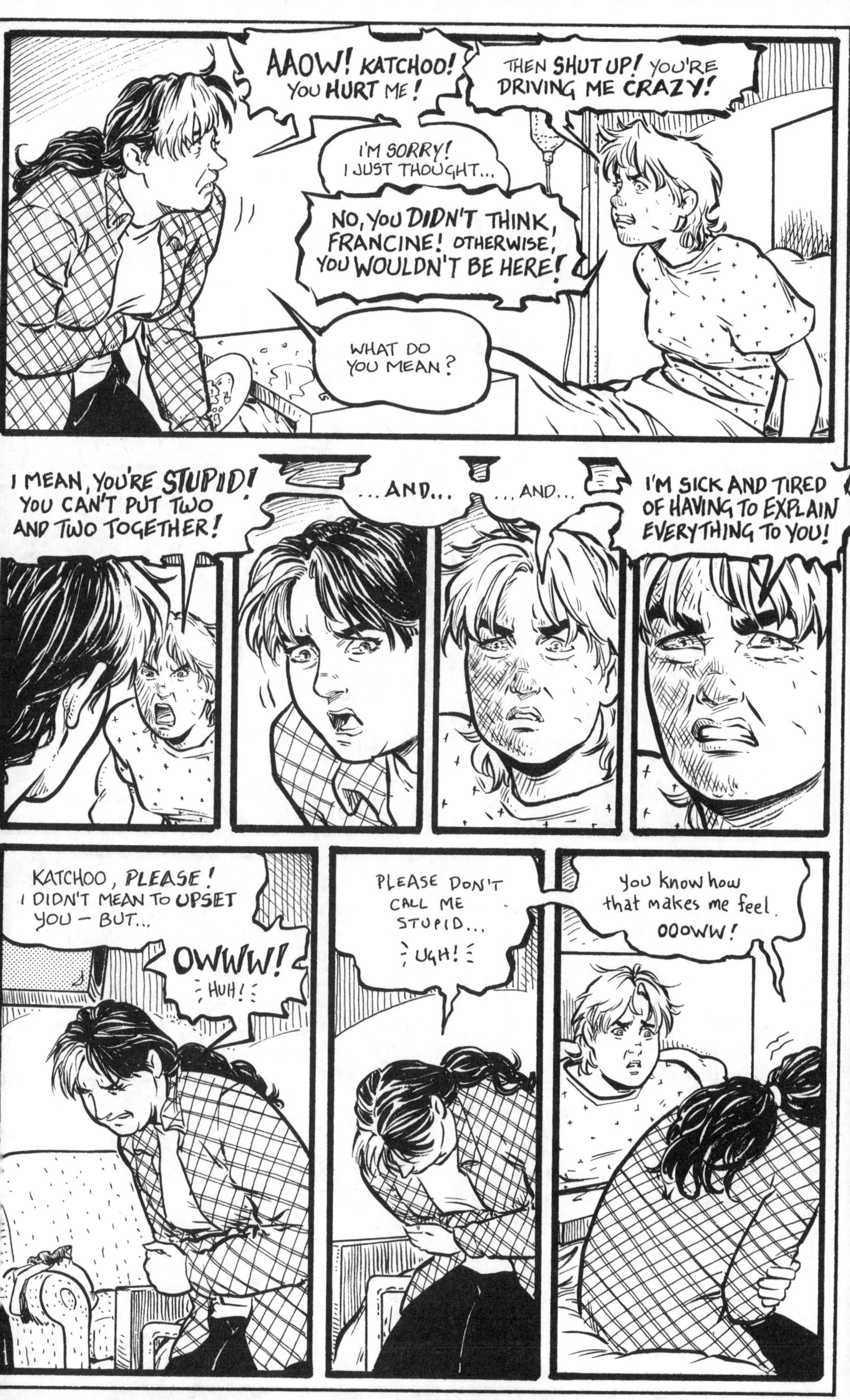
AAOW! KATCHOO! YOU HURT ME!
THEN SHUT UP! YOU'RE DRIVING ME CRAZY!
I'M SORRY! I JUST THOUGHT...
NO, YOU DIDN'T THINK, FRANCINE! OTHERWISE, YOU WOULDN'T BE HERE!
WHAT DO YOU MEAN?
I MEAN, YOU'RE STUPID! YOU CAN'T PUT TWO AND TWO TOGETHER!
...AND...
...AND...
I'M SICK AND TIRED OF HAVING TO EXPLAIN EVERYTHING TO YOU!
KATCHOO, PLEASE! I DIDN'T MEAN TO UPSET YOU — BUT...
OWWW!
HUH!
PLEASE DON'T CALL ME STUPID...
UGH!
You know how that makes me feel.
OOOWW!

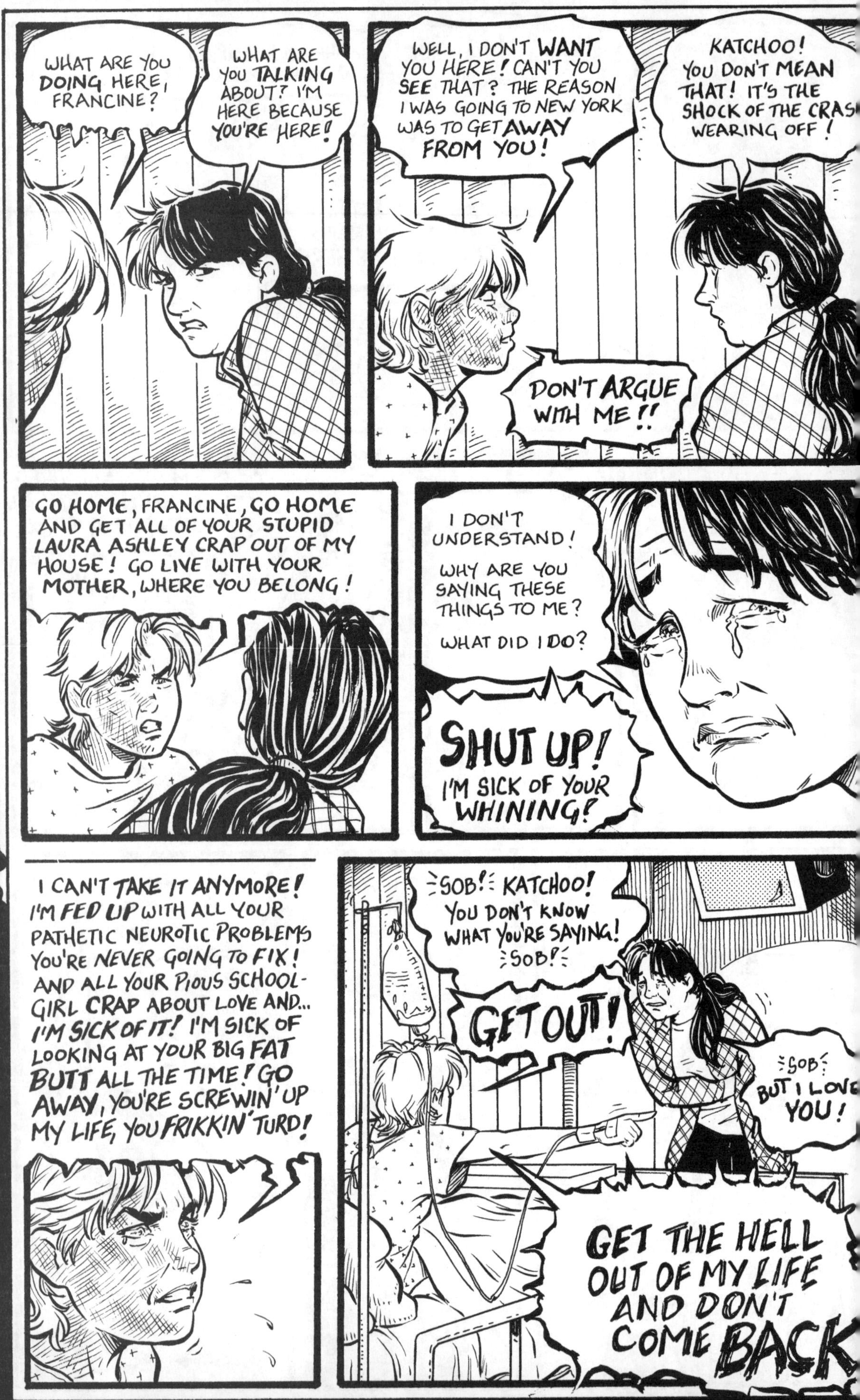
WHAT ARE YOU DOING HERE, FRANCINE?
WHAT ARE YOU TALKING ABOUT? I'M HERE BECAUSE YOU'RE HERE!
WELL, I DON'T WANT YOU HERE! CAN'T YOU SEE THAT? THE REASON I WAS GOING TO NEW YORK WAS TO GET AWAY FROM YOU!
KATCHOO! YOU DON'T MEAN THAT! IT'S THE SHOCK OF THE CRAS WEARING OFF!
DON'T ARGUE WITH ME!!
GO HOME, FRANCINE, GO HOME AND GET ALL OF YOUR STUPID LAURA ASHLEY CRAP OUT OF MY HOUSE! GO LIVE WITH YOUR MOTHER, WHERE YOU BELONG!
I DON'T UNDERSTAND!
WHY ARE YOU SAYING THESE THINGS TO ME?
WHAT DID I DO?
SHUT UP! I'M SICK OF YOUR WHINING!
I CAN'T TAKE IT ANYMORE! I'M FED UP WITH ALL YOUR PATHETIC NEUROTIC PROBLEMS YOU'RE NEVER GOING TO FIX! AND ALL YOUR PIOUS SCHOOL-GIRL CRAP ABOUT LOVE AND... I'M SICK OF IT! I'M SICK OF LOOKING AT YOUR BIG FAT BUTT ALL THE TIME! GO AWAY, YOU'RE SCREWIN' UP MY LIFE, YOU FRIKKIN' TURD!
SOB! KATCHOO! YOU DON'T KNOW WHAT YOU'RE SAYING! SOB!
GET OUT!
SOB BUT I LOVE YOU!
GET THE HELL OUT OF MY LIFE AND DON'T COME BACK

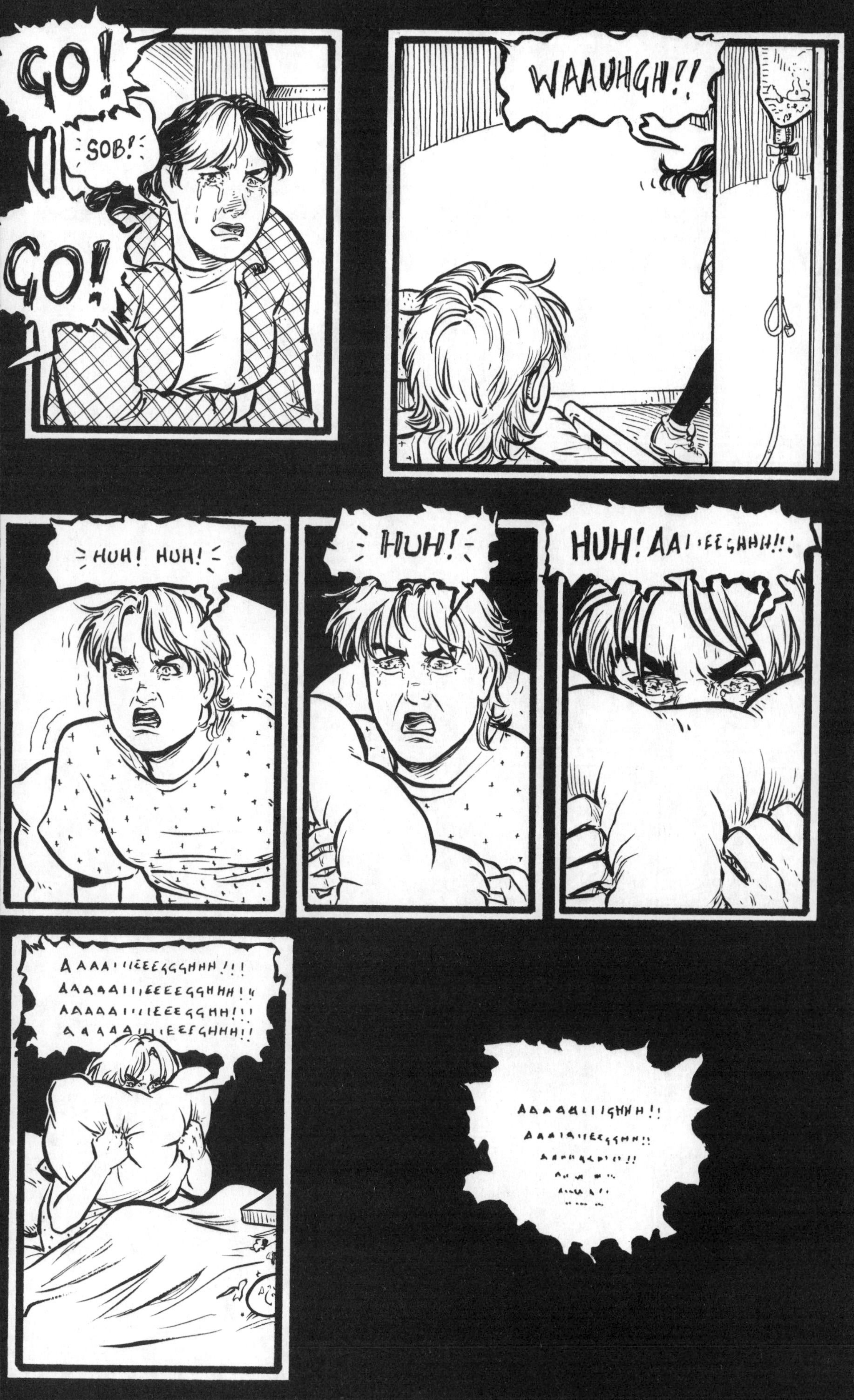
GO!
SOB!
GO!
WAAUHGH!!
HUH! HUH!
HUH!
HUH! AAIEEGHHH!!!
AAAAIIIEEEGGGHHH!!!
AAAAAIIIEEEEEGGHHH!!!
AAAAAIIIIEEEGGHH!!!
AAAAAIIIIEEEGHHH!!
AAAAALIIGHHH!!

ABSTRACT
STUDIO

29

2.75 U.S.
3.80 CAN

STRANGERS IN PARADISE

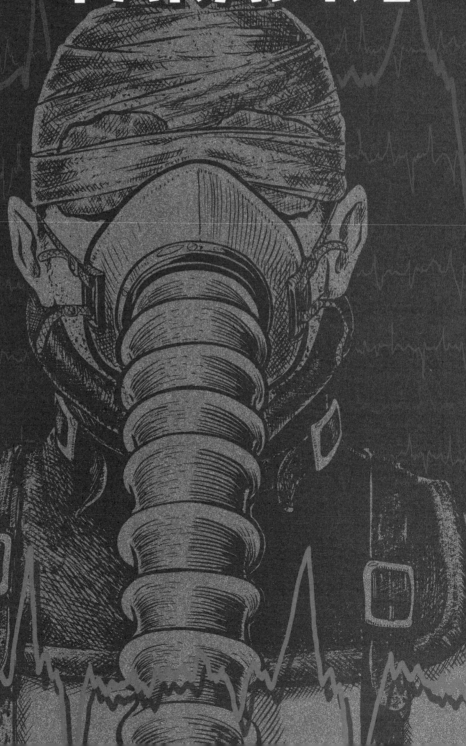

When I wake up at night
Remembering my other life,
I scream.
If I could find a way don't you believe
That I'd be there today?
But for my clever mind, to punish me,
I'm trapped inside this black design
My eyes are gallows and my heart's a nervous wreck
Trapped in confusion all around me I forget
My real name,
But they call me profane.

When I had angry eyes
To see beyond the veil of lies was nothing,
But now they're baby blue and don't see any answers,
I'm as blind as you.
If what they say is true then anything can happen
There are no border lines.
Tho' deep inside I hold the child I think I am,
My hands were midwife to the hell I'm living in.
Oh believe me,
I'm running out of time.

When I wake up at night
Remembering my other life,
I scream.
But every dawning day the faith in me
beyond my reach more distant fades.
My eyes are gallows and my heart's a nervous wreck;
My cries are fondled by the hangman's deadly kiss.
Oh believe me,
I'm running out of

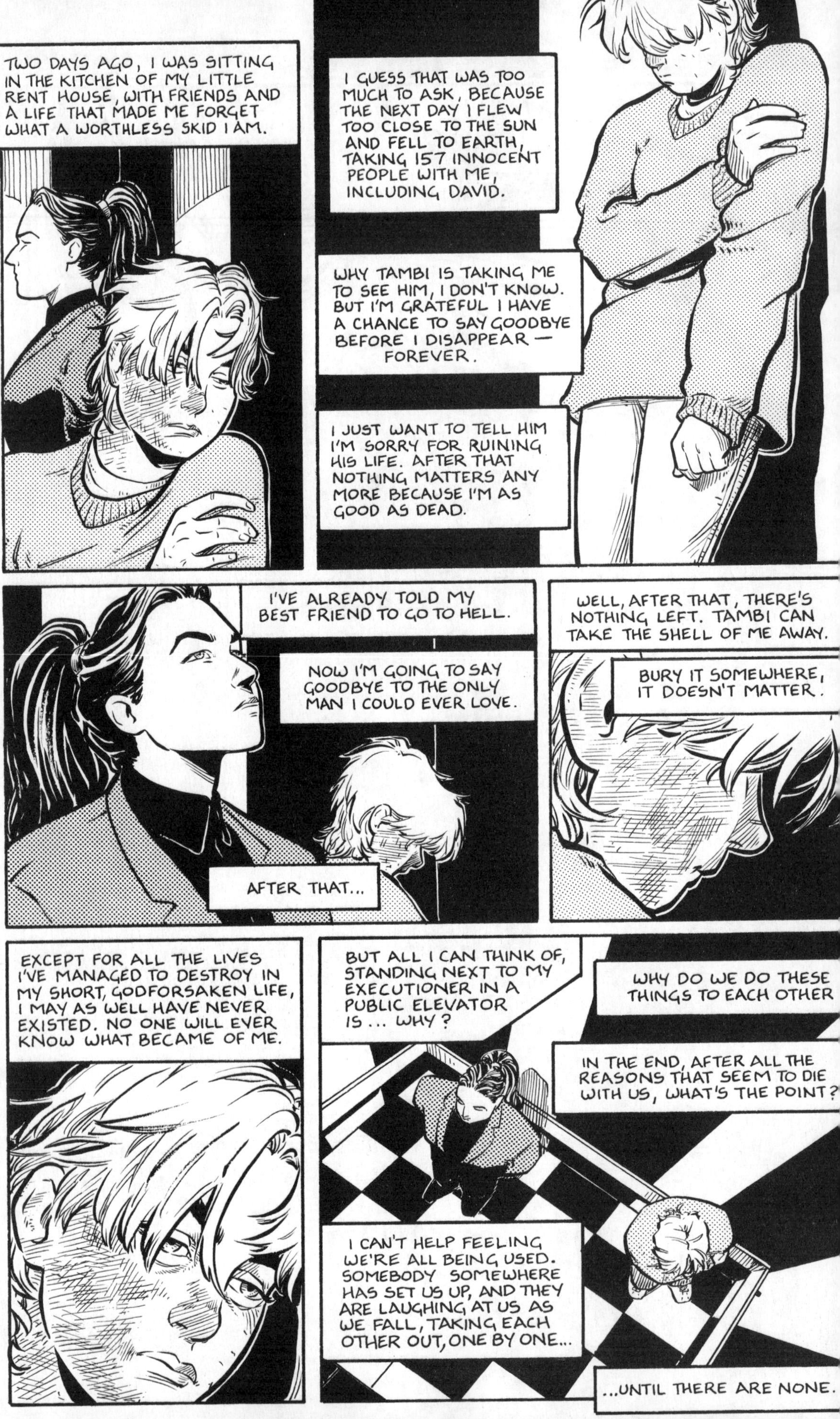
TWO DAYS AGO, I WAS SITTING IN THE KITCHEN OF MY LITTLE RENT HOUSE, WITH FRIENDS AND A LIFE THAT MADE ME FORGET WHAT A WORTHLESS SKID I AM.
I GUESS THAT WAS TOO MUCH TO ASK, BECAUSE THE NEXT DAY I FLEW TOO CLOSE TO THE SUN AND FELL TO EARTH, TAKING 157 INNOCENT PEOPLE WITH ME, INCLUDING DAVID.
WHY TAMBI IS TAKING ME TO SEE HIM, I DON'T KNOW. BUT I'M GRATEFUL I HAVE A CHANCE TO SAY GOODBYE BEFORE I DISAPPEAR — FOREVER.
I JUST WANT TO TELL HIM I'M SORRY FOR RUINING HIS LIFE. AFTER THAT NOTHING MATTERS ANY MORE BECAUSE I'M AS GOOD AS DEAD.
I'VE ALREADY TOLD MY BEST FRIEND TO GO TO HELL.
NOW I'M GOING TO SAY GOODBYE TO THE ONLY MAN I COULD EVER LOVE.
AFTER THAT...
WELL, AFTER THAT, THERE'S NOTHING LEFT. TAMBI CAN TAKE THE SHELL OF ME AWAY.
BURY IT SOMEWHERE, IT DOESN'T MATTER.
EXCEPT FOR ALL THE LIVES I'VE MANAGED TO DESTROY IN MY SHORT, GODFORSAKEN LIFE, I MAY AS WELL HAVE NEVER EXISTED. NO ONE WILL EVER KNOW WHAT BECAME OF ME.
BUT ALL I CAN THINK OF, STANDING NEXT TO MY EXECUTIONER IN A PUBLIC ELEVATOR IS ... WHY?
WHY DO WE DO THESE THINGS TO EACH OTHER
IN THE END, AFTER ALL THE REASONS THAT SEEM TO DIE WITH US, WHAT'S THE POINT?
I CAN'T HELP FEELING WE'RE ALL BEING USED. SOMEBODY SOMEWHERE HAS SET US UP, AND THEY ARE LAUGHING AT US AS WE FALL, TAKING EACH OTHER OUT, ONE BY ONE...
...UNTIL THERE ARE NONE.

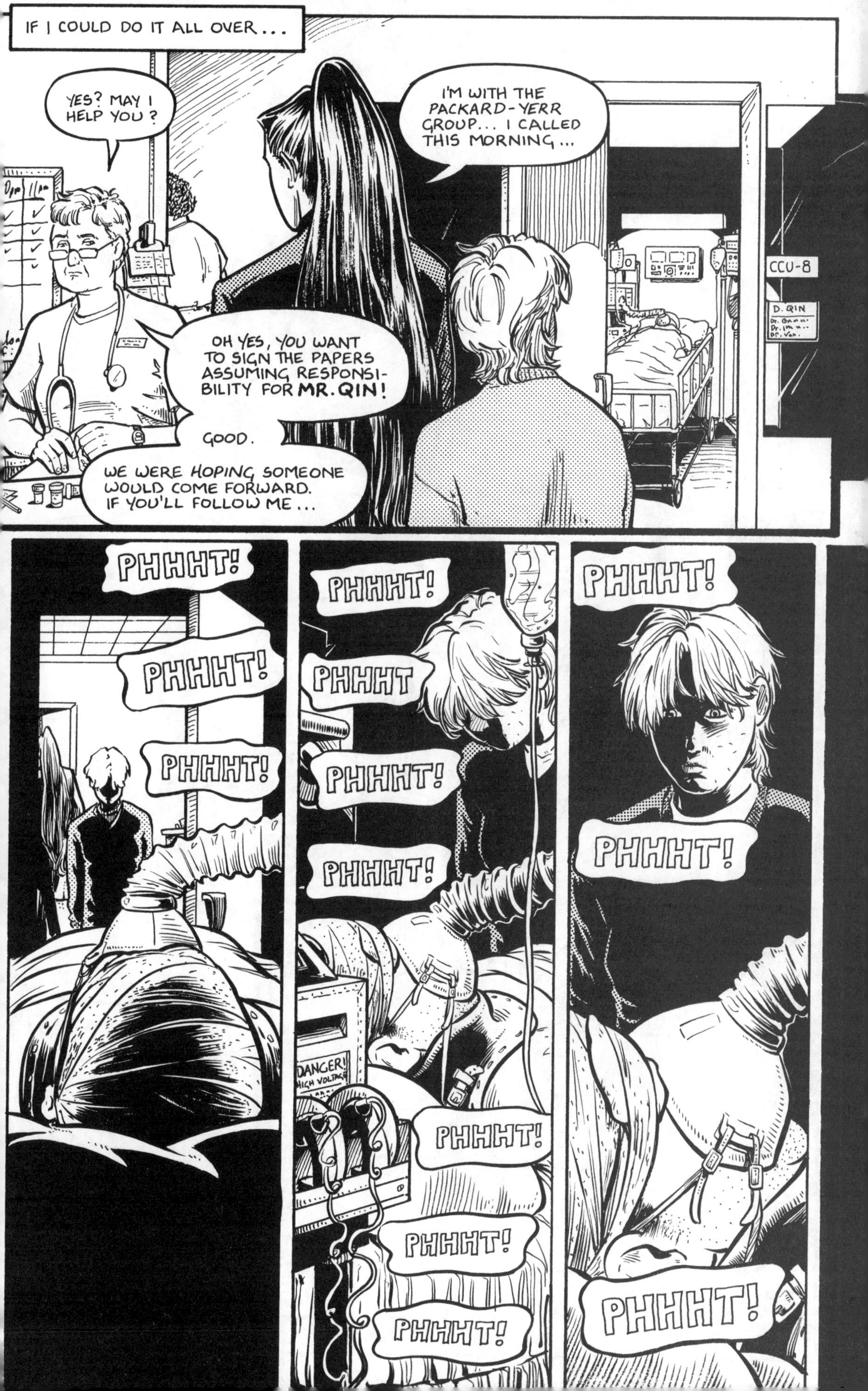
IF I COULD DO IT ALL OVER...
YES? MAY I HELP YOU?
I'M WITH THE PACKARD-YERR GROUP... I CALLED THIS MORNING...
CCU-8
D. QIN
OH YES, YOU WANT TO SIGN THE PAPERS ASSUMING RESPONSIBILITY FOR MR. QIN!
GOOD.
WE WERE HOPING SOMEONE WOULD COME FORWARD. IF YOU'LL FOLLOW ME...
PHHHT!
PHHHT!
PHHHT!
PHHHT!
PHHHT
PHHHT!
PHHHT!
DANGER! HIGH VOLTAGE
PHHHT!
PHHHT!
PHHHT!
PHHHT!
PHHHT!
PHHHT!

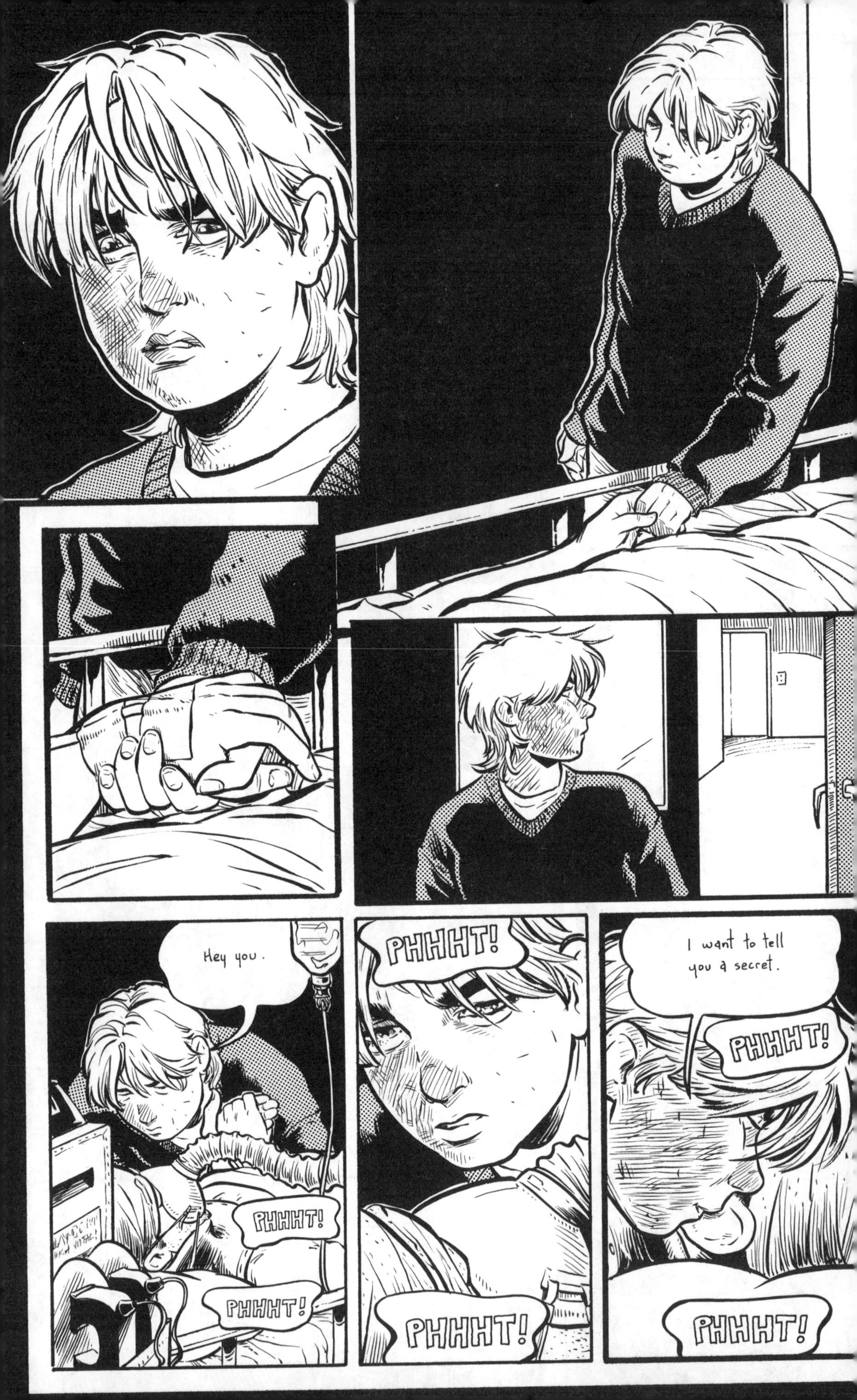
Hey you.
PHHHT!
PHHHT!
PHHHT!
PHHHT!
I want to tell you a secret.
PHHHT!
PHHHT!

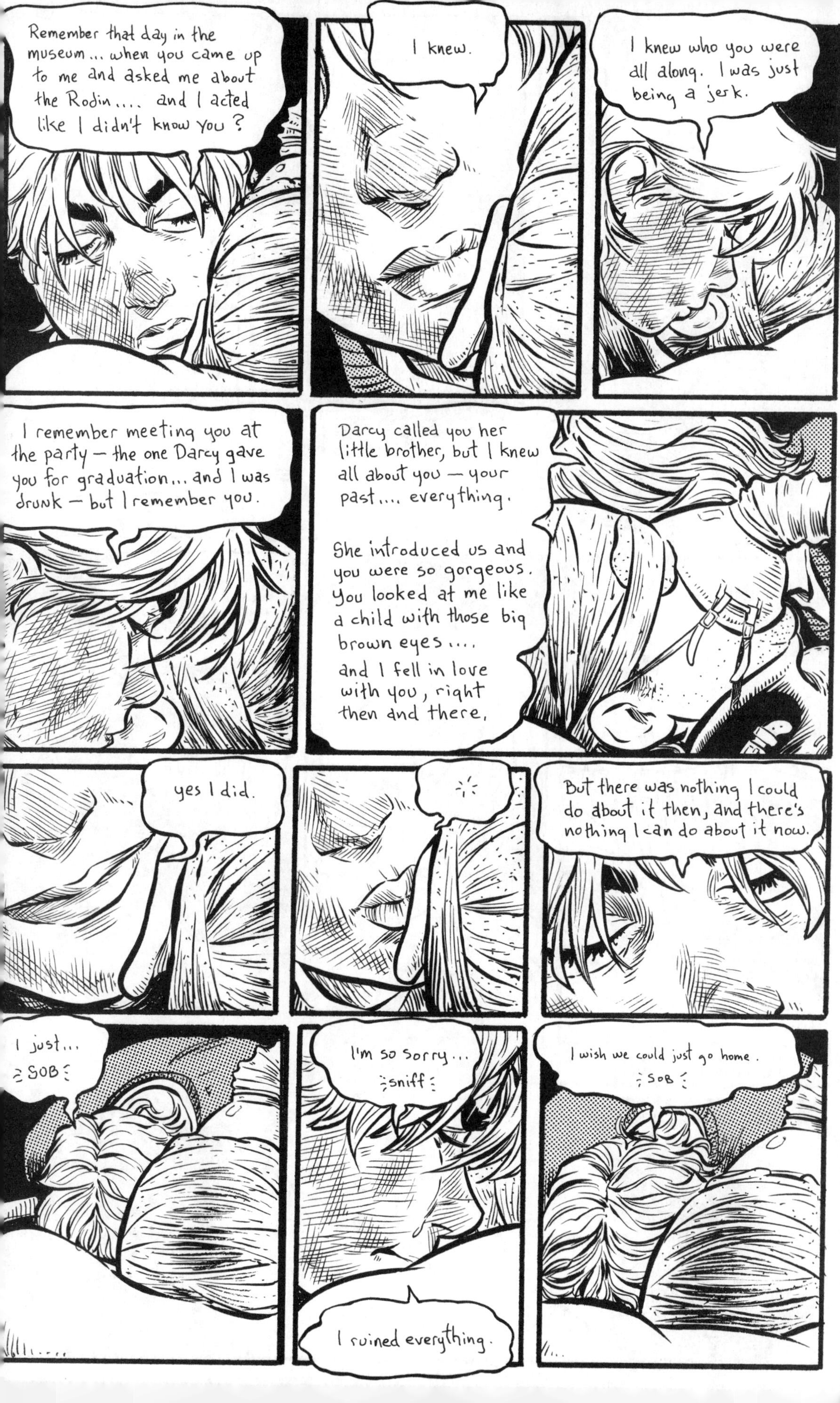
Remember that day in the museum... when you came up to me and asked me about the Rodin.... and I acted like I didn't know you?
I knew.
I knew who you were all along. I was just being a jerk.
I remember meeting you at the party — the one Darcy gave you for graduation... and I was drunk — but I remember you.
Darcy called you her little brother, but I knew all about you — your past.... everything.
She introduced us and you were so gorgeous. You looked at me like a child with those big brown eyes....
and I fell in love with you, right then and there,
yes I did.
But there was nothing I could do about it then, and there's nothing I can do about it now.
I just...
SOB
I'm so sorry...
sniff
I ruined everything.
I wish we could just go home.
SOB

IT'S TIME.

I guess this is goodbye, sweetheart.

⸝ SNIFF ⸝

PHHHT!

PHHHT!

Anataka suki desu. Yousaka Takahashi.

Itsumo.

Itsumademo.

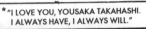

* "I LOVE YOU, YOUSAKA TAKAHASHI. I ALWAYS HAVE, I ALWAYS WILL."

REMEMBER THAT, OR I'LL COME BACK AND KICK YOUR BUTT. YOU HEAR?

PHHHT!

PHHHT!

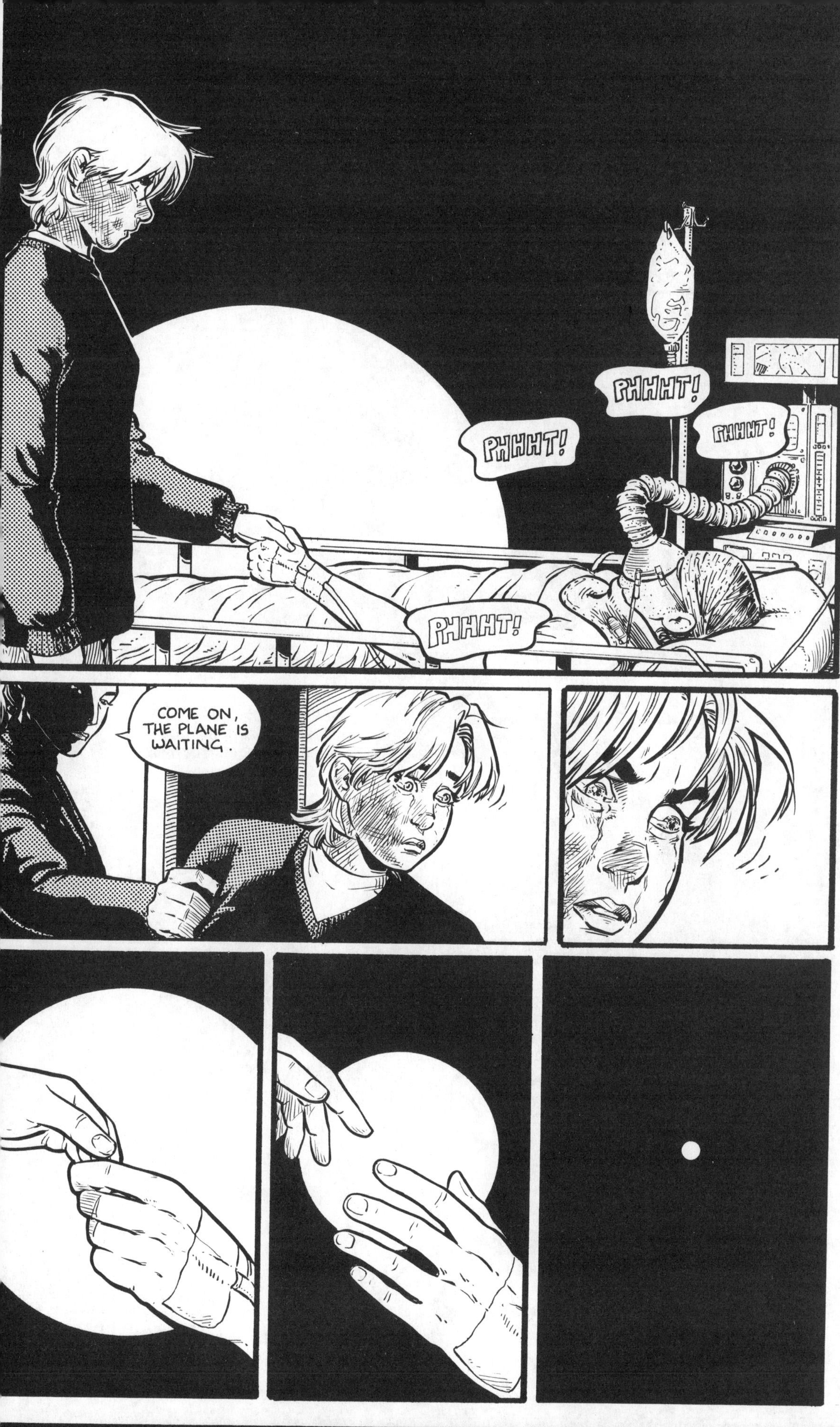
PHHHT!
PHHHT!
PHHHT!
PHHHT!
COME ON, THE PLANE IS WAITING.

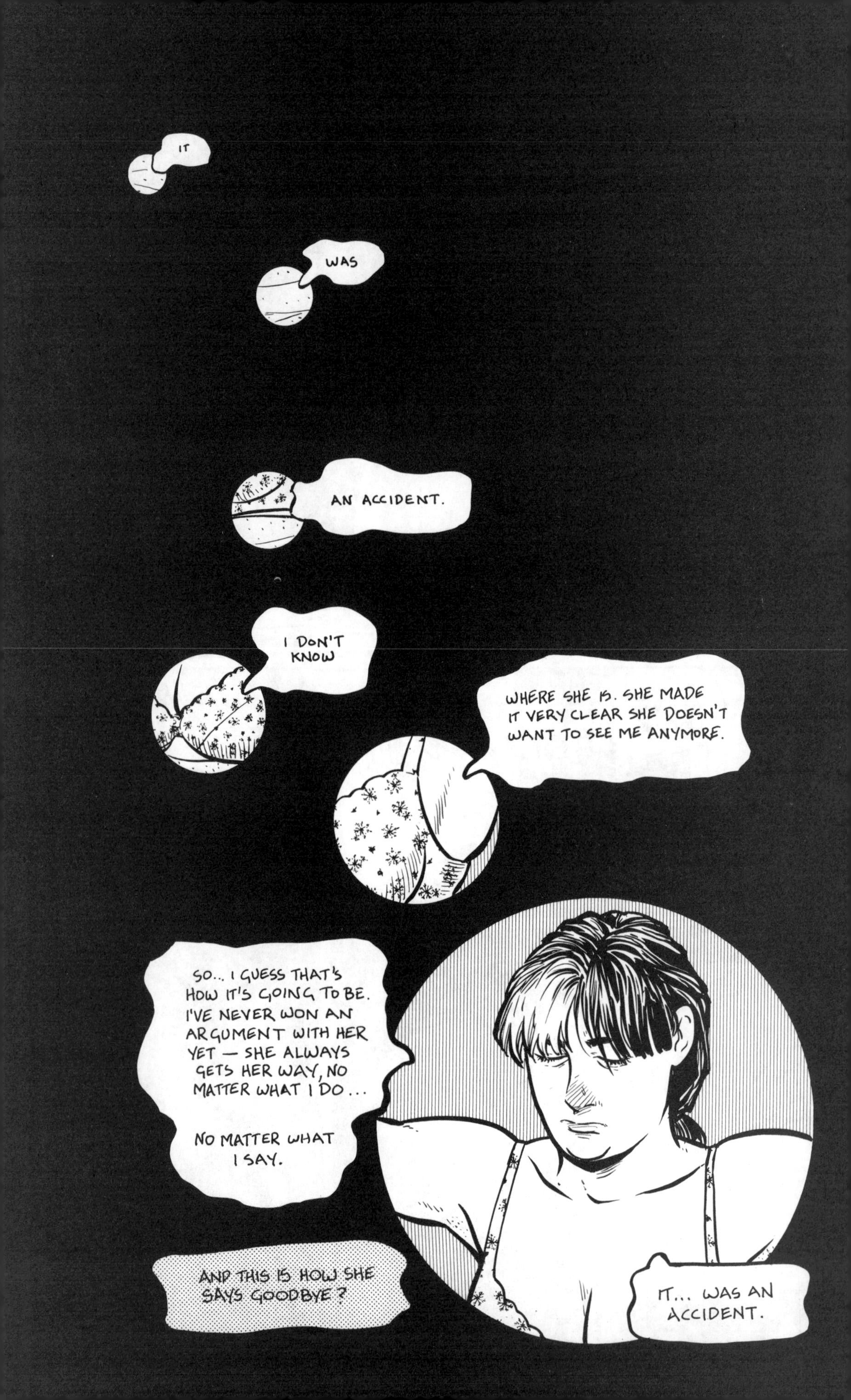
IT
WAS
AN ACCIDENT.
I DON'T KNOW
WHERE SHE IS. SHE MADE IT VERY CLEAR SHE DOESN'T WANT TO SEE ME ANYMORE.
SO... I GUESS THAT'S HOW IT'S GOING TO BE. I'VE NEVER WON AN ARGUMENT WITH HER YET — SHE ALWAYS GETS HER WAY, NO MATTER WHAT I DO...
NO MATTER WHAT I SAY.
AND THIS IS HOW SHE SAYS GOODBYE?
IT... WAS AN ACCIDENT.

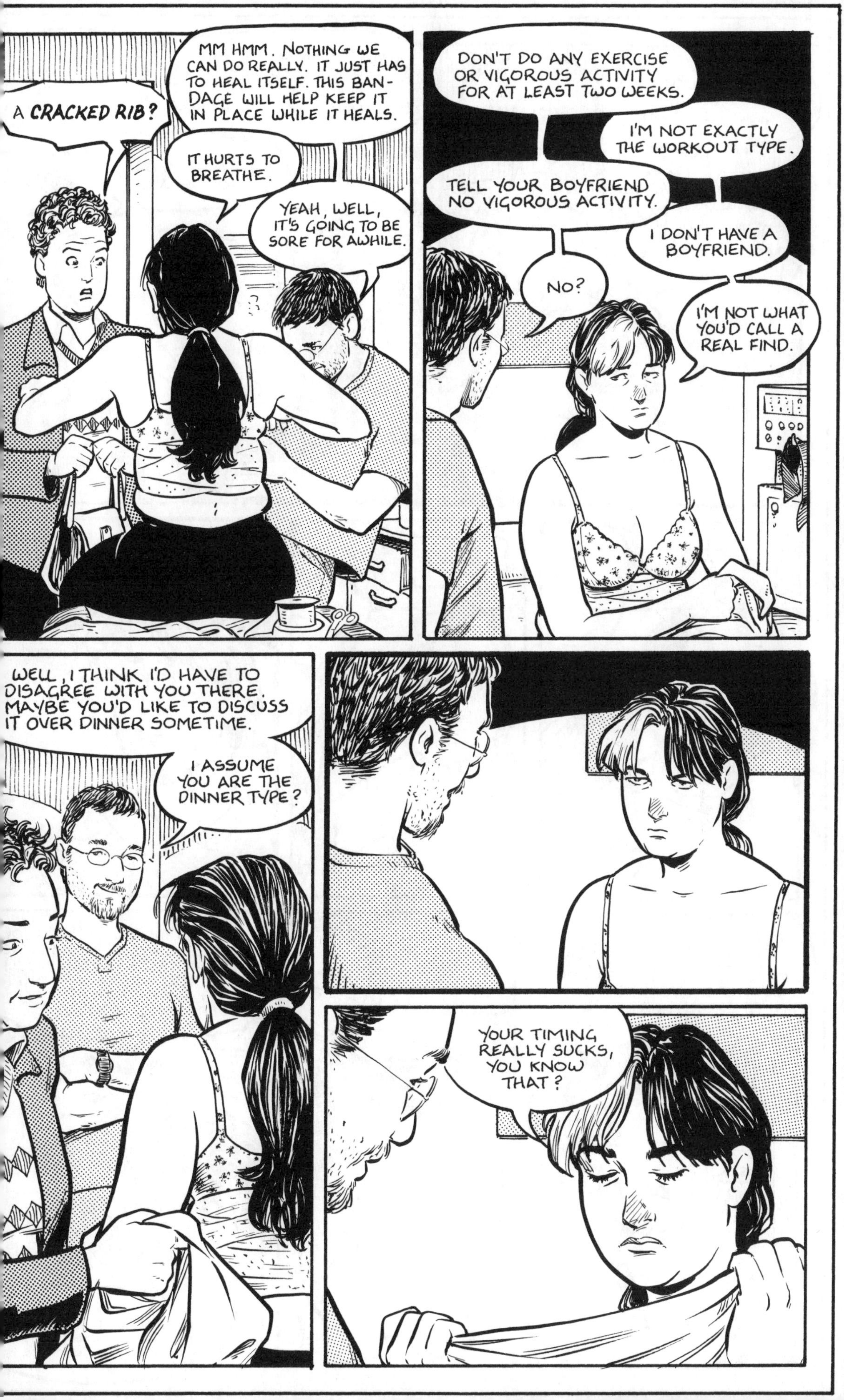
A CRACKED RIB?
MM HMM. NOTHING WE CAN DO REALLY. IT JUST HAS TO HEAL ITSELF. THIS BANDAGE WILL HELP KEEP IT IN PLACE WHILE IT HEALS.
IT HURTS TO BREATHE.
YEAH, WELL, IT'S GOING TO BE SORE FOR AWHILE.
DON'T DO ANY EXERCISE OR VIGOROUS ACTIVITY FOR AT LEAST TWO WEEKS.
I'M NOT EXACTLY THE WORKOUT TYPE.
TELL YOUR BOYFRIEND NO VIGOROUS ACTIVITY.
I DON'T HAVE A BOYFRIEND.
NO?
I'M NOT WHAT YOU'D CALL A REAL FIND.
WELL, I THINK I'D HAVE TO DISAGREE WITH YOU THERE. MAYBE YOU'D LIKE TO DISCUSS IT OVER DINNER SOMETIME.
I ASSUME YOU ARE THE DINNER TYPE?
YOUR TIMING REALLY SUCKS, YOU KNOW THAT?

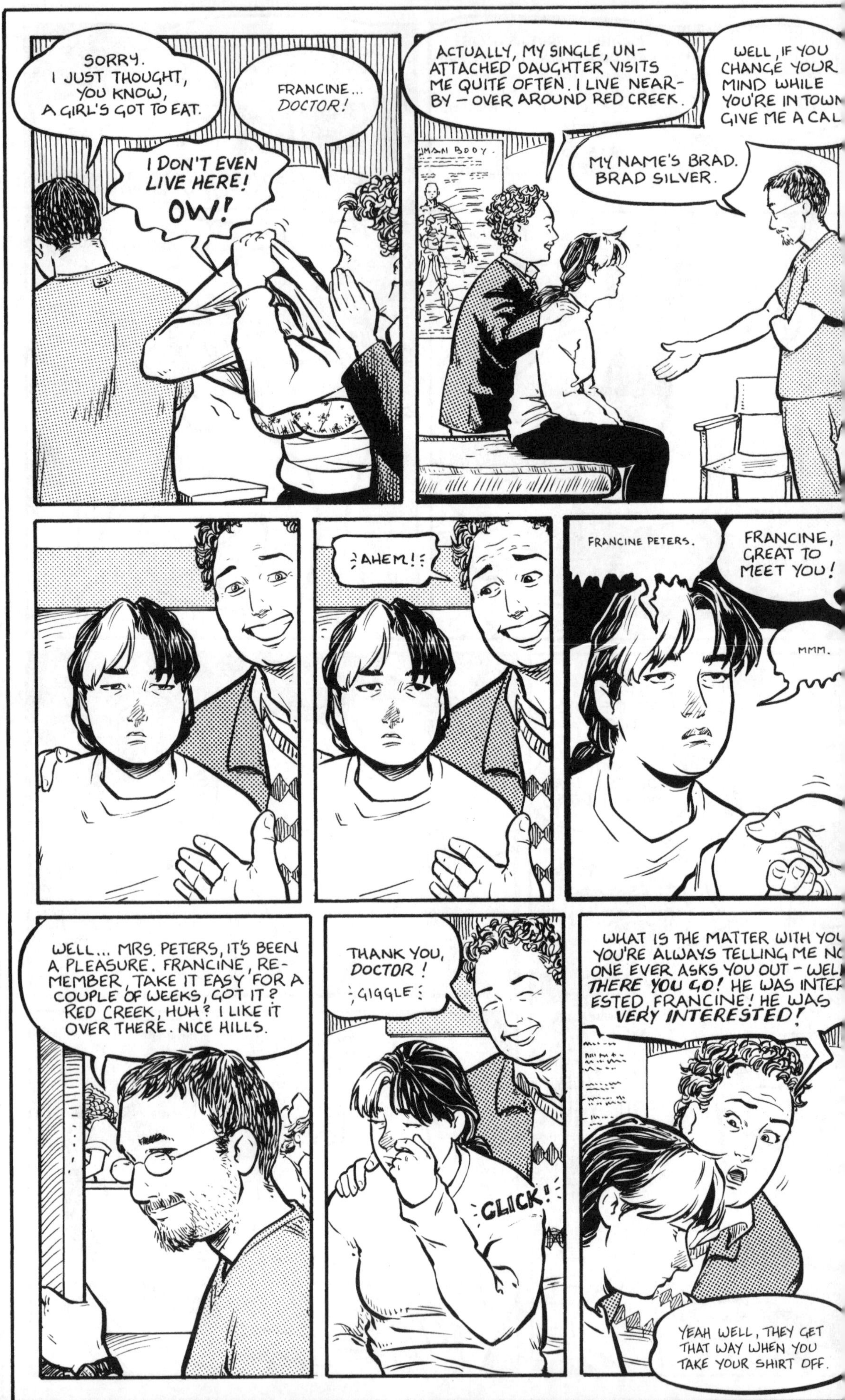
SORRY. I JUST THOUGHT, YOU KNOW, A GIRL'S GOT TO EAT.
FRANCINE... DOCTOR!
I DON'T EVEN LIVE HERE! OW!
ACTUALLY, MY SINGLE, UN-ATTACHED DAUGHTER VISITS ME QUITE OFTEN. I LIVE NEAR-BY – OVER AROUND RED CREEK.
WELL, IF YOU CHANGE YOUR MIND WHILE YOU'RE IN TOWN GIVE ME A CAL
MY NAME'S BRAD. BRAD SILVER.
AHEM!
FRANCINE PETERS.
FRANCINE, GREAT TO MEET YOU!
MMM.
WELL... MRS. PETERS, IT'S BEEN A PLEASURE. FRANCINE, RE-MEMBER, TAKE IT EASY FOR A COUPLE OF WEEKS, GOT IT? RED CREEK, HUH? I LIKE IT OVER THERE. NICE HILLS.
THANK YOU, DOCTOR!
GIGGLE
CLICK!
WHAT IS THE MATTER WITH YO YOU'RE ALWAYS TELLING ME N ONE EVER ASKS YOU OUT – WEL THERE YOU GO! HE WAS INTER-ESTED, FRANCINE! HE WAS VERY INTERESTED!
YEAH WELL, THEY GET THAT WAY WHEN YOU TAKE YOUR SHIRT OFF.

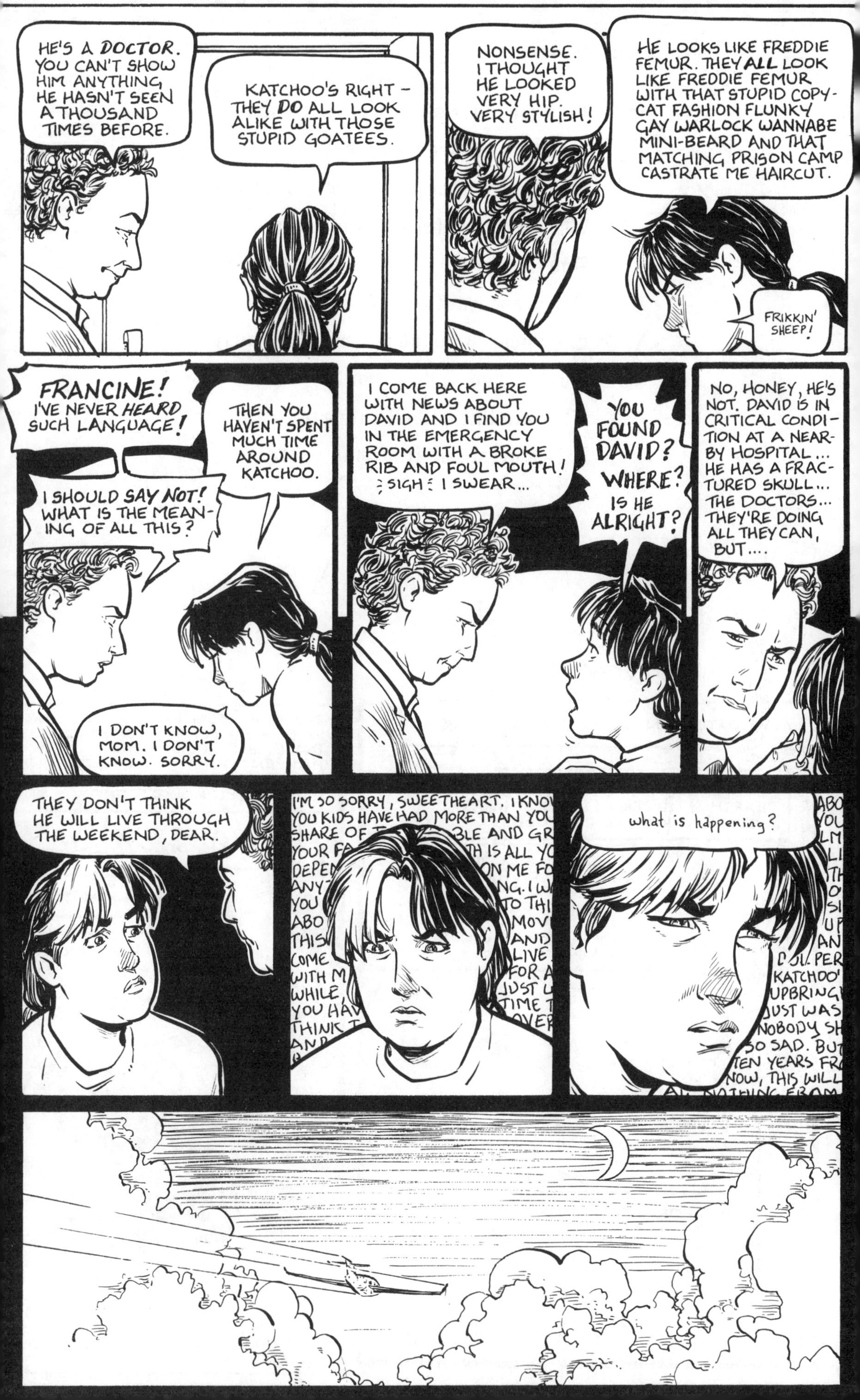

HE'S A **DOCTOR**. YOU CAN'T SHOW HIM ANYTHING HE HASN'T SEEN A THOUSAND TIMES BEFORE.
KATCHOO'S RIGHT - THEY **DO** ALL LOOK ALIKE WITH THOSE STUPID GOATEES.
NONSENSE. I THOUGHT HE LOOKED VERY HIP. VERY STYLISH!
HE LOOKS LIKE FREDDIE FEMUR. THEY **ALL** LOOK LIKE FREDDIE FEMUR WITH THAT STUPID COPY-CAT FASHION FLUNKY GAY WARLOCK WANNABE MINI-BEARD AND THAT MATCHING PRISON CAMP CASTRATE ME HAIRCUT.
FRIKKIN' SHEEP!
FRANCINE! I'VE NEVER **HEARD** SUCH LANGUAGE!
THEN YOU HAVEN'T SPENT MUCH TIME AROUND KATCHOO.
I SHOULD **SAY NOT**! WHAT IS THE MEANING OF ALL THIS?
I DON'T KNOW, MOM. I DON'T KNOW. SORRY.
I COME BACK HERE WITH NEWS ABOUT DAVID AND I FIND YOU IN THE EMERGENCY ROOM WITH A BROKE RIB AND FOUL MOUTH! :SIGH: I SWEAR...
YOU FOUND DAVID? WHERE? IS HE ALRIGHT?
NO, HONEY, HE'S NOT. DAVID IS IN CRITICAL CONDITION AT A NEARBY HOSPITAL... HE HAS A FRACTURED SKULL... THE DOCTORS... THEY'RE DOING ALL THEY CAN, BUT....
THEY DON'T THINK HE WILL LIVE THROUGH THE WEEKEND, DEAR.
I'M SO SORRY, SWEETHEART.
what is happening?

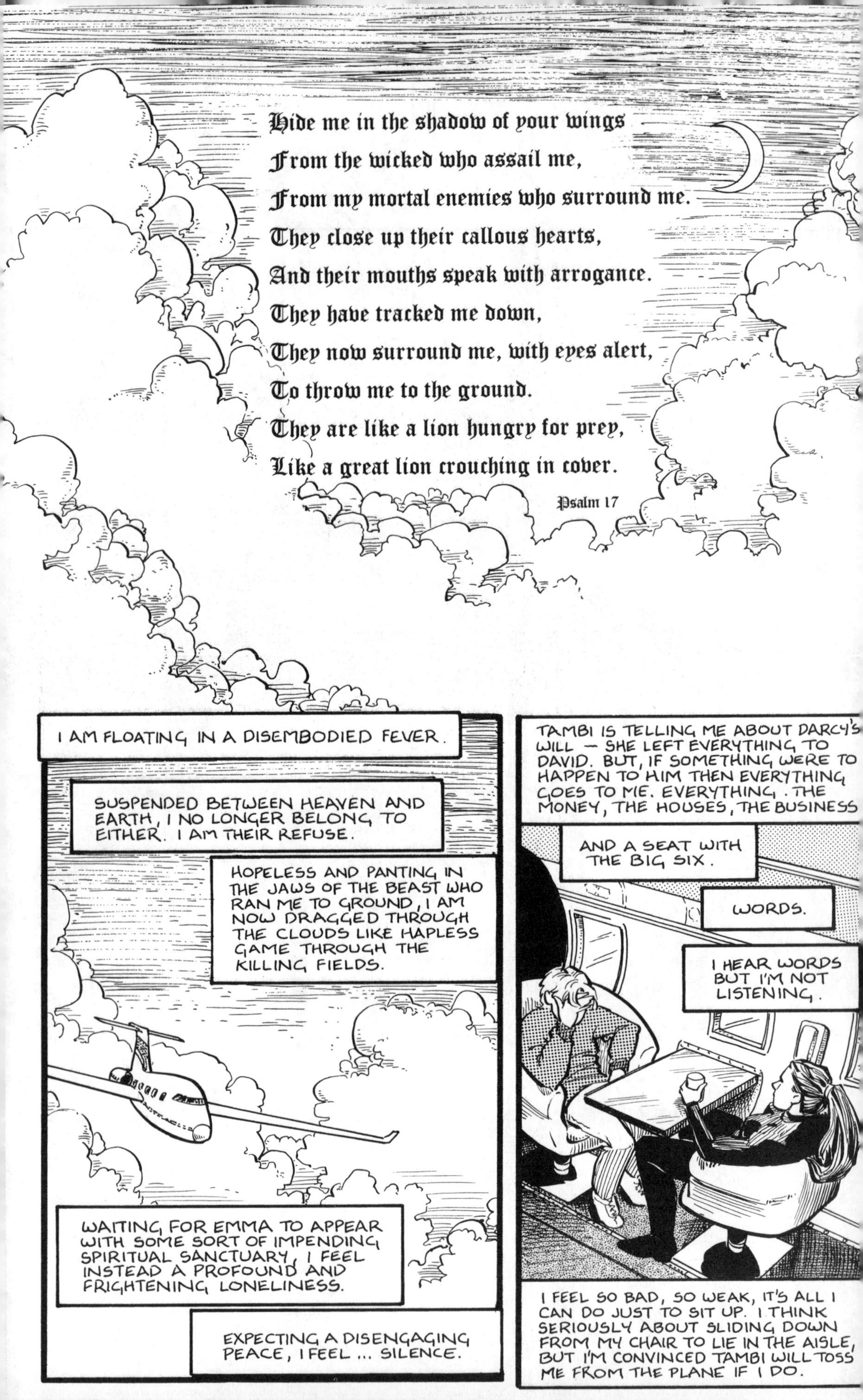
Hide me in the shadow of your wings
From the wicked who assail me,
From my mortal enemies who surround me.
They close up their callous hearts,
And their mouths speak with arrogance.
They have tracked me down,
They now surround me, with eyes alert,
To throw me to the ground.
They are like a lion hungry for prey,
Like a great lion crouching in cover.
Psalm 17
I AM FLOATING IN A DISEMBODIED FEVER.
SUSPENDED BETWEEN HEAVEN AND EARTH, I NO LONGER BELONG TO EITHER. I AM THEIR REFUSE.
HOPELESS AND PANTING IN THE JAWS OF THE BEAST WHO RAN ME TO GROUND, I AM NOW DRAGGED THROUGH THE CLOUDS LIKE HAPLESS GAME THROUGH THE KILLING FIELDS.
WAITING FOR EMMA TO APPEAR WITH SOME SORT OF IMPENDING SPIRITUAL SANCTUARY, I FEEL INSTEAD A PROFOUND AND FRIGHTENING LONELINESS.
EXPECTING A DISENGAGING PEACE, I FEEL ... SILENCE.
TAMBI IS TELLING ME ABOUT DARCY'S WILL — SHE LEFT EVERYTHING TO DAVID. BUT, IF SOMETHING WERE TO HAPPEN TO HIM THEN EVERYTHING GOES TO ME. EVERYTHING. THE MONEY, THE HOUSES, THE BUSINESS
AND A SEAT WITH THE BIG SIX.
WORDS.
I HEAR WORDS BUT I'M NOT LISTENING.
I FEEL SO BAD, SO WEAK, IT'S ALL I CAN DO JUST TO SIT UP. I THINK SERIOUSLY ABOUT SLIDING DOWN FROM MY CHAIR TO LIE IN THE AISLE, BUT I'M CONVINCED TAMBI WILL TOSS ME FROM THE PLANE IF I DO.

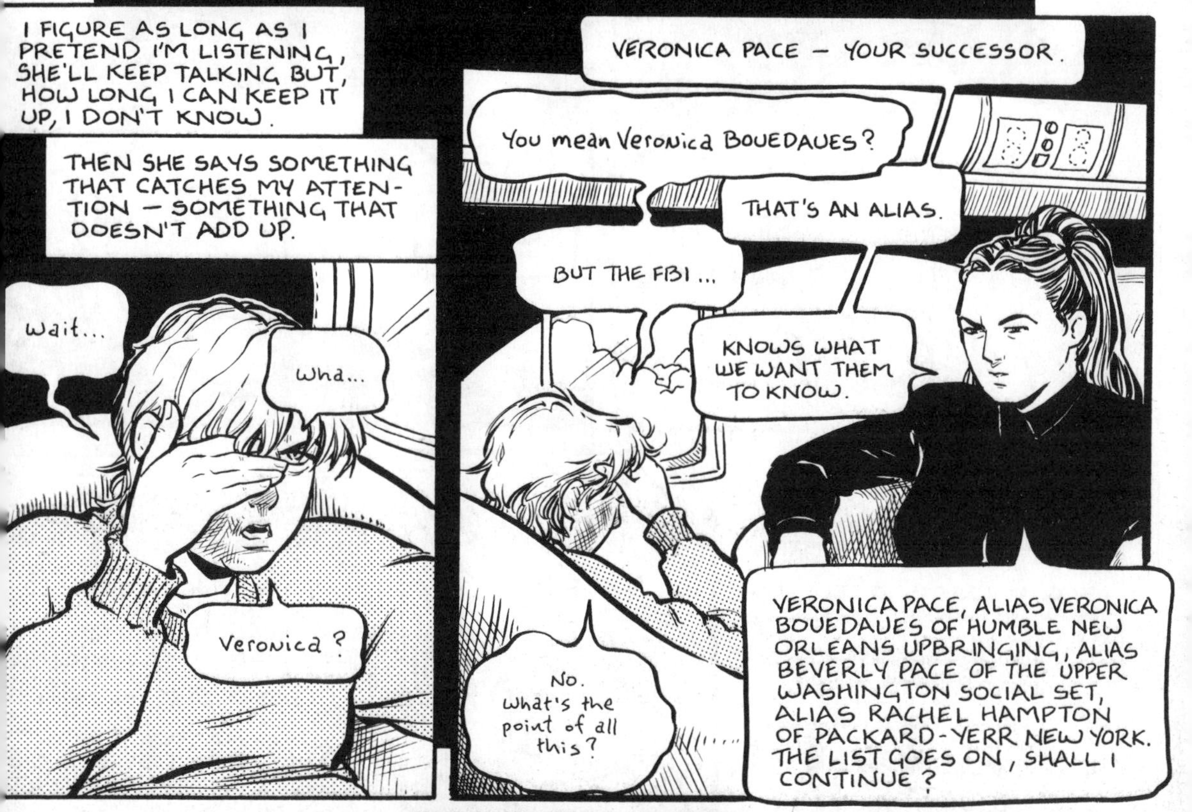
I FIGURE AS LONG AS I PRETEND I'M LISTENING, SHE'LL KEEP TALKING BUT, HOW LONG I CAN KEEP IT UP, I DON'T KNOW.
THEN SHE SAYS SOMETHING THAT CATCHES MY ATTENTION — SOMETHING THAT DOESN'T ADD UP.
wait...
wha...
Veronica?
VERONICA PACE — YOUR SUCCESSOR.
You mean Veronica BOUEDAUES?
THAT'S AN ALIAS.
BUT THE FBI...
KNOWS WHAT WE WANT THEM TO KNOW.
No. what's the point of all this?
VERONICA PACE, ALIAS VERONICA BOUEDAUES OF HUMBLE NEW ORLEANS UPBRINGING, ALIAS BEVERLY PACE OF THE UPPER WASHINGTON SOCIAL SET, ALIAS RACHEL HAMPTON OF PACKARD-YERR NEW YORK. THE LIST GOES ON, SHALL I CONTINUE?

/ERONICA WANTS TO RESURRECT THE PARKER GIRLS — AND SHE WANTS TO SPEARHEAD THE OPERATION.

PRETTY AMBITIOUS FOR A CHAUFFEUR.

NEVER TRUST THE QUIET, CONTRITE ONES.

HOW LONG HAS THIS BEEN GOING ON?

THIS GOES BACK TO BEFORE YOU CAME IN. VERONICA AND SAM WERE PLANNING A COUP D'ETAT TO SEIZE THE OPERATION FROM DARCY. THEY KNEW THAT SAL UCCIANI AND THE OTHERS IN THE BIG SIX WERE NOT HAPPY WITH DARCY'S LACK OF RESPECT AND... DISCRETION, SO THEY OFFERED HIM A DEAL... HELP THEM REMOVE DARCY AND SANCTION THEIR NEW MANAGEMENT AND, IN RETURN, THEY ASSURED HIM A SIGNIFICANT INCREASE IN BRANCH COOPERATION, PLUS A HIGHER PERCENTAGE OF THE TAKE.

:SIGH: IDIOTS.

THAT'S WHEN SAL SENT ME IN.

TO HELP THEM?

TO WATCH THEM. SAL'S NOT STUPID, HE WASN'T ABOUT TO WASTE TIME WITH A COUPLE OF ZEALOUS FOOT SOLDIERS, BUT HE KNEW THEY WERE A

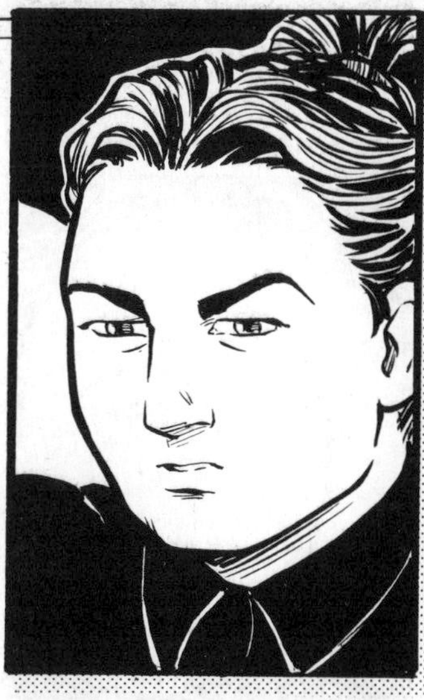

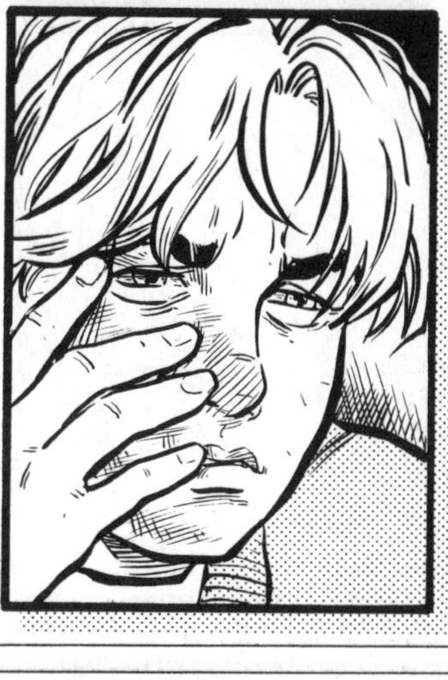

PRECURSOR OF THINGS TO COME. MY JOB WAS TO PROTECT THE INTERESTS OF THE COMPANY — WHATEVER THAT REQUIRED.

AND DARCY NEVER KNEW.

I DON'T THINK SO.

WHY ARE YOU TELLING ME ALL THIS?

BECAUSE THAT'S WHEN YOU CAME IN. YOU CHANGED EVERYTHING.

ME?

ALL OF THIS WAS IN PLACE WHEN EMMA INTRODUCED YOU TO DARCY. SHE KNEW DARCY HAD A FETISH FOR TEENAGE GIRLS...

WAIT A MINUTE...

AND EMMA NEEDED THE MONEY FOR CRANK...

THAT'S A ***DAMN LIE!***

IS IT? WHY DO YOU THINK EMMA GOT YOU INTO PROSTITUTION? WHAT HAPPENED TO ALL THE MONEY YOU MADE?

I... EMMA HANDLED ALL THAT.

WHY DO YOU THINK SHE PULLED YOU OFF THE STREETS — BECAUSE SHE FELT ***SORRY*** FOR YOU? YOU WERE A CASH COW TO HER. DON'T TELL ME YOU'VE BEEN HARBORING SOME SORT OF ROMANTIC ILLUSION ABOUT HER. NOT ***YOU!***

HMM.

I DIDN'T KNOW THAT.

LOOK, I'M NOT IN A HURRY TO DIE BUT, WHY ARE WE HAVING THIS CONVERSATION?

MY GOAL HERE IS TO TELL YOU THE TRUTH...ABOUT EVERYTHING.

WHY? WHAT DIFFERENCE DOES IT MAKE NOW?

DARCY FELL IN LOVE WITH YOU, SHE TRUSTED YOU, SHE EVEN CONFIDED IN YOU. YOU BEGAN TO OFFER YOUR OPINION AND YOUR OBSERVATIONS WERE ASTUTE. YOU DIRECTED HER THROUGH SEVERAL COMPLICATED SITUATIONS AND YOUR INFLUENCE EVENTUALLY MADE THE PARKER OPERATION MORE POWERFUL AND COMPLEX THAN ANYONE THOUGHT POSSIBLE. IN SHORT, TO EVERYONE'S SURPRISE, IT TURNS OUT YOU HAVE A GIFT FOR THIS LINE OF WORK. THAT'S WHY SAMANTHA AND VERONICA SET YOU UP.

THAT'S WHAT I'VE BEEN SAYING, AND YOU KNEW THIS ALL ALONG?

I TOLD YOU, MY JOB WAS TO PROTECT THE COMPANY, NOT FIX YOUR PROBLEMS. DARCY HAD A PARTY FOR DAVID AND INVITED SENATOR CHALMERS, WHO WAS BRINGING HER A PAYMENT FOR A BLACKMAIL DEAL SHE WAS WORKING ON HIM. SHE SENT YOU AND EMMA UPSTAIRS UNDER THE PRETEXT OF REWARDING HIS COOPERATION, BUT THE HIDDEN CAMERAS WOULD SERVE TO PERPETUATE HIS SERVITUDE. THE SENATOR HAD THE MONEY ON HIM. WHEN SAMANTHA WENT TO SWEEP THE ROOM OF LIABILITIES AFTER YOU AND EMMA FINISHED, SHE INTENDED TO TAKE THE MONEY AND HIDE IT. YOU AND EMMA WOULD BE ACCUSED OF THE CRIME AND, IF ALL WENT ACCORDING TO PLAN, THE TWO OF YOU WOULD NEVER SEE THE LIGHT OF DAY AGAIN. SIMPLE ENOUGH, RIGHT? WHAT COULD POSSIBLY GO WRONG?

BUT YOU BEAT THEM TO THE PUNCH — YOU DISAPPEARED WITH THE MONEY BEFORE THEY HAD A CHANCE TO NAIL YOU. I MUST SAY, I WAS IMPRESSED. YOUR TIMING HAS ALWAYS BEEN IMPECCABLE, MISS CHOOVANSKI.

I DIDN'T TAKE THE MONEY.

I KNOW. EMMA TOOK IT, DIDN'T SHE? YOU DIDN'T EVEN KNOW SHE HAD IT UNTIL SHE SHOWED YOU IN HAWAII, DID YOU? YOU JUST WANTED TO RUN AWAY — BUT SHE COMPLICATED MATTERS. HOW AM I DOING SO FAR?

IT'S PISSING ME OFF YOU KNEW ALL THIS AND DIDN'T SAY SOMETHING.

YOU FLEW TO ZURICH AND OPENED AN ACCOUNT IN SAMANTHA'S NAME — A BRILLIANT MOVE BY THE WAY, VERY FARSIGHTED — AND WHEN YOU REJOINED EMMA IN HAWAII, WE WERE WAITING FOR YOU. THE MONEY WAS NOWHERE TO BE FOUND. YOU ACTED LIKE YOU DIDN'T KNOW WHAT WE WERE TALKING ABOUT, EMMA OVERDOSES ON HER NEW CRANK AND NEARLY DROWNS, SAM AND VERONICA WANT TO CRUCIFY YOU AND DARCY WANTS THE PRODIGAL DAUGHTER TO COME HOME. WOULD YOU CARE FOR A DRINK?

NO.

DARCY WOULDN'T LET THEM KILL YOU, SO THEY LET YOU GO. YOU AND EMMA SPLIT UP TO FORK THE TRAIL — SHE GOES HOME TO TORONTO AND YOU TO HOUSTON. SAM'S PLAN WAS TO FOLLOW YOU CONVINCED YOU'D LEAD THEM TO THE MONEY. THEN SHE COULD USE THE WHOLE MESS TO DISCREDIT DARCY AND GET WHAT SHE WANTED. BUT YOU DO NOTHING. YOU LAY LOW, AND SAM GROWS IMPATIENT. THE MONEY SHE'S SIPHONING OFF THE COMPANY ISN'T ENOUGH. SHE VILIFIES YOU TO PARKER— SO THEY SEND DAVID.

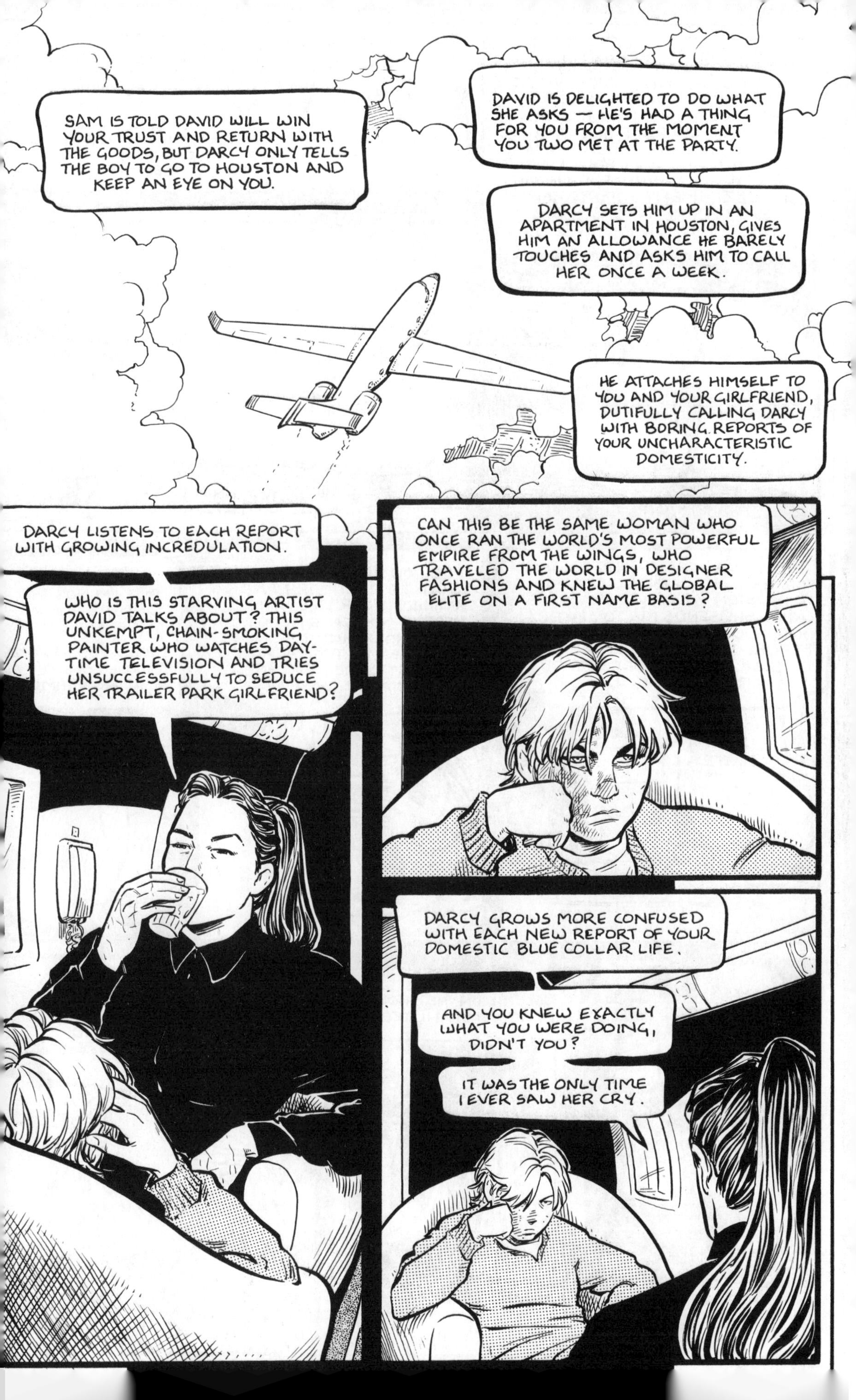
SAM IS TOLD DAVID WILL WIN YOUR TRUST AND RETURN WITH THE GOODS, BUT DARCY ONLY TELLS THE BOY TO GO TO HOUSTON AND KEEP AN EYE ON YOU.
DAVID IS DELIGHTED TO DO WHAT SHE ASKS — HE'S HAD A THING FOR YOU FROM THE MOMENT YOU TWO MET AT THE PARTY.
DARCY SETS HIM UP IN AN APARTMENT IN HOUSTON, GIVES HIM AN ALLOWANCE HE BARELY TOUCHES AND ASKS HIM TO CALL HER ONCE A WEEK.
HE ATTACHES HIMSELF TO YOU AND YOUR GIRLFRIEND, DUTIFULLY CALLING DARCY WITH BORING REPORTS OF YOUR UNCHARACTERISTIC DOMESTICITY.
DARCY LISTENS TO EACH REPORT WITH GROWING INCREDULATION.
WHO IS THIS STARVING ARTIST DAVID TALKS ABOUT? THIS UNKEMPT, CHAIN-SMOKING PAINTER WHO WATCHES DAY-TIME TELEVISION AND TRIES UNSUCCESSFULLY TO SEDUCE HER TRAILER PARK GIRLFRIEND?
CAN THIS BE THE SAME WOMAN WHO ONCE RAN THE WORLD'S MOST POWERFUL EMPIRE FROM THE WINGS, WHO TRAVELED THE WORLD IN DESIGNER FASHIONS AND KNEW THE GLOBAL ELITE ON A FIRST NAME BASIS?
DARCY GROWS MORE CONFUSED WITH EACH NEW REPORT OF YOUR DOMESTIC BLUE COLLAR LIFE.
AND YOU KNEW EXACTLY WHAT YOU WERE DOING, DIDN'T YOU?
IT WAS THE ONLY TIME I EVER SAW HER CRY.

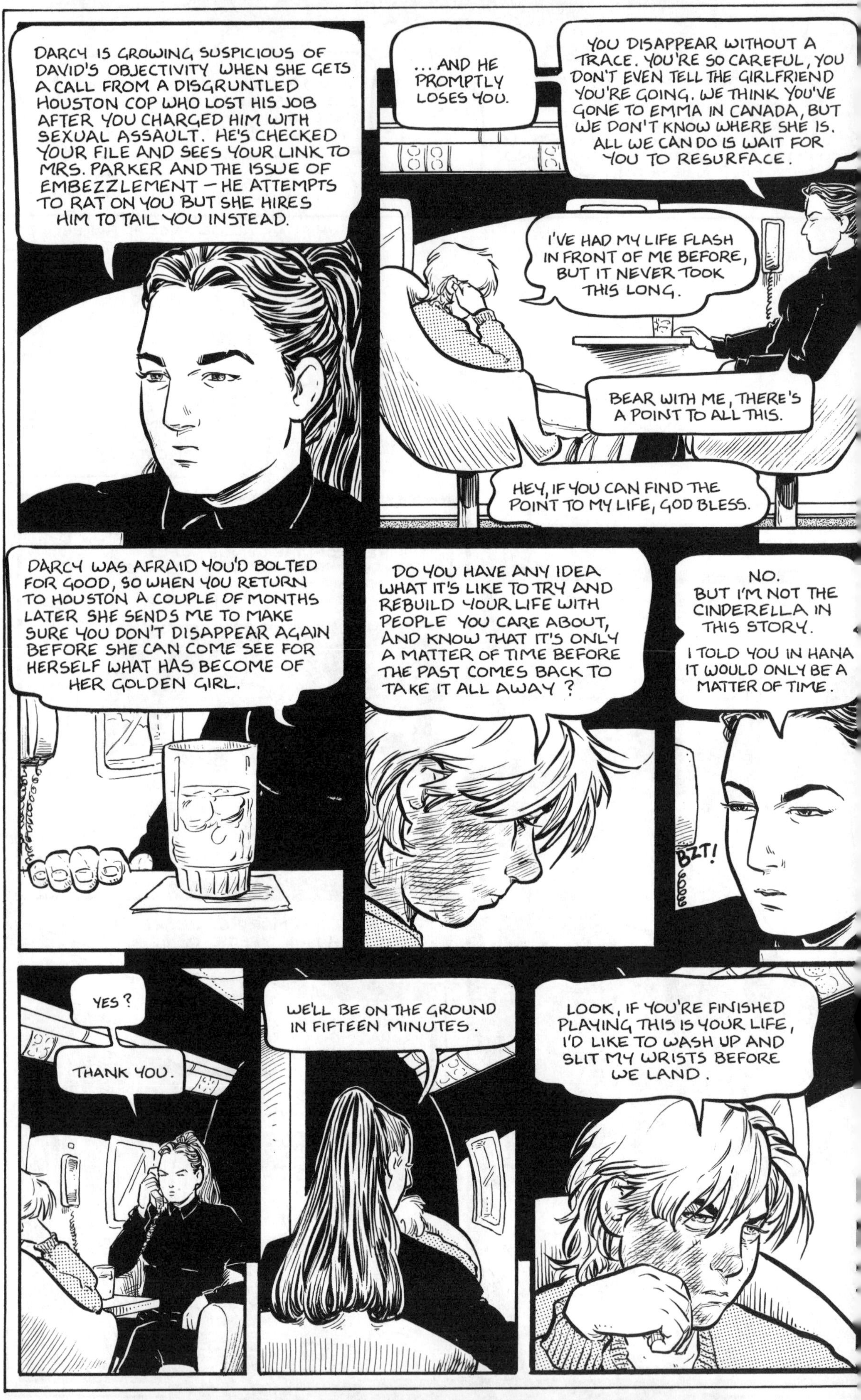
DARCY IS GROWING SUSPICIOUS OF DAVID'S OBJECTIVITY WHEN SHE GETS A CALL FROM A DISGRUNTLED HOUSTON COP WHO LOST HIS JOB AFTER YOU CHARGED HIM WITH SEXUAL ASSAULT. HE'S CHECKED YOUR FILE AND SEES YOUR LINK TO MRS. PARKER AND THE ISSUE OF EMBEZZLEMENT – HE ATTEMPTS TO RAT ON YOU BUT SHE HIRES HIM TO TAIL YOU INSTEAD.
...AND HE PROMPTLY LOSES YOU.
YOU DISAPPEAR WITHOUT A TRACE. YOU'RE SO CAREFUL, YOU DON'T EVEN TELL THE GIRLFRIEND YOU'RE GOING. WE THINK YOU'VE GONE TO EMMA IN CANADA, BUT WE DON'T KNOW WHERE SHE IS. ALL WE CAN DO IS WAIT FOR YOU TO RESURFACE.
I'VE HAD MY LIFE FLASH IN FRONT OF ME BEFORE, BUT IT NEVER TOOK THIS LONG.
BEAR WITH ME, THERE'S A POINT TO ALL THIS.
HEY, IF YOU CAN FIND THE POINT TO MY LIFE, GOD BLESS.
DARCY WAS AFRAID YOU'D BOLTED FOR GOOD, SO WHEN YOU RETURN TO HOUSTON A COUPLE OF MONTHS LATER SHE SENDS ME TO MAKE SURE YOU DON'T DISAPPEAR AGAIN BEFORE SHE CAN COME SEE FOR HERSELF WHAT HAS BECOME OF HER GOLDEN GIRL.
DO YOU HAVE ANY IDEA WHAT IT'S LIKE TO TRY AND REBUILD YOUR LIFE WITH PEOPLE YOU CARE ABOUT, AND KNOW THAT IT'S ONLY A MATTER OF TIME BEFORE THE PAST COMES BACK TO TAKE IT ALL AWAY?
NO. BUT I'M NOT THE CINDERELLA IN THIS STORY.
I TOLD YOU IN HANA IT WOULD ONLY BE A MATTER OF TIME.
BZT!
YES?
THANK YOU.
WE'LL BE ON THE GROUND IN FIFTEEN MINUTES.
LOOK, IF YOU'RE FINISHED PLAYING THIS IS YOUR LIFE, I'D LIKE TO WASH UP AND SLIT MY WRISTS BEFORE WE LAND.

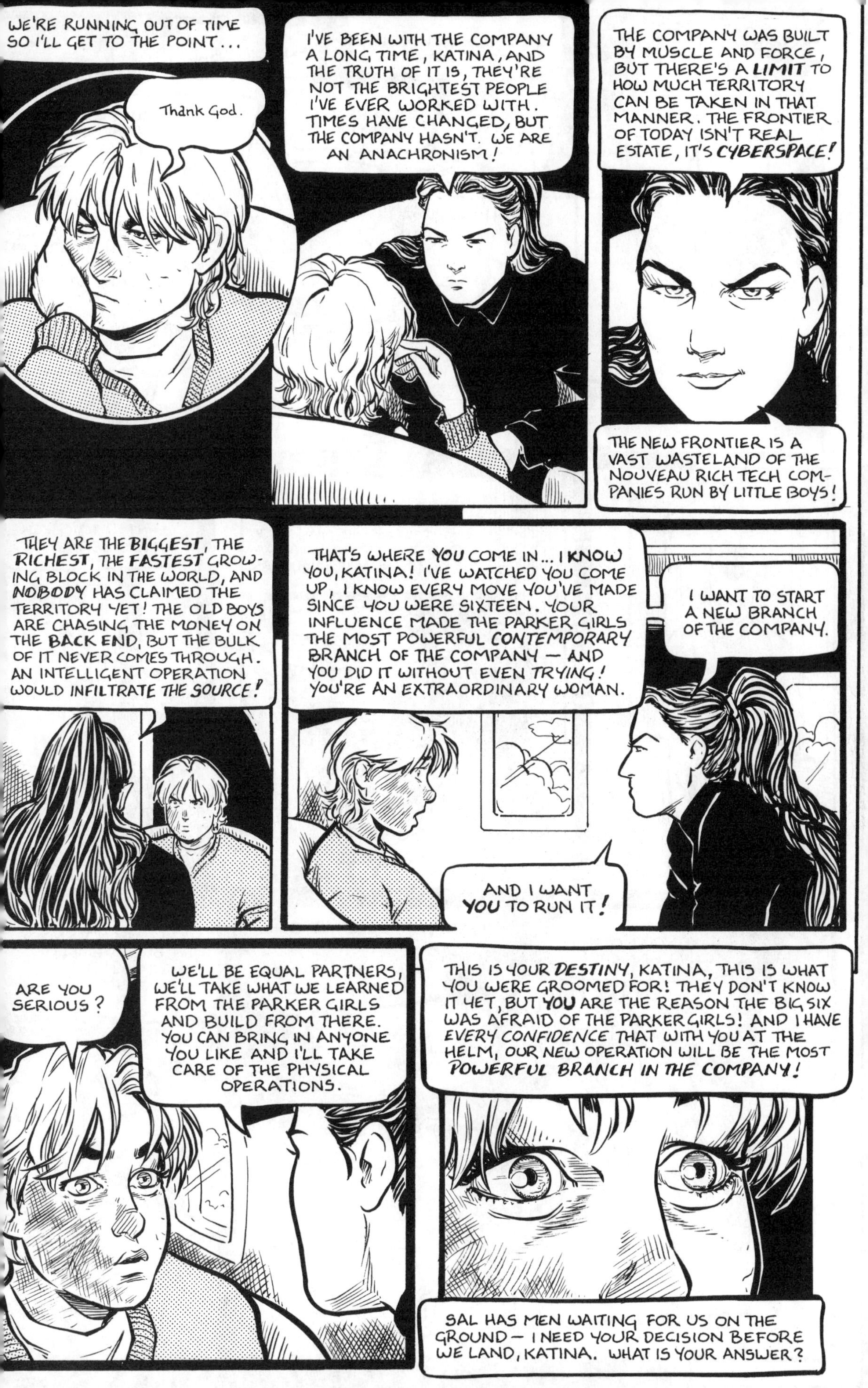
WE'RE RUNNING OUT OF TIME SO I'LL GET TO THE POINT...
Thank God.
I'VE BEEN WITH THE COMPANY A LONG TIME, KATINA, AND THE TRUTH OF IT IS, THEY'RE NOT THE BRIGHTEST PEOPLE I'VE EVER WORKED WITH. TIMES HAVE CHANGED, BUT THE COMPANY HASN'T. WE ARE AN ANACHRONISM!
THE COMPANY WAS BUILT BY MUSCLE AND FORCE, BUT THERE'S A LIMIT TO HOW MUCH TERRITORY CAN BE TAKEN IN THAT MANNER. THE FRONTIER OF TODAY ISN'T REAL ESTATE, IT'S CYBERSPACE!
THE NEW FRONTIER IS A VAST WASTELAND OF THE NOUVEAU RICH TECH COMPANIES RUN BY LITTLE BOYS!
THEY ARE THE BIGGEST, THE RICHEST, THE FASTEST GROWING BLOCK IN THE WORLD, AND NOBODY HAS CLAIMED THE TERRITORY YET! THE OLD BOYS ARE CHASING THE MONEY ON THE BACK END, BUT THE BULK OF IT NEVER COMES THROUGH. AN INTELLIGENT OPERATION WOULD INFILTRATE THE SOURCE!
THAT'S WHERE YOU COME IN... I KNOW YOU, KATINA! I'VE WATCHED YOU COME UP, I KNOW EVERY MOVE YOU'VE MADE SINCE YOU WERE SIXTEEN. YOUR INFLUENCE MADE THE PARKER GIRLS THE MOST POWERFUL CONTEMPORARY BRANCH OF THE COMPANY — AND YOU DID IT WITHOUT EVEN TRYING! YOU'RE AN EXTRAORDINARY WOMAN.
I WANT TO START A NEW BRANCH OF THE COMPANY.
AND I WANT YOU TO RUN IT!
ARE YOU SERIOUS?
WE'LL BE EQUAL PARTNERS, WE'LL TAKE WHAT WE LEARNED FROM THE PARKER GIRLS AND BUILD FROM THERE. YOU CAN BRING IN ANYONE YOU LIKE AND I'LL TAKE CARE OF THE PHYSICAL OPERATIONS.
THIS IS YOUR DESTINY, KATINA, THIS IS WHAT YOU WERE GROOMED FOR! THEY DON'T KNOW IT YET, BUT YOU ARE THE REASON THE BIG SIX WAS AFRAID OF THE PARKER GIRLS! AND I HAVE EVERY CONFIDENCE THAT WITH YOU AT THE HELM, OUR NEW OPERATION WILL BE THE MOST POWERFUL BRANCH IN THE COMPANY!
SAL HAS MEN WAITING FOR US ON THE GROUND — I NEED YOUR DECISION BEFORE WE LAND, KATINA. WHAT IS YOUR ANSWER?

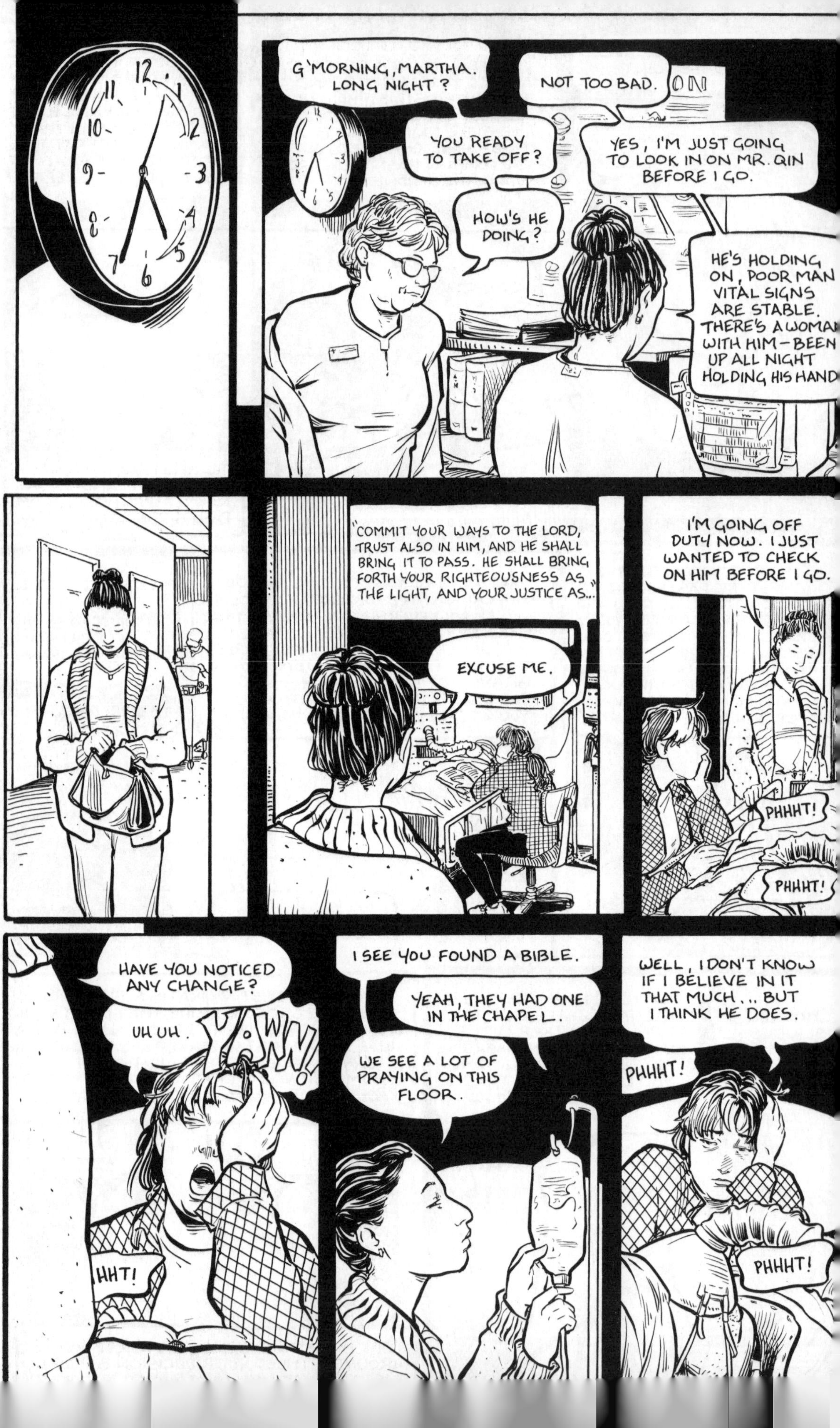
G'MORNING, MARTHA. LONG NIGHT?
NOT TOO BAD.
YOU READY TO TAKE OFF?
YES, I'M JUST GOING TO LOOK IN ON MR. QIN BEFORE I GO.
HOW'S HE DOING?
HE'S HOLDING ON, POOR MAN VITAL SIGNS ARE STABLE. THERE'S A WOMAN WITH HIM—BEEN UP ALL NIGHT HOLDING HIS HAND
"COMMIT YOUR WAYS TO THE LORD, TRUST ALSO IN HIM, AND HE SHALL BRING IT TO PASS. HE SHALL BRING FORTH YOUR RIGHTEOUSNESS AS THE LIGHT, AND YOUR JUSTICE AS..."
EXCUSE ME.
I'M GOING OFF DUTY NOW. I JUST WANTED TO CHECK ON HIM BEFORE I GO.
PHHHT!
PHHHT!
HAVE YOU NOTICED ANY CHANGE?
UH UH.
YAWN!
HHT!
I SEE YOU FOUND A BIBLE.
YEAH, THEY HAD ONE IN THE CHAPEL.
WE SEE A LOT OF PRAYING ON THIS FLOOR.
WELL, I DON'T KNOW IF I BELIEVE IN IT THAT MUCH... BUT I THINK HE DOES.
PHHHT!
PHHHT!

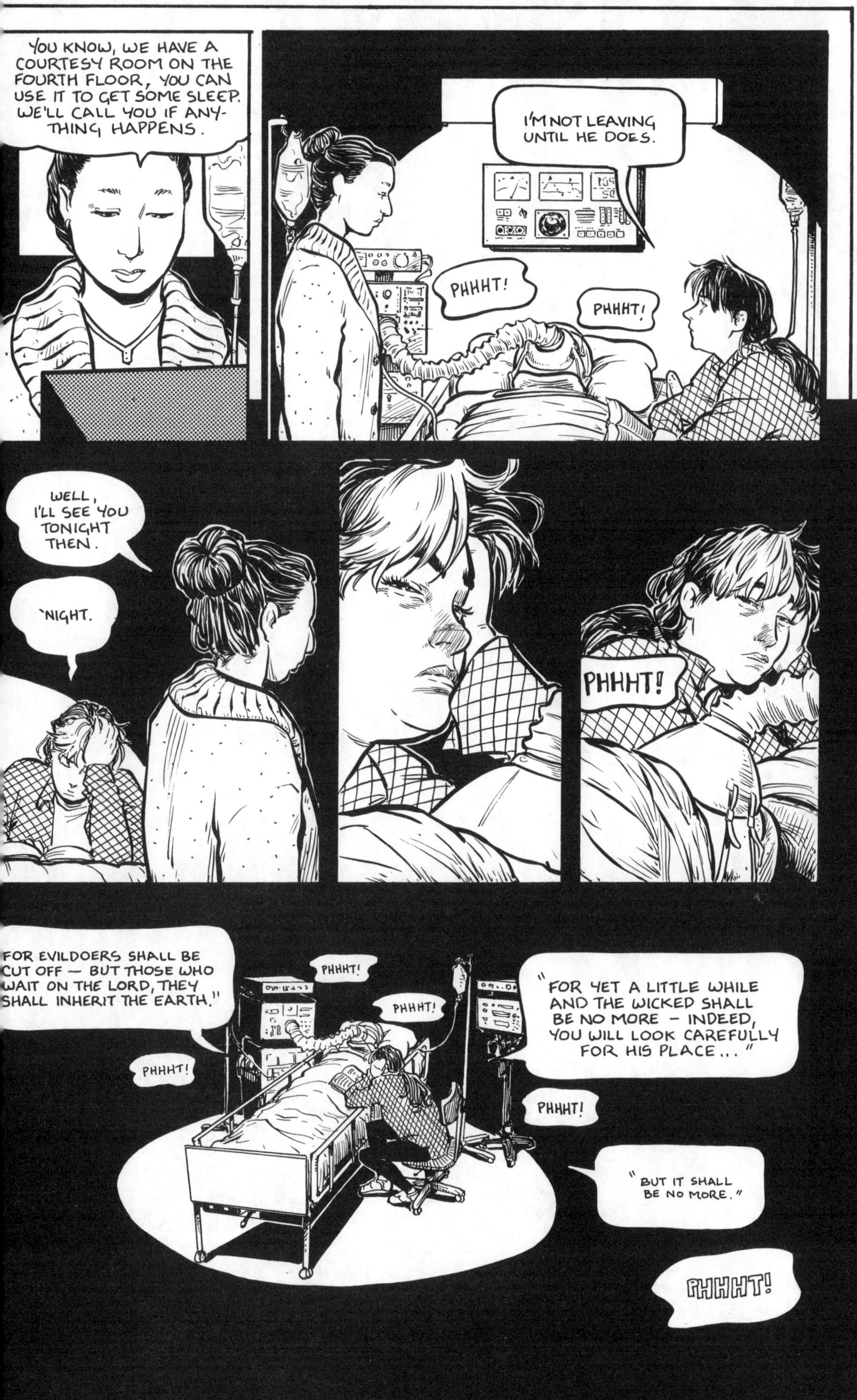
YOU KNOW, WE HAVE A COURTESY ROOM ON THE FOURTH FLOOR, YOU CAN USE IT TO GET SOME SLEEP. WE'LL CALL YOU IF ANY-THING HAPPENS.
I'M NOT LEAVING UNTIL HE DOES.
PHHHT!
PHHHT!
WELL, I'LL SEE YOU TONIGHT THEN.
'NIGHT.
PHHHT!
FOR EVILDOERS SHALL BE CUT OFF — BUT THOSE WHO WAIT ON THE LORD, THEY SHALL INHERIT THE EARTH."
PHHHT!
PHHHT!
PHHHT!
"FOR YET A LITTLE WHILE AND THE WICKED SHALL BE NO MORE - INDEED, YOU WILL LOOK CAREFULLY FOR HIS PLACE..."
PHHHT!
"BUT IT SHALL BE NO MORE."
PHHHT!

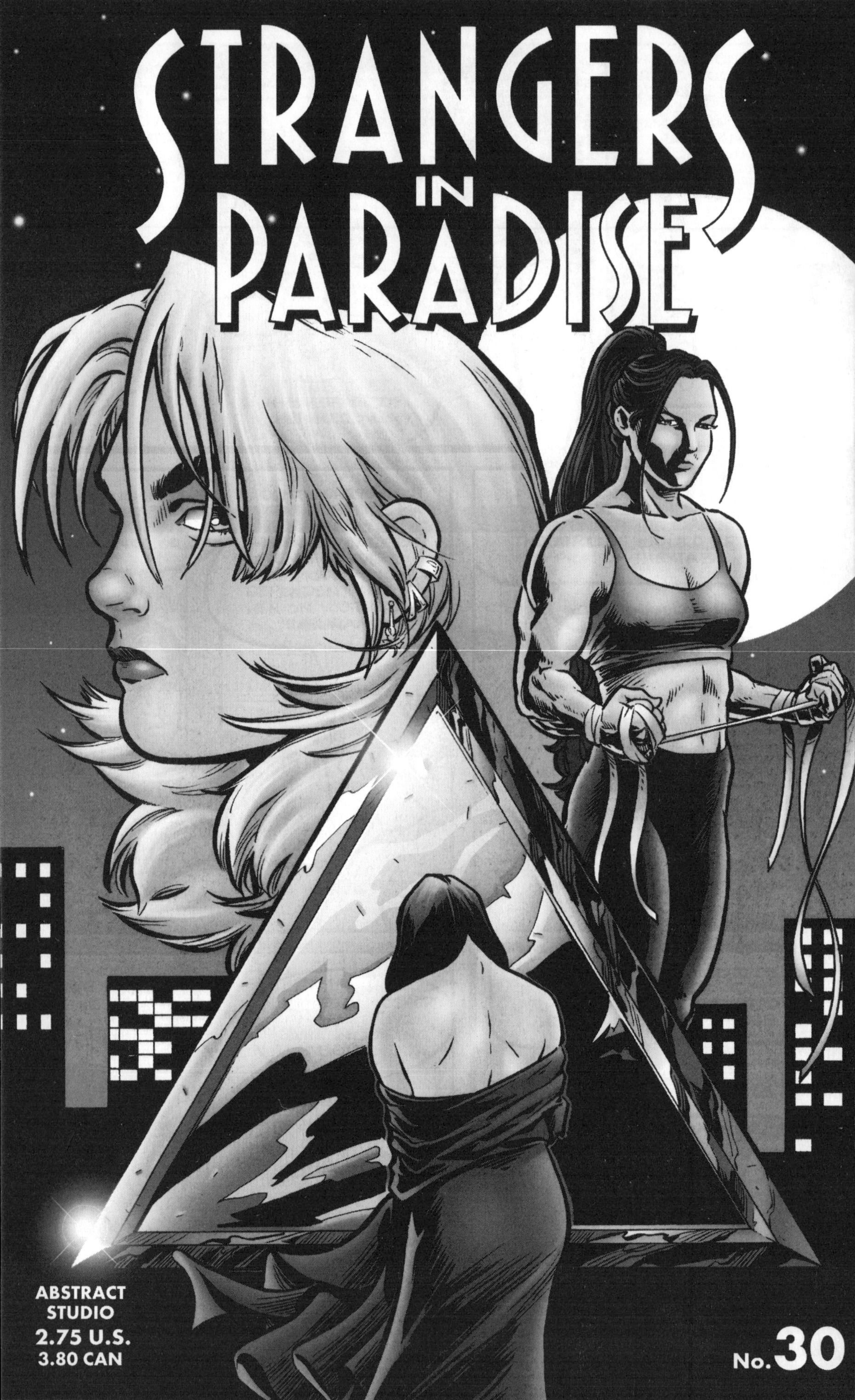
STRANGERS IN PARADISE
ABSTRACT STUDIO
2.75 U.S.
3.80 CAN
No. 30

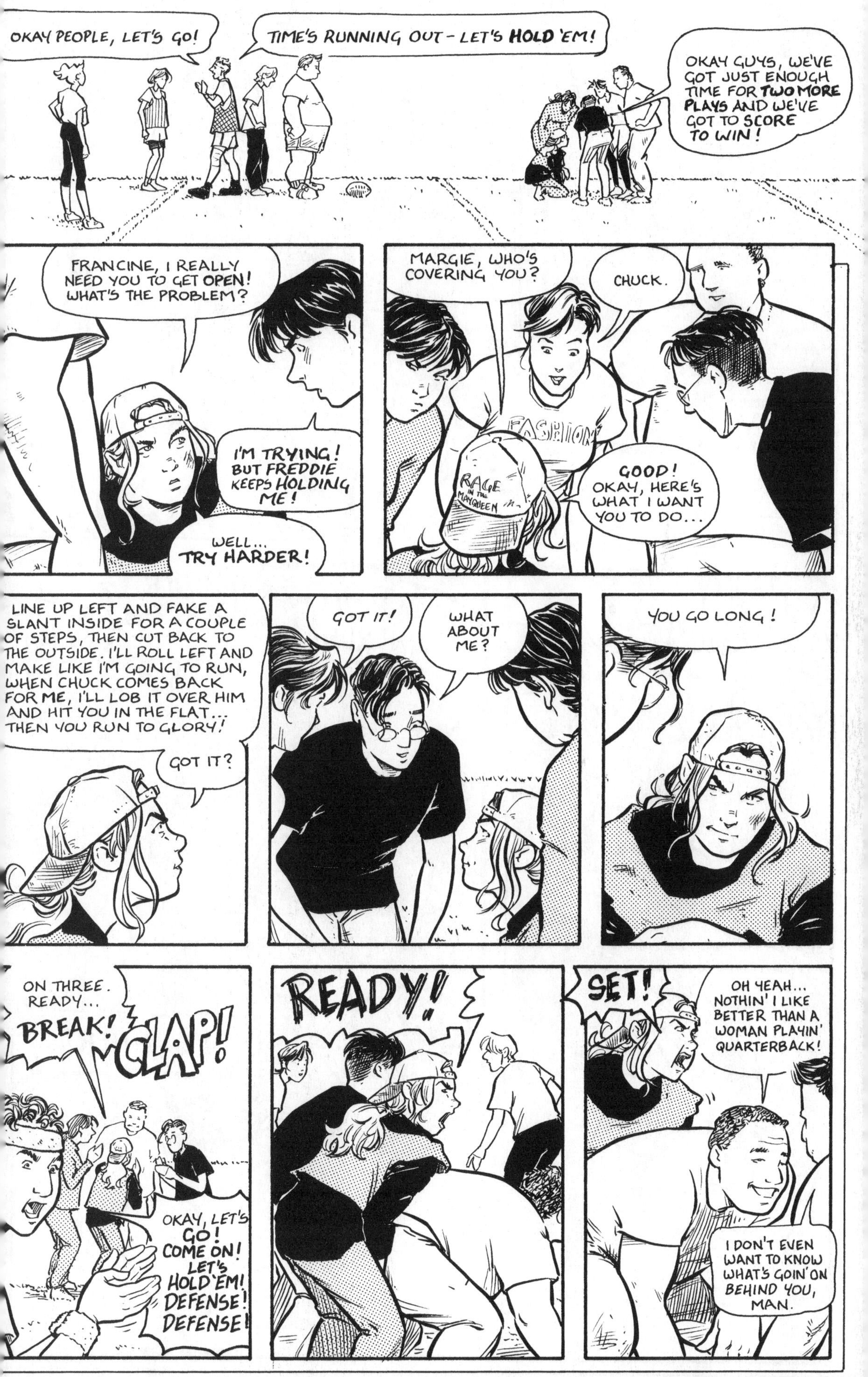
OKAY PEOPLE, LET'S GO!
TIME'S RUNNING OUT - LET'S HOLD 'EM!
OKAY GUYS, WE'VE GOT JUST ENOUGH TIME FOR TWO MORE PLAYS AND WE'VE GOT TO SCORE TO WIN!
FRANCINE, I REALLY NEED YOU TO GET OPEN! WHAT'S THE PROBLEM?
I'M TRYING! BUT FREDDIE KEEPS HOLDING ME!
WELL... TRY HARDER!
MARGIE, WHO'S COVERING YOU?
CHUCK.
FASHION
RAGE IN THE MAYQUEEN
GOOD! OKAY, HERE'S WHAT I WANT YOU TO DO...
LINE UP LEFT AND FAKE A SLANT INSIDE FOR A COUPLE OF STEPS, THEN CUT BACK TO THE OUTSIDE. I'LL ROLL LEFT AND MAKE LIKE I'M GOING TO RUN, WHEN CHUCK COMES BACK FOR ME, I'LL LOB IT OVER HIM AND HIT YOU IN THE FLAT... THEN YOU RUN TO GLORY!
GOT IT?
GOT IT!
WHAT ABOUT ME?
YOU GO LONG!
ON THREE. READY...
BREAK!
CLAP!
OKAY, LET'S GO! COME ON! LET'S HOLD 'EM! DEFENSE! DEFENSE!
READY!
SET!
OH YEAH... NOTHIN' I LIKE BETTER THAN A WOMAN PLAYIN' QUARTERBACK!
I DON'T EVEN WANT TO KNOW WHAT'S GOIN' ON BEHIND YOU, MAN.

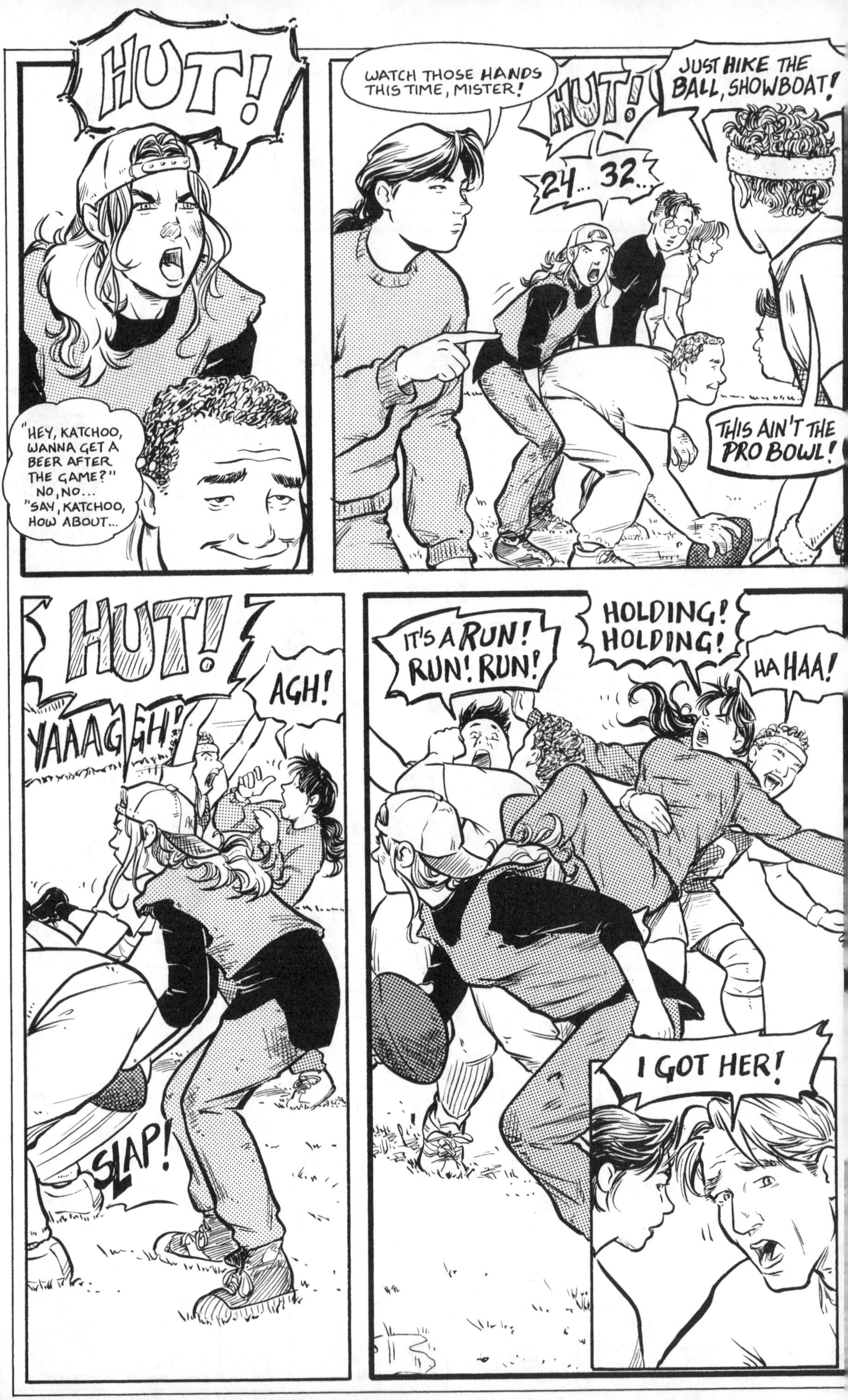

HUT!
"HEY, KATCHOO, WANNA GET A BEER AFTER THE GAME?" NO, NO... "SAY, KATCHOO, HOW ABOUT...
WATCH THOSE HANDS THIS TIME, MISTER!
HUT!
24... 32...
JUST HIKE THE BALL, SHOWBOAT!
THIS AIN'T THE PRO BOWL!
HUT!
YAAAGGH!
AGH!
SLAP!
IT'S A RUN! RUN! RUN!
HOLDING! HOLDING!
HA HAA!
I GOT HER!

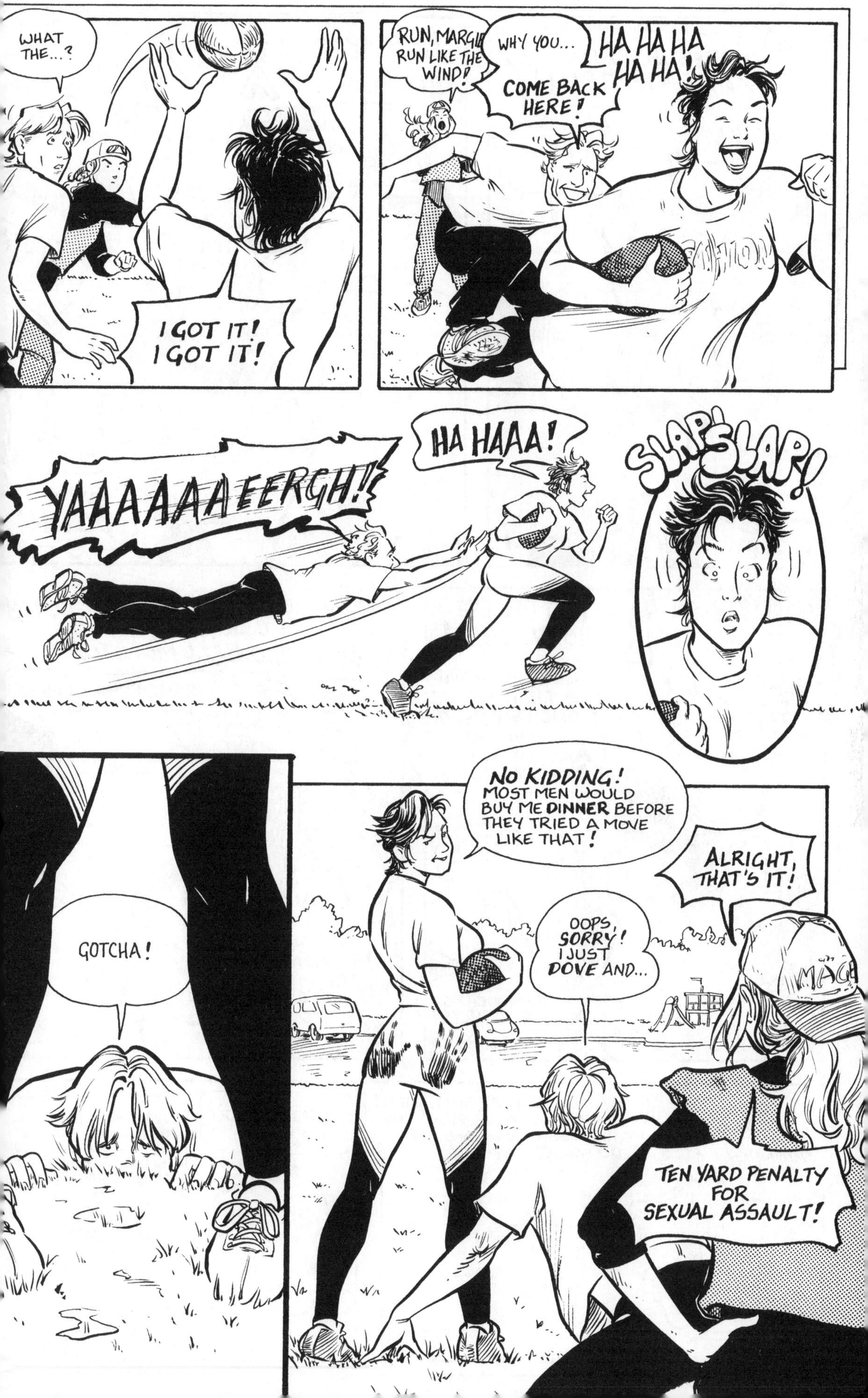
WHAT THE...?
I GOT IT! I GOT IT!
RUN, MARGIE RUN LIKE THE WIND!
WHY YOU...
COME BACK HERE!
HA HA HA HA HA!
YAAAAAAEERGH!!
HA HAAA!
SLAP! SLAP!
GOTCHA!
NO KIDDING! MOST MEN WOULD BUY ME DINNER BEFORE THEY TRIED A MOVE LIKE THAT!
ALRIGHT, THAT'S IT!
OOPS, SORRY! I JUST DOVE AND...
TEN YARD PENALTY FOR SEXUAL ASSAULT!

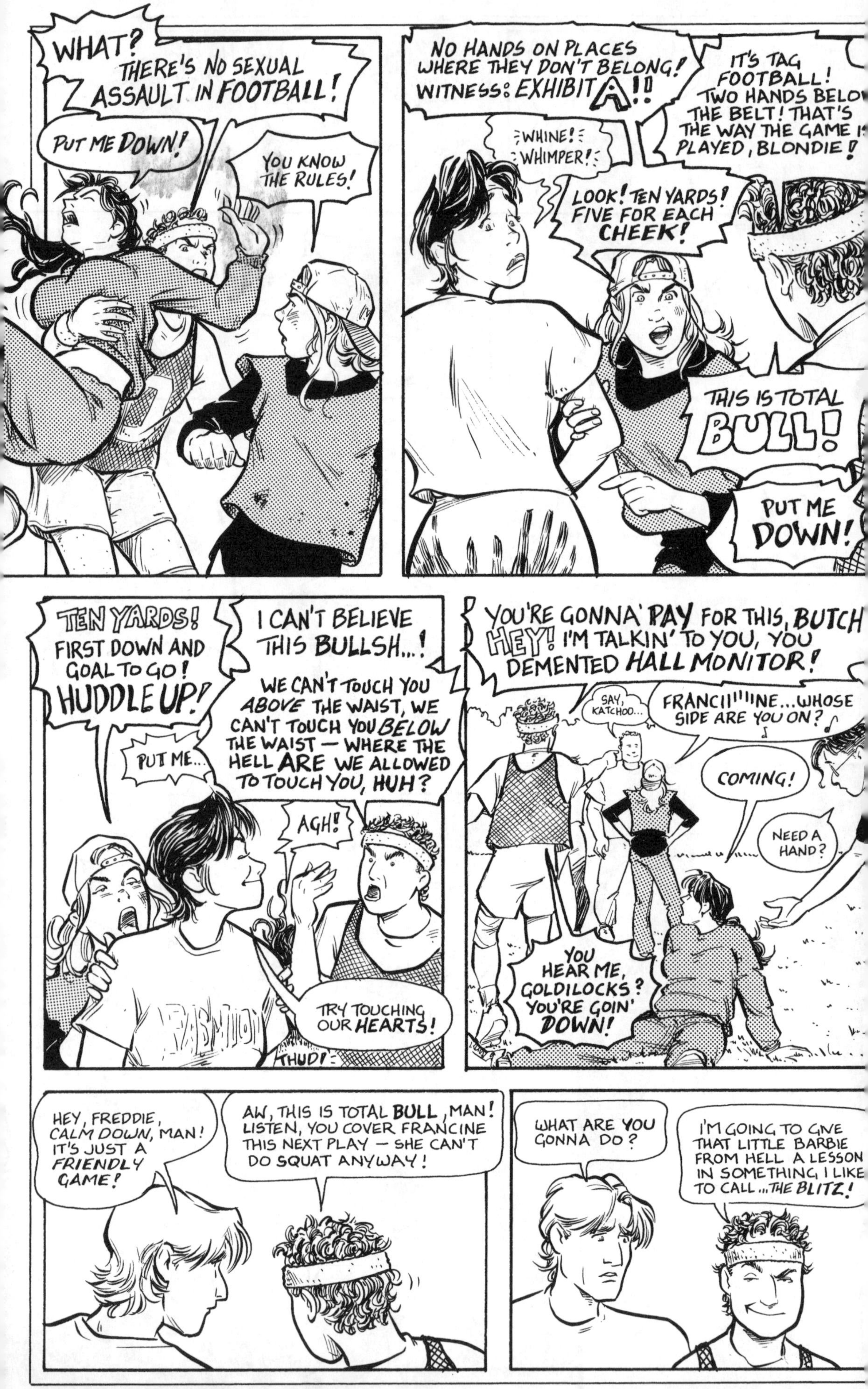
WHAT? THERE'S NO SEXUAL ASSAULT IN FOOTBALL!
PUT ME DOWN!
YOU KNOW THE RULES!
NO HANDS ON PLACES WHERE THEY DON'T BELONG! WITNESS: EXHIBIT A!!
WHINE! WHIMPER!
IT'S TAG FOOTBALL! TWO HANDS BELO THE BELT! THAT'S THE WAY THE GAME I PLAYED, BLONDIE!
LOOK! TEN YARDS! FIVE FOR EACH CHEEK!
THIS IS TOTAL BULL!
PUT ME DOWN!
TEN YARDS! FIRST DOWN AND GOAL TO GO! HUDDLE UP!
I CAN'T BELIEVE THIS BULLSH...!
WE CAN'T TOUCH YOU ABOVE THE WAIST, WE CAN'T TOUCH YOU BELOW THE WAIST — WHERE THE HELL ARE WE ALLOWED TO TOUCH YOU, HUH?
PUT ME...
AGH!
TRY TOUCHING OUR HEARTS!
THUD!
YOU'RE GONNA' PAY FOR THIS, BUTCH
HEY! I'M TALKIN' TO YOU, YOU DEMENTED HALL MONITOR!
SAY, KATCHOO...
FRANCIIIIINE... WHOSE SIDE ARE YOU ON?
COMING!
NEED A HAND?
YOU HEAR ME, GOLDILOCKS? YOU'RE GOIN' DOWN!
HEY, FREDDIE, CALM DOWN, MAN! IT'S JUST A FRIENDLY GAME!
AW, THIS IS TOTAL BULL, MAN! LISTEN, YOU COVER FRANCINE THIS NEXT PLAY — SHE CAN'T DO SQUAT ANYWAY!
WHAT ARE YOU GONNA DO?
I'M GOING TO GIVE THAT LITTLE BARBIE FROM HELL A LESSON IN SOMETHING I LIKE TO CALL... THE BLITZ!

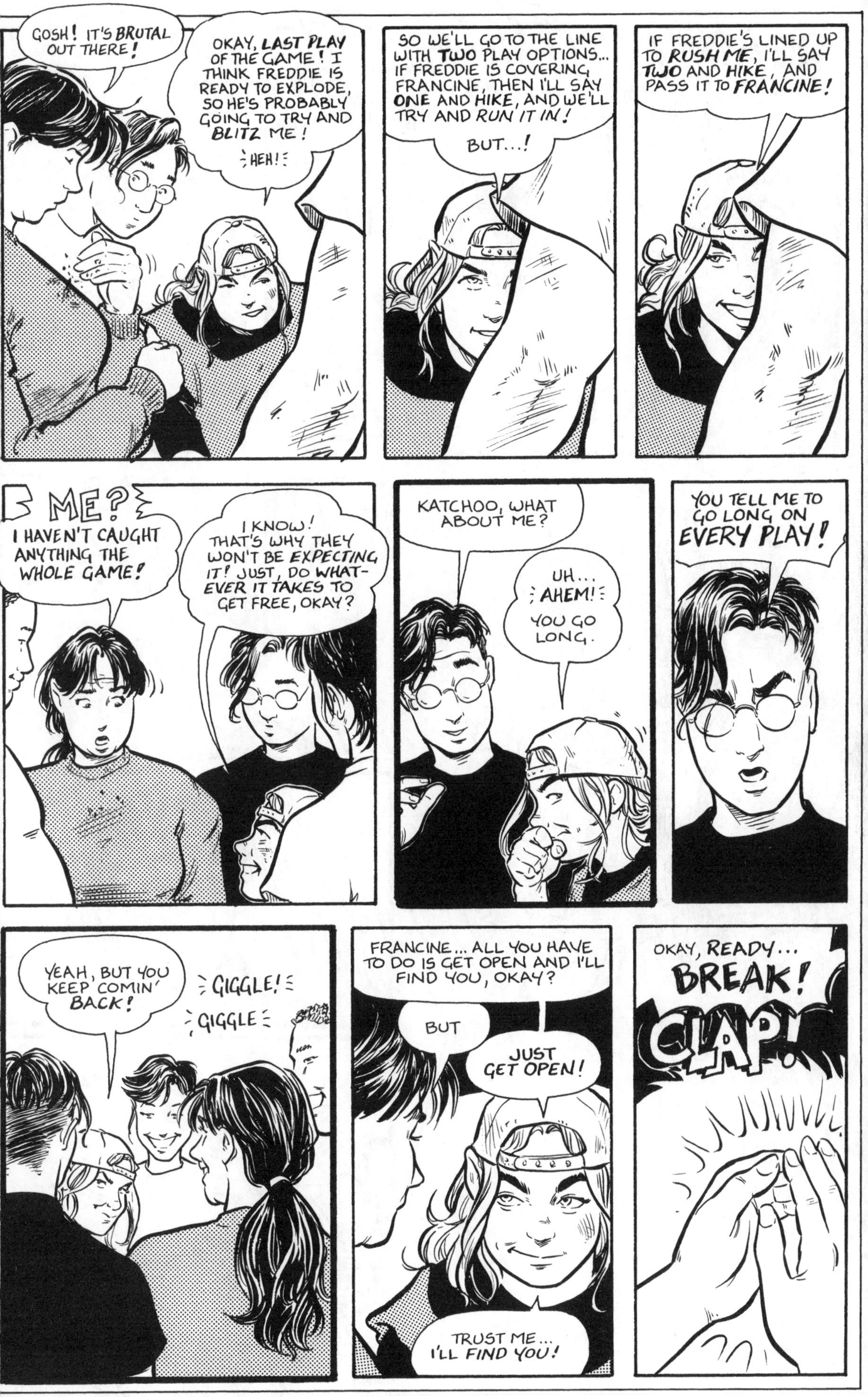
GOSH! IT'S BRUTAL OUT THERE!
OKAY, LAST PLAY OF THE GAME! I THINK FREDDIE IS READY TO EXPLODE, SO HE'S PROBABLY GOING TO TRY AND BLITZ ME!
HEH!
SO WE'LL GO TO THE LINE WITH TWO PLAY OPTIONS... IF FREDDIE IS COVERING FRANCINE, THEN I'LL SAY ONE AND HIKE, AND WE'LL TRY AND RUN IT IN!
BUT...!
IF FREDDIE'S LINED UP TO RUSH ME, I'LL SAY TWO AND HIKE, AND PASS IT TO FRANCINE!
ME?
I HAVEN'T CAUGHT ANYTHING THE WHOLE GAME!
I KNOW! THAT'S WHY THEY WON'T BE EXPECTING IT! JUST, DO WHATEVER IT TAKES TO GET FREE, OKAY?
KATCHOO, WHAT ABOUT ME?
UH... AHEM! YOU GO LONG.
YOU TELL ME TO GO LONG ON EVERY PLAY!
YEAH, BUT YOU KEEP COMIN' BACK!
GIGGLE!
GIGGLE
FRANCINE... ALL YOU HAVE TO DO IS GET OPEN AND I'LL FIND YOU, OKAY?
BUT
JUST GET OPEN!
TRUST ME... I'LL FIND YOU!
OKAY, READY... BREAK!
CLAP!

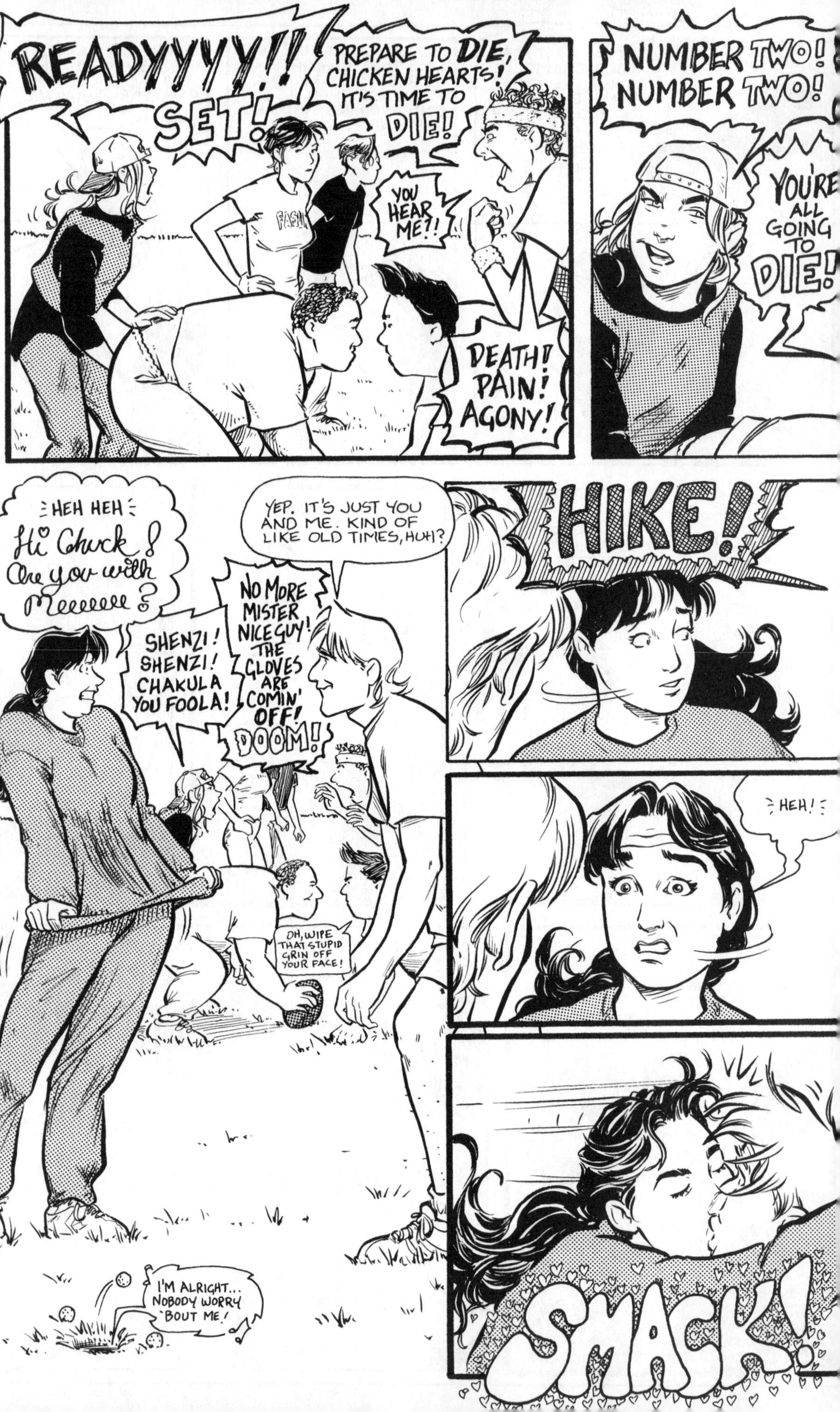
READYYYY!!
SET!
PREPARE TO DIE, CHICKEN HEARTS! IT'S TIME TO DIE!
YOU HEAR ME?!
DEATH! PAIN! AGONY!
NUMBER TWO! NUMBER TWO!
YOU'RE ALL GOING TO DIE!
HEH HEH
Hi Chuck! Are you with Meeeeee?
YEP. IT'S JUST YOU AND ME. KIND OF LIKE OLD TIMES, HUH?
SHENZI! SHENZI! CHAKULA YOU FOOLA!
NO MORE MISTER NICE GUY! THE GLOVES ARE COMIN' OFF! DOOM!
OH, WIPE THAT STUPID GRIN OFF YOUR FACE!
I'M ALRIGHT... NOBODY WORRY 'BOUT ME!
HIKE!
HEH!
SMACK!

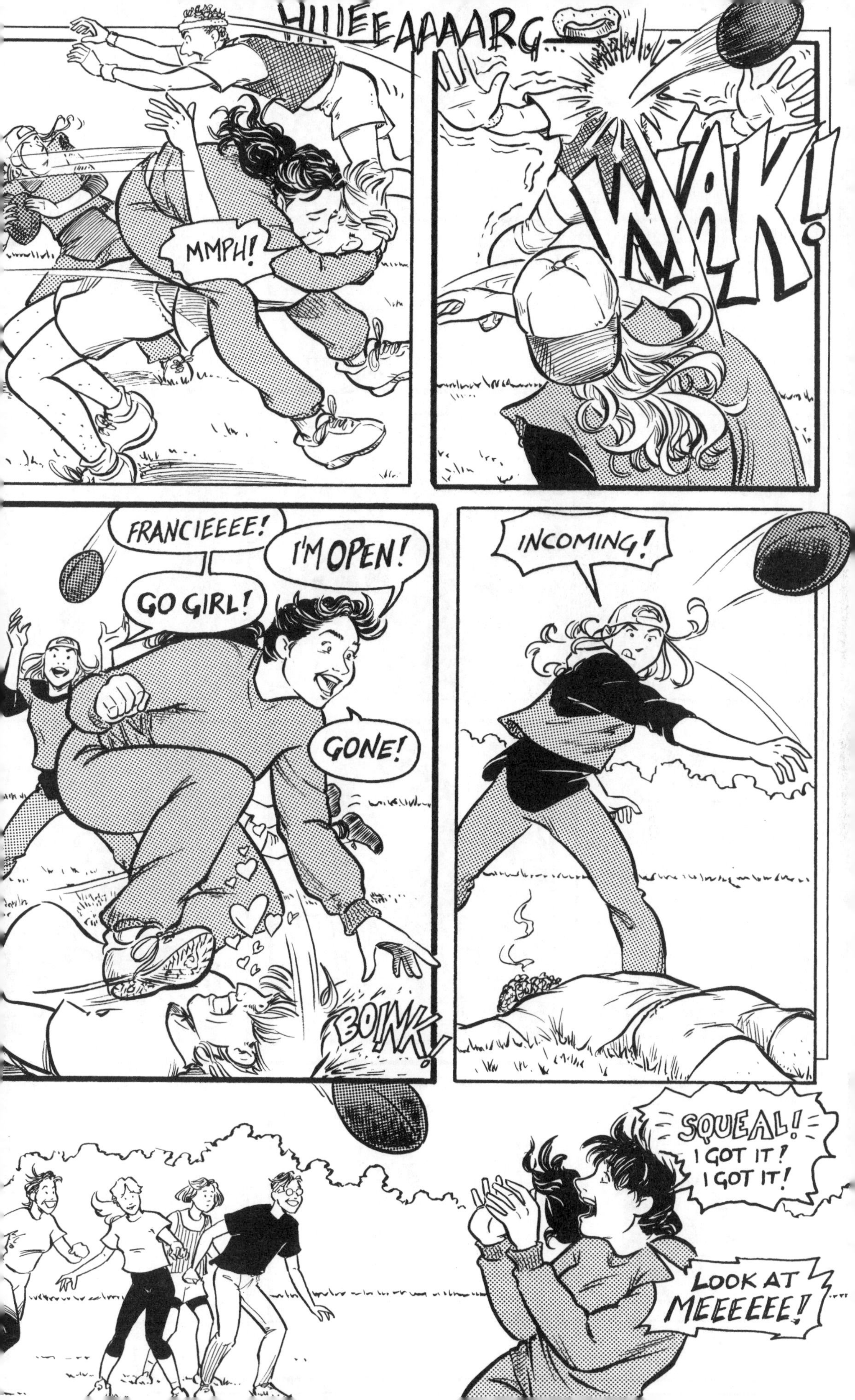
HIIIEEAAAARG
MMPH!
WAK!
FRANCIEEEE!
GO GIRL!
I'M OPEN!
GONE!
BOINK!
INCOMING!
SQUEAL!
I GOT IT!
I GOT IT!
LOOK AT
MEEEEEE!

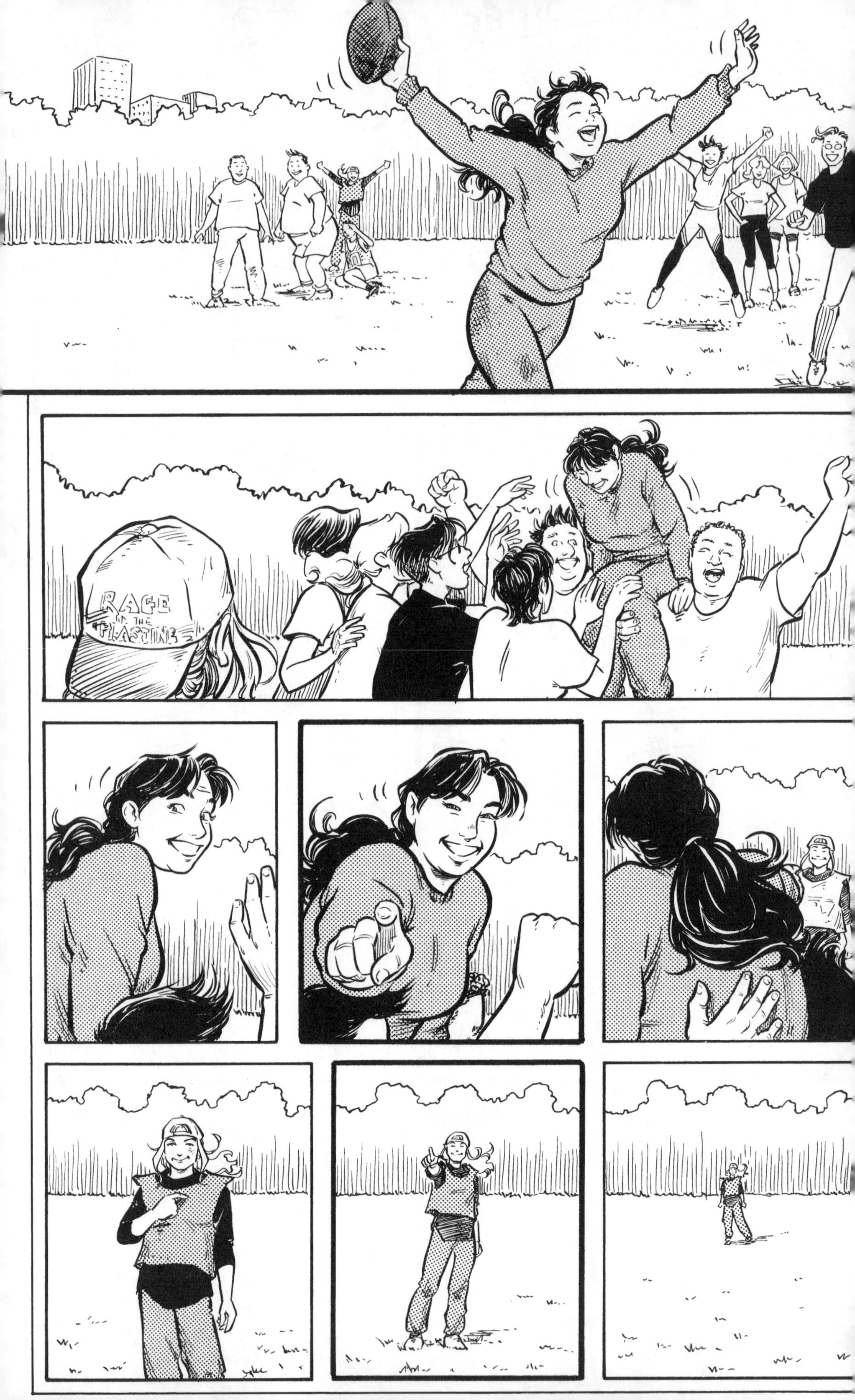
RAGE IN THE PLASTINE

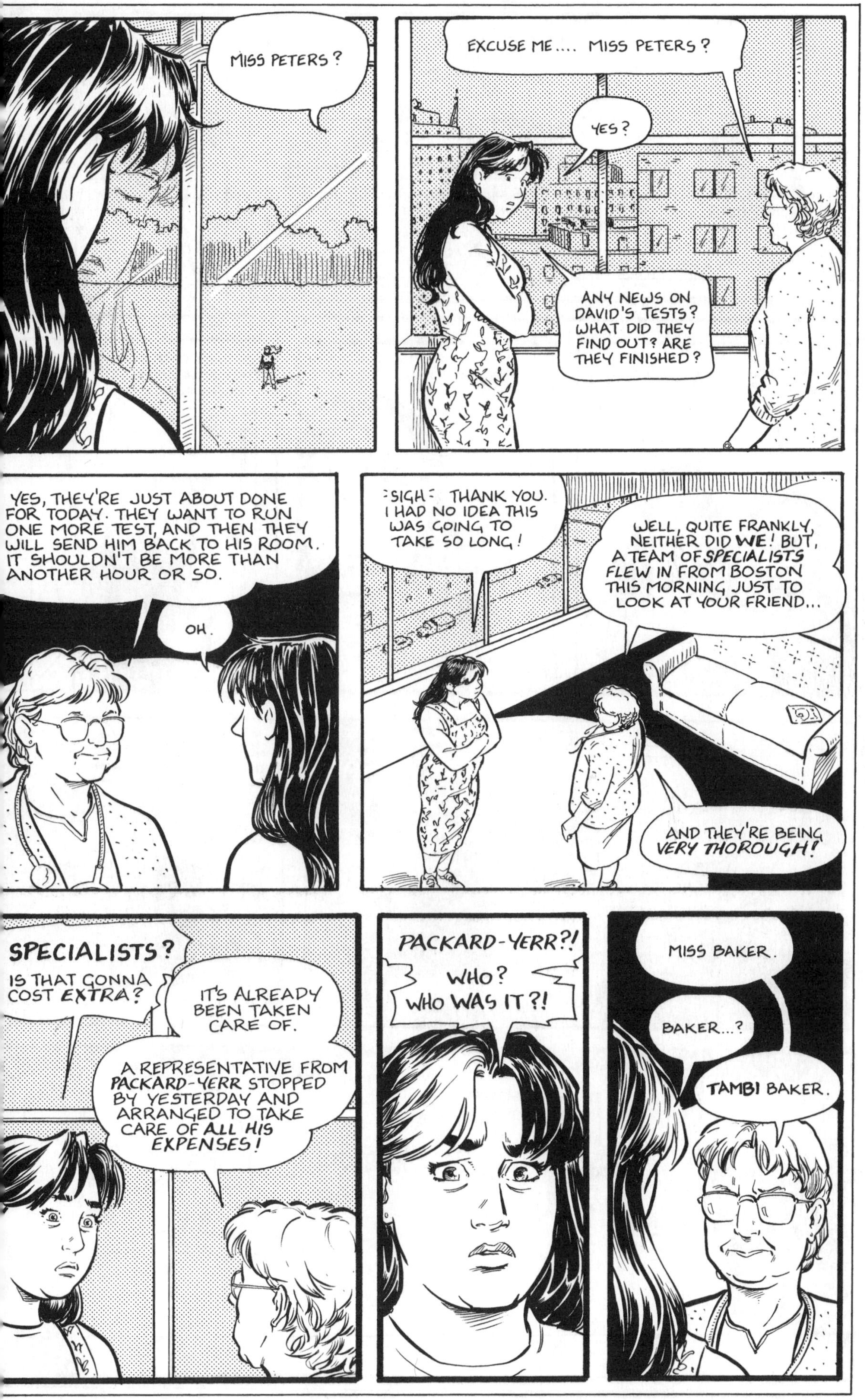
MISS PETERS?
EXCUSE ME.... MISS PETERS?
YES?
ANY NEWS ON DAVID'S TESTS? WHAT DID THEY FIND OUT? ARE THEY FINISHED?
YES, THEY'RE JUST ABOUT DONE FOR TODAY. THEY WANT TO RUN ONE MORE TEST, AND THEN THEY WILL SEND HIM BACK TO HIS ROOM. IT SHOULDN'T BE MORE THAN ANOTHER HOUR OR SO.
OH.
:SIGH: THANK YOU. I HAD NO IDEA THIS WAS GOING TO TAKE SO LONG!
WELL, QUITE FRANKLY, NEITHER DID WE! BUT, A TEAM OF SPECIALISTS FLEW IN FROM BOSTON THIS MORNING JUST TO LOOK AT YOUR FRIEND...
AND THEY'RE BEING VERY THOROUGH!
SPECIALISTS? IS THAT GONNA COST EXTRA?
IT'S ALREADY BEEN TAKEN CARE OF.
A REPRESENTATIVE FROM PACKARD-YERR STOPPED BY YESTERDAY AND ARRANGED TO TAKE CARE OF ALL HIS EXPENSES!
PACKARD-YERR?!
WHO? WHO WAS IT?!
MISS BAKER.
BAKER...?
TAMBI BAKER.

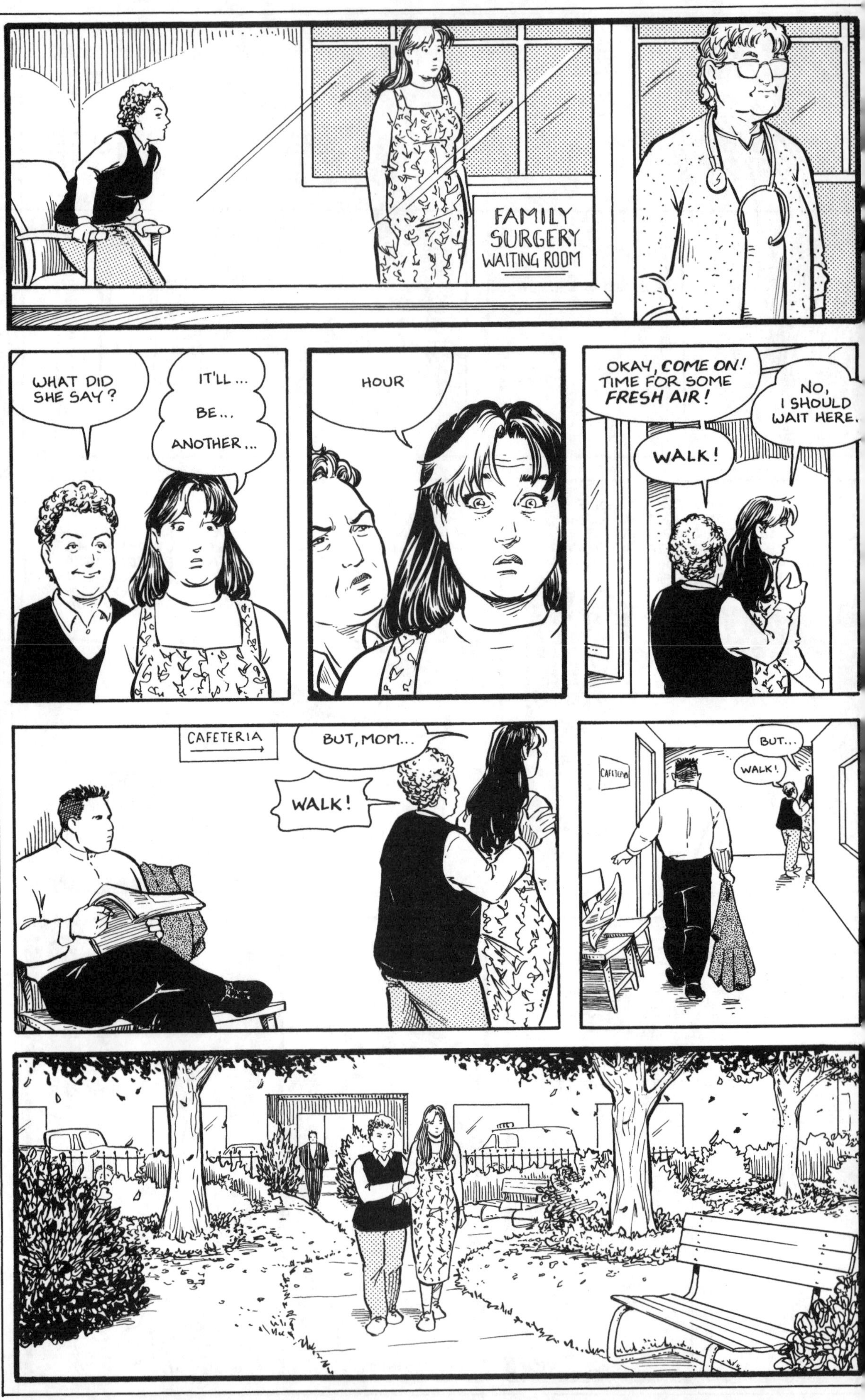
FAMILY
SURGERY
WAITING ROOM
WHAT DID SHE SAY?
IT'LL... BE... ANOTHER...
HOUR
OKAY, COME ON! TIME FOR SOME FRESH AIR!
WALK!
NO, I SHOULD WAIT HERE.
CAFETERIA
BUT, MOM...
WALK!
BUT...
WALK!

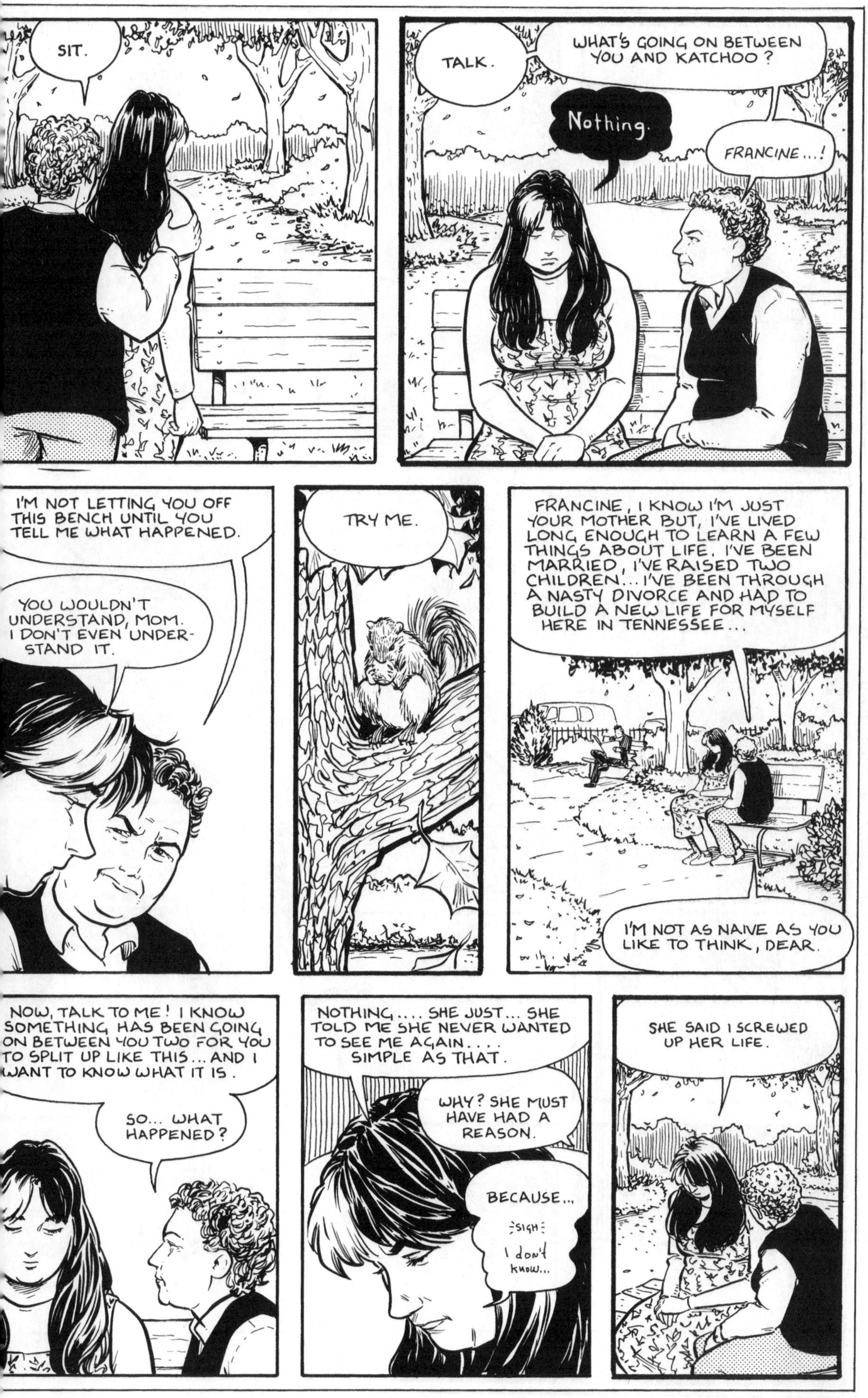
SIT.
TALK.
WHAT'S GOING ON BETWEEN YOU AND KATCHOO?
Nothing.
FRANCINE...!
I'M NOT LETTING YOU OFF THIS BENCH UNTIL YOU TELL ME WHAT HAPPENED.
YOU WOULDN'T UNDERSTAND, MOM. I DON'T EVEN UNDERSTAND IT.
TRY ME.
FRANCINE, I KNOW I'M JUST YOUR MOTHER BUT, I'VE LIVED LONG ENOUGH TO LEARN A FEW THINGS ABOUT LIFE. I'VE BEEN MARRIED, I'VE RAISED TWO CHILDREN... I'VE BEEN THROUGH A NASTY DIVORCE AND HAD TO BUILD A NEW LIFE FOR MYSELF HERE IN TENNESSEE...
I'M NOT AS NAIVE AS YOU LIKE TO THINK, DEAR.
NOW, TALK TO ME! I KNOW SOMETHING HAS BEEN GOING ON BETWEEN YOU TWO FOR YOU TO SPLIT UP LIKE THIS... AND I WANT TO KNOW WHAT IT IS.
SO... WHAT HAPPENED?
NOTHING.... SHE JUST... SHE TOLD ME SHE NEVER WANTED TO SEE ME AGAIN.... SIMPLE AS THAT.
WHY? SHE MUST HAVE HAD A REASON.
BECAUSE...
SIGH
I don't know...
SHE SAID I SCREWED UP HER LIFE.

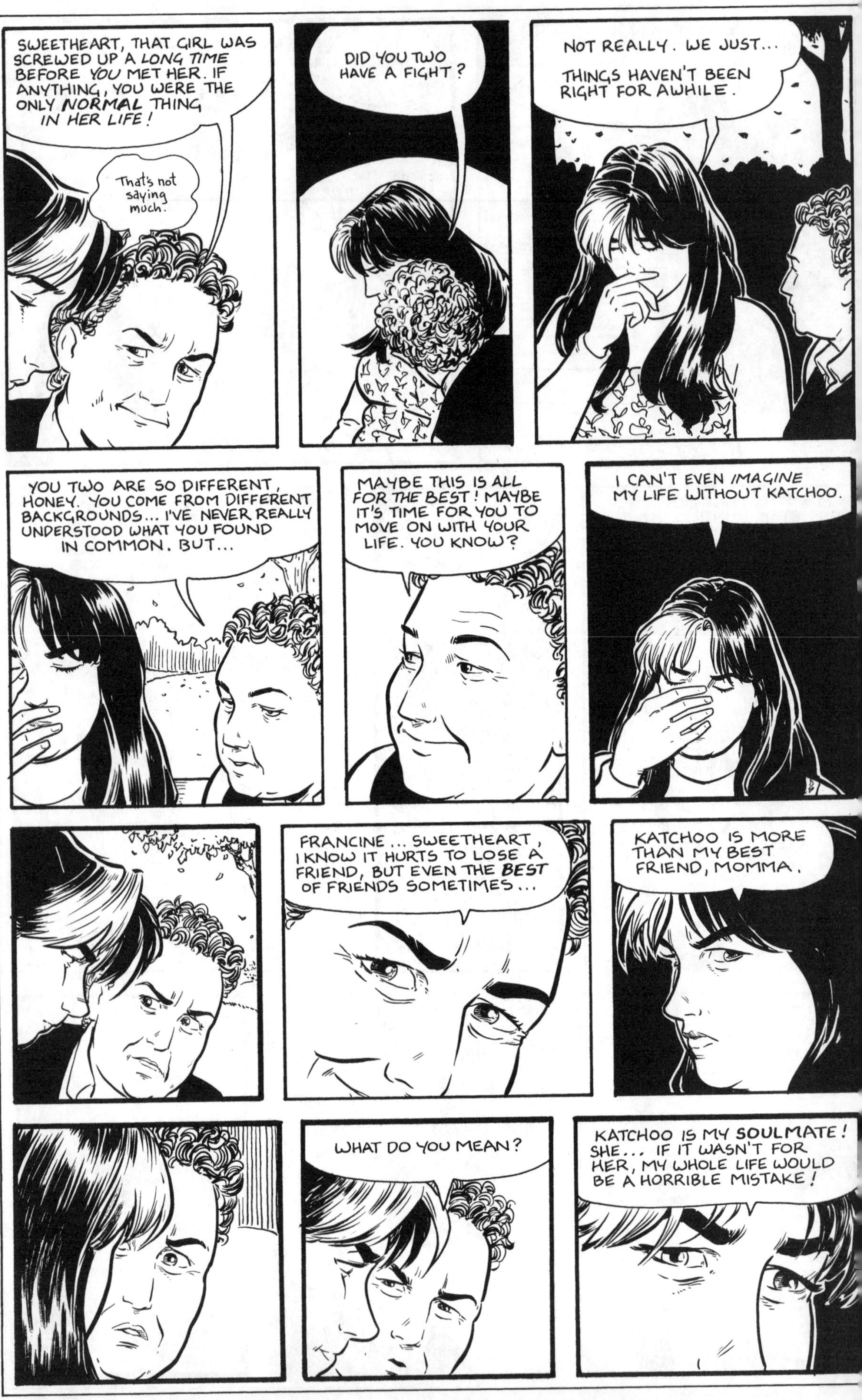
SWEETHEART, THAT GIRL WAS SCREWED UP A LONG TIME BEFORE YOU MET HER. IF ANYTHING, YOU WERE THE ONLY NORMAL THING IN HER LIFE!
That's not saying much.
DID YOU TWO HAVE A FIGHT?
NOT REALLY. WE JUST...
THINGS HAVEN'T BEEN RIGHT FOR AWHILE.
YOU TWO ARE SO DIFFERENT, HONEY. YOU COME FROM DIFFERENT BACKGROUNDS... I'VE NEVER REALLY UNDERSTOOD WHAT YOU FOUND IN COMMON. BUT...
MAYBE THIS IS ALL FOR THE BEST! MAYBE IT'S TIME FOR YOU TO MOVE ON WITH YOUR LIFE. YOU KNOW?
I CAN'T EVEN IMAGINE MY LIFE WITHOUT KATCHOO.
FRANCINE... SWEETHEART, I KNOW IT HURTS TO LOSE A FRIEND, BUT EVEN THE BEST OF FRIENDS SOMETIMES...
KATCHOO IS MORE THAN MY BEST FRIEND, MOMMA.
WHAT DO YOU MEAN?
KATCHOO IS MY SOULMATE! SHE... IF IT WASN'T FOR HER, MY WHOLE LIFE WOULD BE A HORRIBLE MISTAKE!

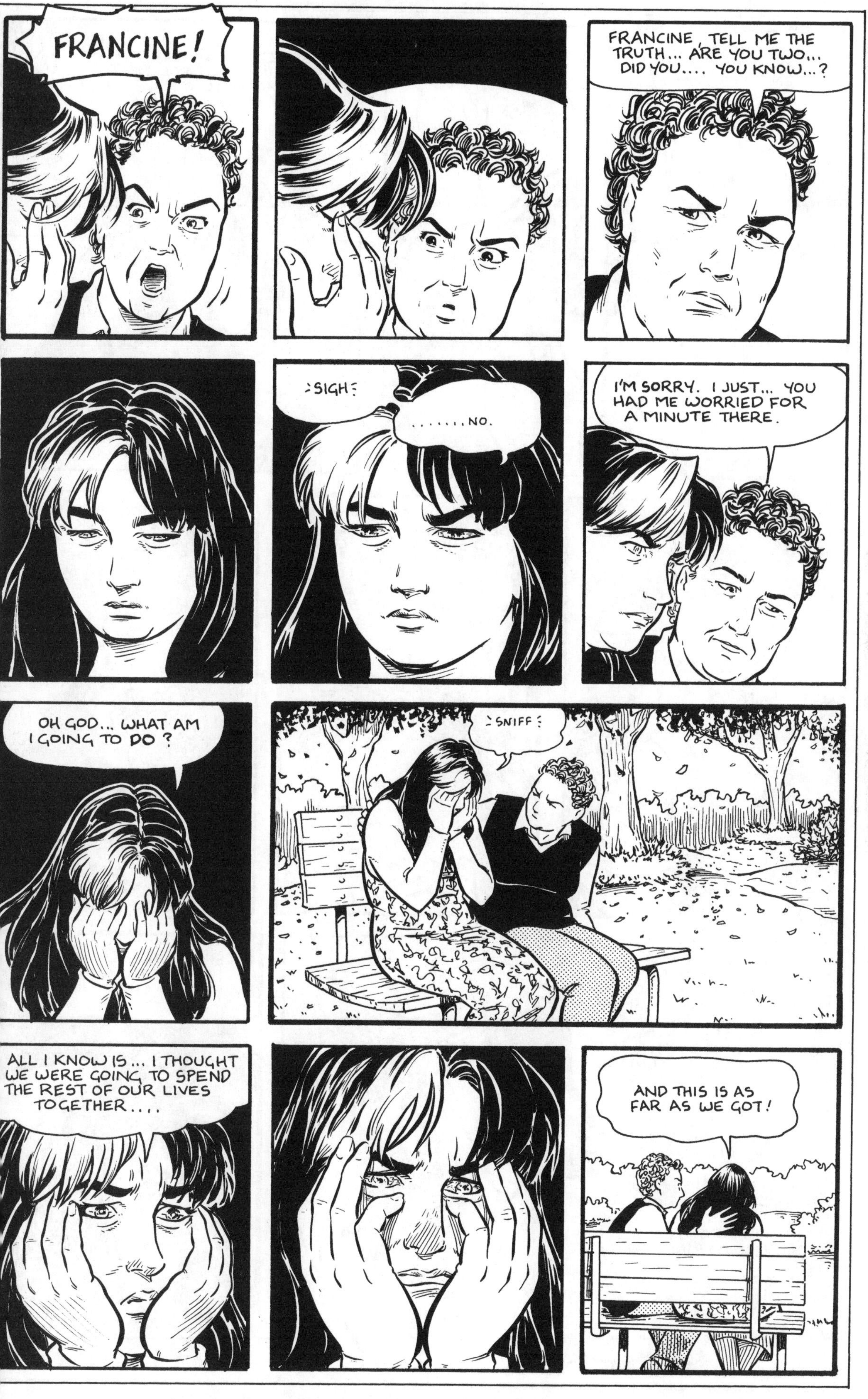
FRANCINE!
FRANCINE, TELL ME THE TRUTH... ARE YOU TWO... DID YOU.... YOU KNOW...?
SIGH
.......NO.
I'M SORRY. I JUST... YOU HAD ME WORRIED FOR A MINUTE THERE.
OH GOD... WHAT AM I GOING TO DO?
SNIFF
ALL I KNOW IS... I THOUGHT WE WERE GOING TO SPEND THE REST OF OUR LIVES TOGETHER....
AND THIS IS AS FAR AS WE GOT!

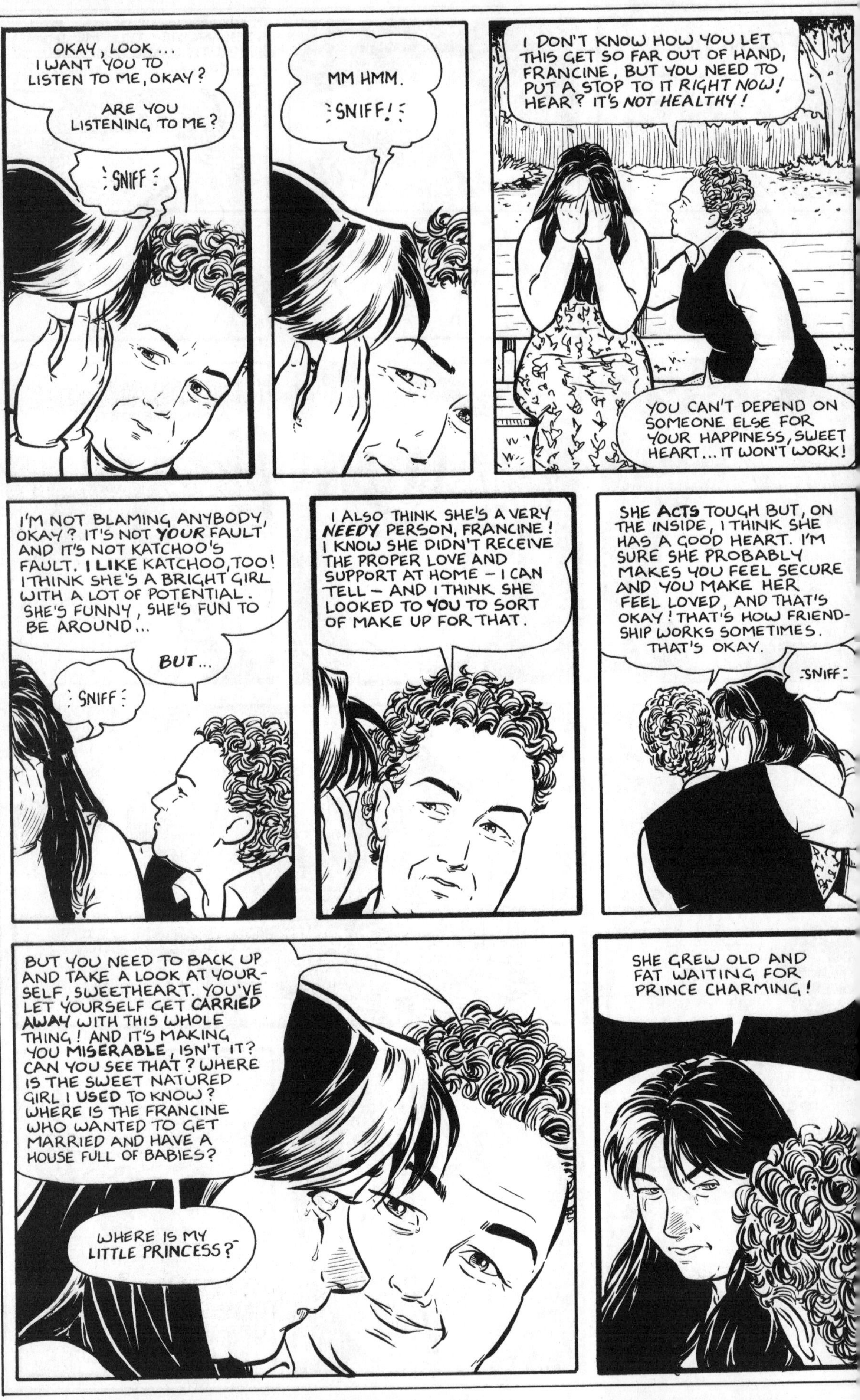

OKAY, LOOK... I WANT YOU TO LISTEN TO ME, OKAY? ARE YOU LISTENING TO ME?
SNIFF
MM HMM. SNIFF!
I DON'T KNOW HOW YOU LET THIS GET SO FAR OUT OF HAND, FRANCINE, BUT YOU NEED TO PUT A STOP TO IT RIGHT NOW! HEAR? IT'S NOT HEALTHY!
YOU CAN'T DEPEND ON SOMEONE ELSE FOR YOUR HAPPINESS, SWEET HEART... IT WON'T WORK!
I'M NOT BLAMING ANYBODY, OKAY? IT'S NOT YOUR FAULT AND IT'S NOT KATCHOO'S FAULT. I LIKE KATCHOO, TOO! I THINK SHE'S A BRIGHT GIRL WITH A LOT OF POTENTIAL. SHE'S FUNNY, SHE'S FUN TO BE AROUND... BUT...
SNIFF
I ALSO THINK SHE'S A VERY NEEDY PERSON, FRANCINE! I KNOW SHE DIDN'T RECEIVE THE PROPER LOVE AND SUPPORT AT HOME - I CAN TELL - AND I THINK SHE LOOKED TO YOU TO SORT OF MAKE UP FOR THAT.
SHE ACTS TOUGH BUT, ON THE INSIDE, I THINK SHE HAS A GOOD HEART. I'M SURE SHE PROBABLY MAKES YOU FEEL SECURE AND YOU MAKE HER FEEL LOVED, AND THAT'S OKAY! THAT'S HOW FRIENDSHIP WORKS SOMETIMES. THAT'S OKAY.
SNIFF
BUT YOU NEED TO BACK UP AND TAKE A LOOK AT YOURSELF, SWEETHEART. YOU'VE LET YOURSELF GET CARRIED AWAY WITH THIS WHOLE THING! AND IT'S MAKING YOU MISERABLE, ISN'T IT? CAN YOU SEE THAT? WHERE IS THE SWEET NATURED GIRL I USED TO KNOW? WHERE IS THE FRANCINE WHO WANTED TO GET MARRIED AND HAVE A HOUSE FULL OF BABIES?
WHERE IS MY LITTLE PRINCESS?
SHE GREW OLD AND FAT WAITING FOR PRINCE CHARMING!

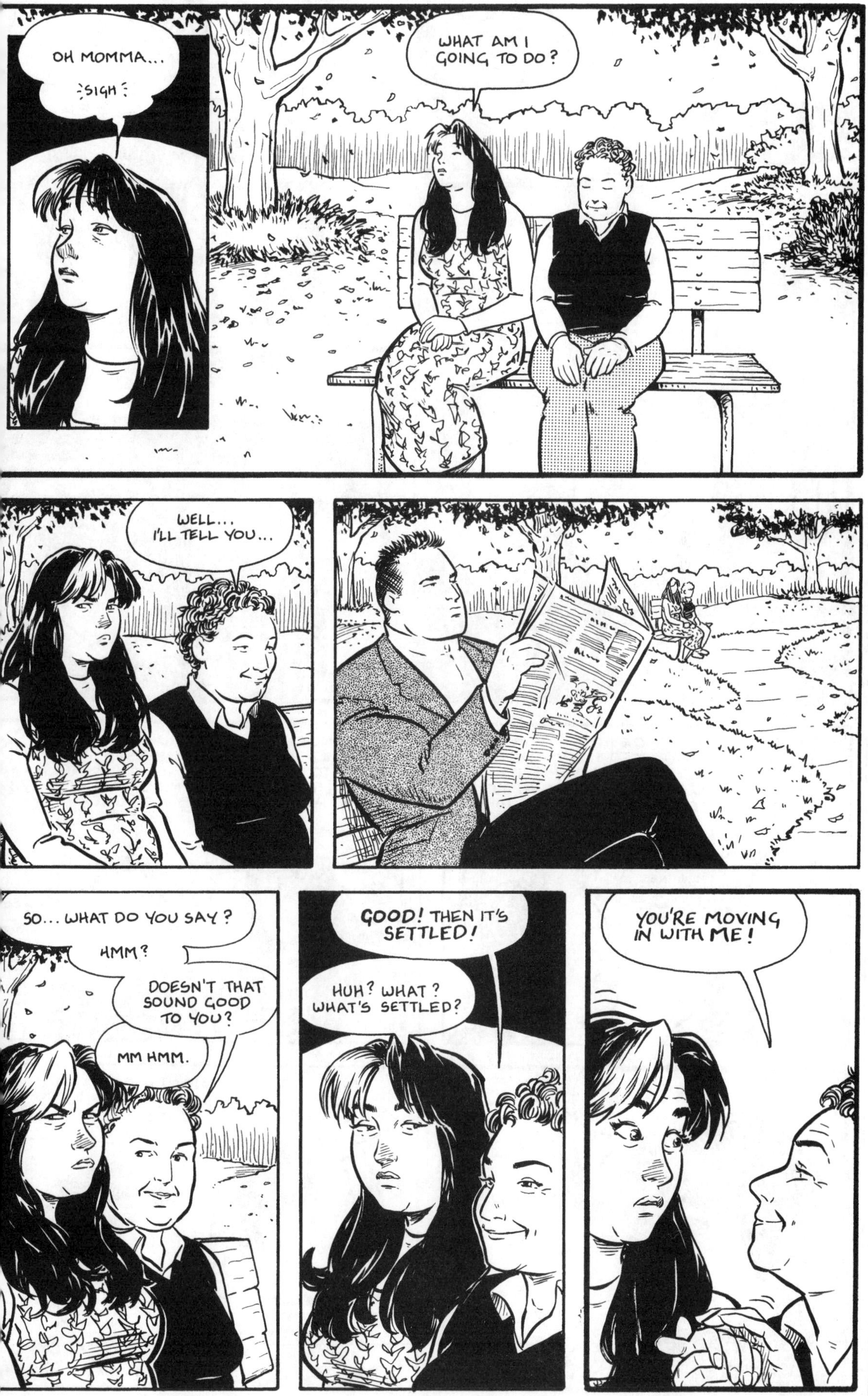
OH MOMMA...
SIGH
WHAT AM I GOING TO DO?
WELL... I'LL TELL YOU...
SO... WHAT DO YOU SAY?
HMM?
DOESN'T THAT SOUND GOOD TO YOU?
MM HMM.
GOOD! THEN IT'S SETTLED!
HUH? WHAT? WHAT'S SETTLED?
YOU'RE MOVING IN WITH ME!

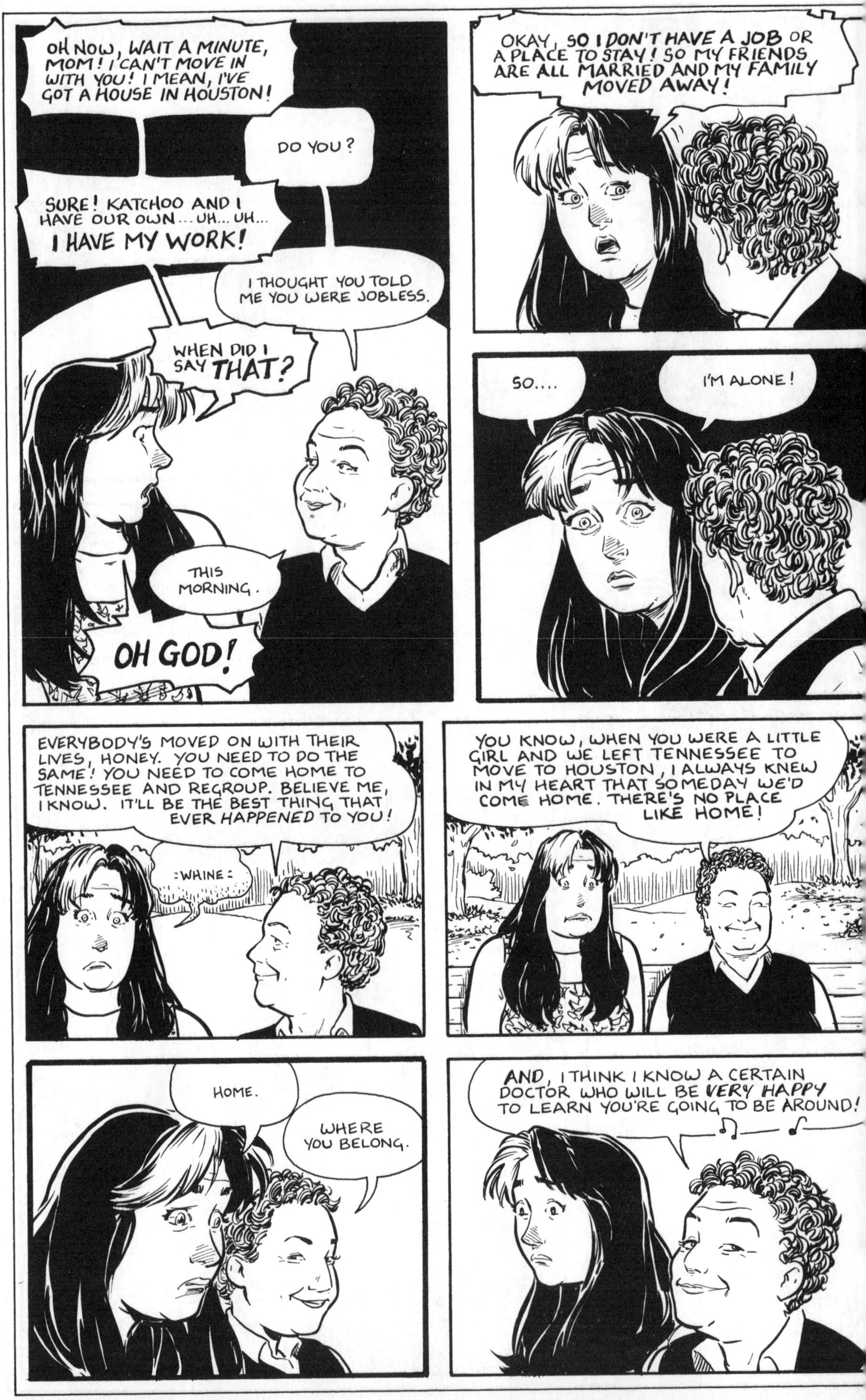
OH NOW, WAIT A MINUTE, MOM! I CAN'T MOVE IN WITH YOU! I MEAN, I'VE GOT A HOUSE IN HOUSTON!
DO YOU?
SURE! KATCHOO AND I HAVE OUR OWN... UH... UH... I HAVE MY WORK!
I THOUGHT YOU TOLD ME YOU WERE JOBLESS.
WHEN DID I SAY THAT?
THIS MORNING.
OH GOD!
OKAY, SO I DON'T HAVE A JOB OR A PLACE TO STAY! SO MY FRIENDS ARE ALL MARRIED AND MY FAMILY MOVED AWAY!
SO....
I'M ALONE!
EVERYBODY'S MOVED ON WITH THEIR LIVES, HONEY. YOU NEED TO DO THE SAME! YOU NEED TO COME HOME TO TENNESSEE AND REGROUP. BELIEVE ME, I KNOW. IT'LL BE THE BEST THING THAT EVER HAPPENED TO YOU!
:WHINE:
YOU KNOW, WHEN YOU WERE A LITTLE GIRL AND WE LEFT TENNESSEE TO MOVE TO HOUSTON, I ALWAYS KNEW IN MY HEART THAT SOMEDAY WE'D COME HOME. THERE'S NO PLACE LIKE HOME!
HOME.
WHERE YOU BELONG.
AND, I THINK I KNOW A CERTAIN DOCTOR WHO WILL BE VERY HAPPY TO LEARN YOU'RE GOING TO BE AROUND!

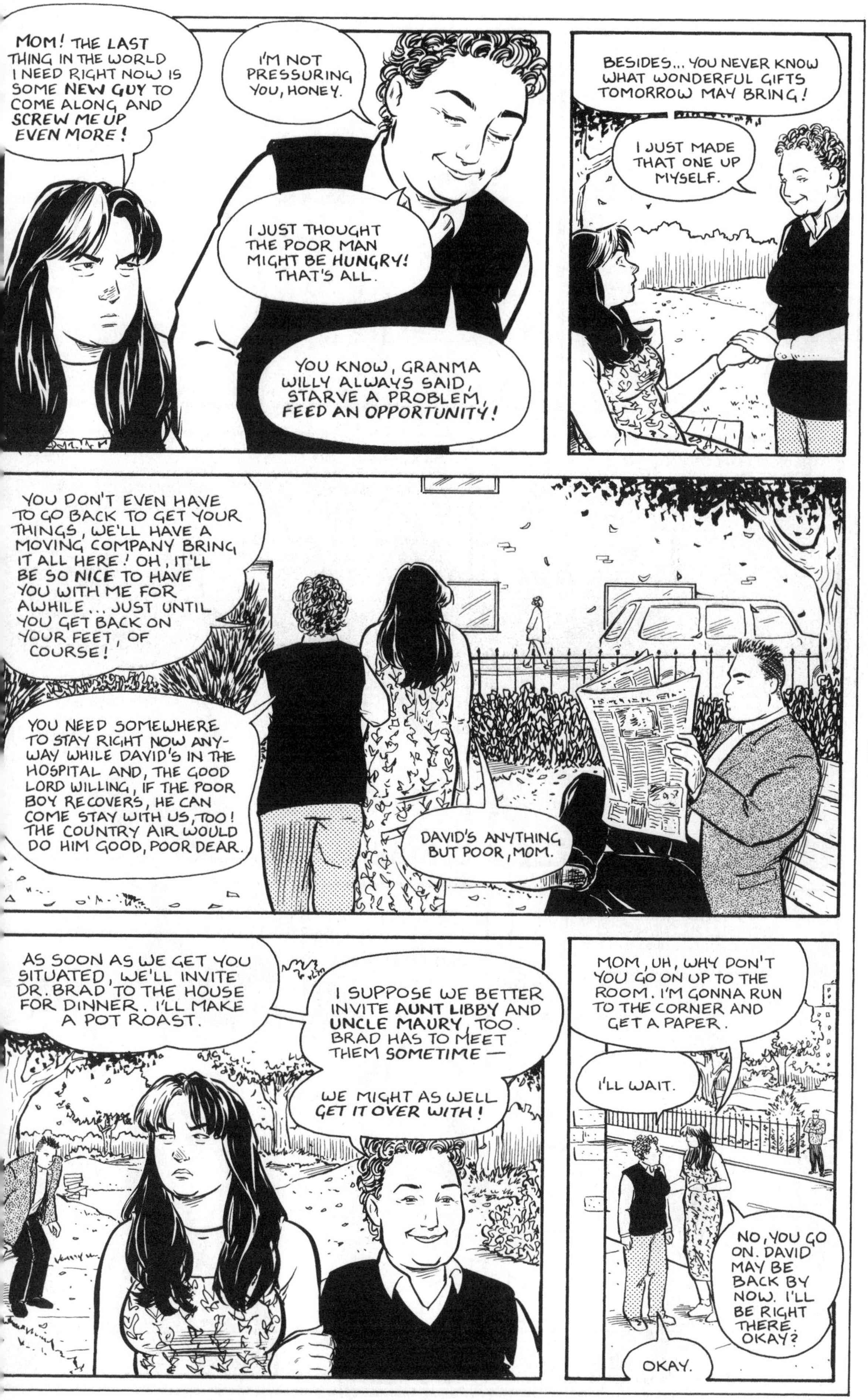
MOM! THE LAST THING IN THE WORLD I NEED RIGHT NOW IS SOME NEW GUY TO COME ALONG AND SCREW ME UP EVEN MORE!
I'M NOT PRESSURING YOU, HONEY.
I JUST THOUGHT THE POOR MAN MIGHT BE HUNGRY! THAT'S ALL.
YOU KNOW, GRANMA WILLY ALWAYS SAID, STARVE A PROBLEM, FEED AN OPPORTUNITY!
BESIDES... YOU NEVER KNOW WHAT WONDERFUL GIFTS TOMORROW MAY BRING!
I JUST MADE THAT ONE UP MYSELF.
YOU DON'T EVEN HAVE TO GO BACK TO GET YOUR THINGS, WE'LL HAVE A MOVING COMPANY BRING IT ALL HERE! OH, IT'LL BE SO NICE TO HAVE YOU WITH ME FOR AWHILE... JUST UNTIL YOU GET BACK ON YOUR FEET, OF COURSE!
YOU NEED SOMEWHERE TO STAY RIGHT NOW ANY-WAY WHILE DAVID'S IN THE HOSPITAL AND, THE GOOD LORD WILLING, IF THE POOR BOY RECOVERS, HE CAN COME STAY WITH US, TOO! THE COUNTRY AIR WOULD DO HIM GOOD, POOR DEAR.
DAVID'S ANYTHING BUT POOR, MOM.
AS SOON AS WE GET YOU SITUATED, WE'LL INVITE DR. BRAD TO THE HOUSE FOR DINNER. I'LL MAKE A POT ROAST.
I SUPPOSE WE BETTER INVITE AUNT LIBBY AND UNCLE MAURY, TOO. BRAD HAS TO MEET THEM SOMETIME—
WE MIGHT AS WELL GET IT OVER WITH!
MOM, UH, WHY DON'T YOU GO ON UP TO THE ROOM. I'M GONNA RUN TO THE CORNER AND GET A PAPER.
I'LL WAIT.
NO, YOU GO ON. DAVID MAY BE BACK BY NOW. I'LL BE RIGHT THERE. OKAY?
OKAY.

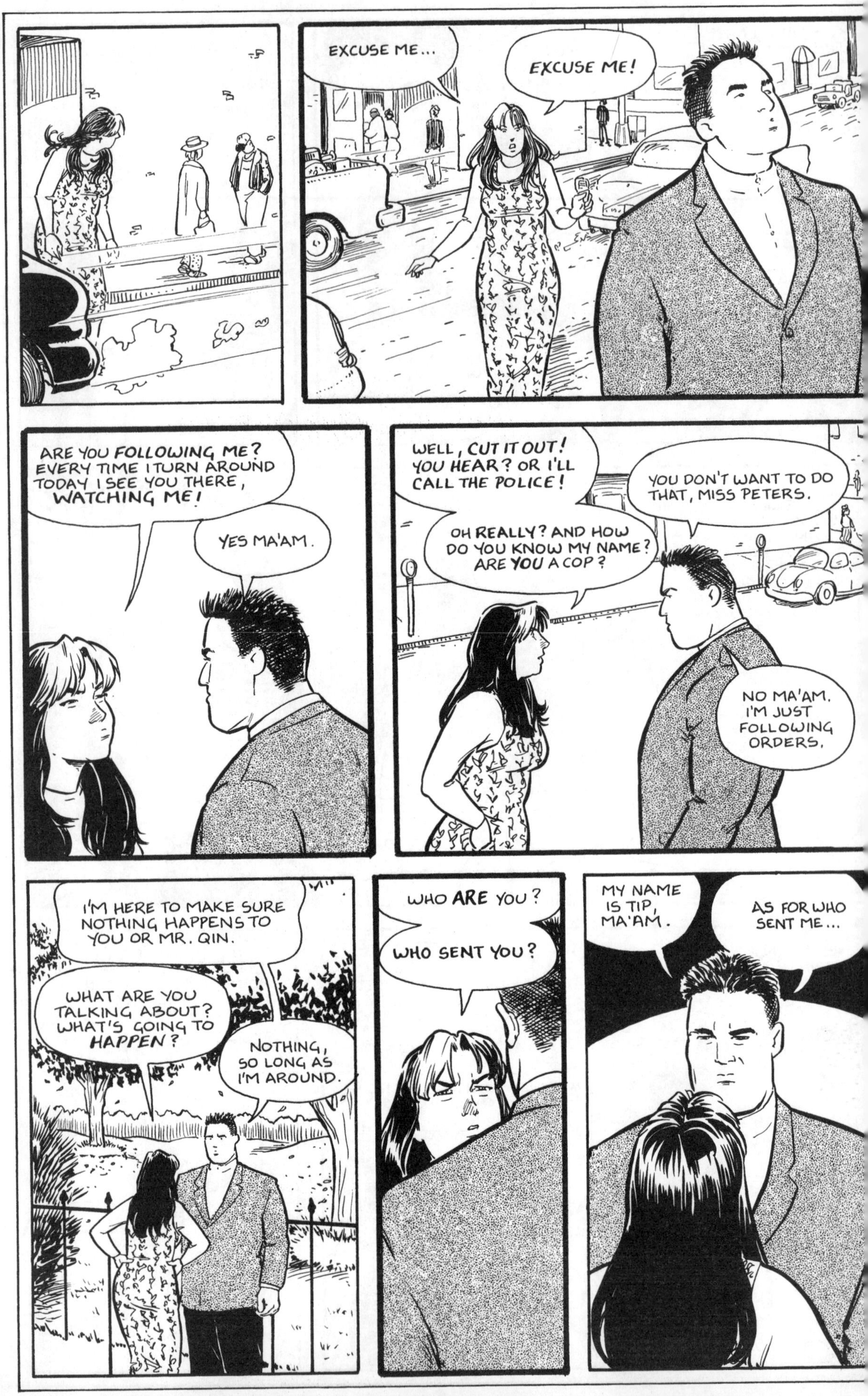
EXCUSE ME...
EXCUSE ME!
ARE YOU FOLLOWING ME? EVERY TIME I TURN AROUND TODAY I SEE YOU THERE, WATCHING ME!
YES MA'AM.
WELL, CUT IT OUT! YOU HEAR? OR I'LL CALL THE POLICE!
YOU DON'T WANT TO DO THAT, MISS PETERS.
OH REALLY? AND HOW DO YOU KNOW MY NAME? ARE YOU A COP?
NO MA'AM. I'M JUST FOLLOWING ORDERS.
I'M HERE TO MAKE SURE NOTHING HAPPENS TO YOU OR MR. QIN.
WHAT ARE YOU TALKING ABOUT? WHAT'S GOING TO HAPPEN?
NOTHING, SO LONG AS I'M AROUND.
WHO ARE YOU?
WHO SENT YOU?
MY NAME IS TIP, MA'AM.
AS FOR WHO SENT ME...

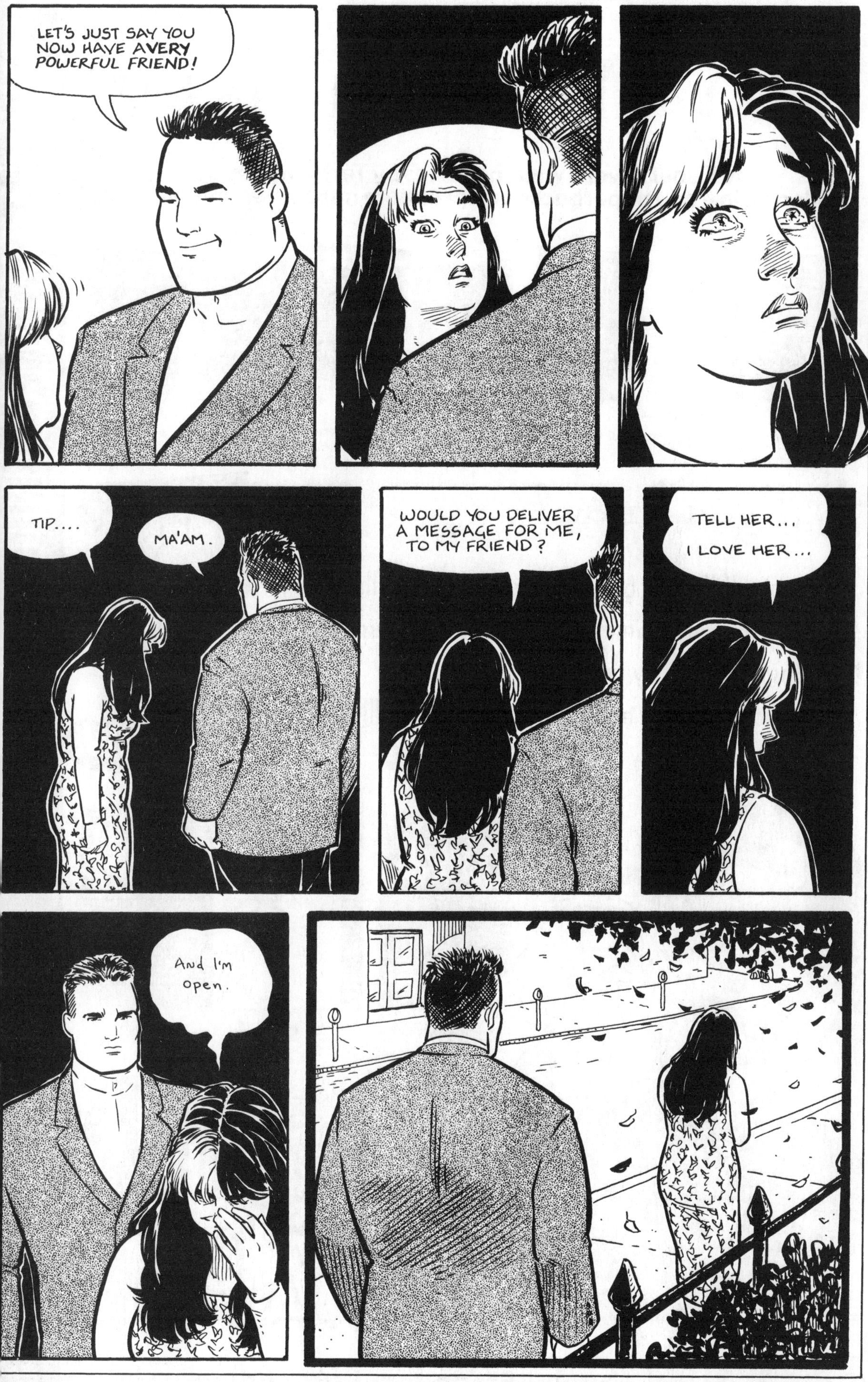
LET'S JUST SAY YOU NOW HAVE A VERY POWERFUL FRIEND!
TIP....
MA'AM.
WOULD YOU DELIVER A MESSAGE FOR ME, TO MY FRIEND?
TELL HER...
I LOVE HER...
And I'm open.

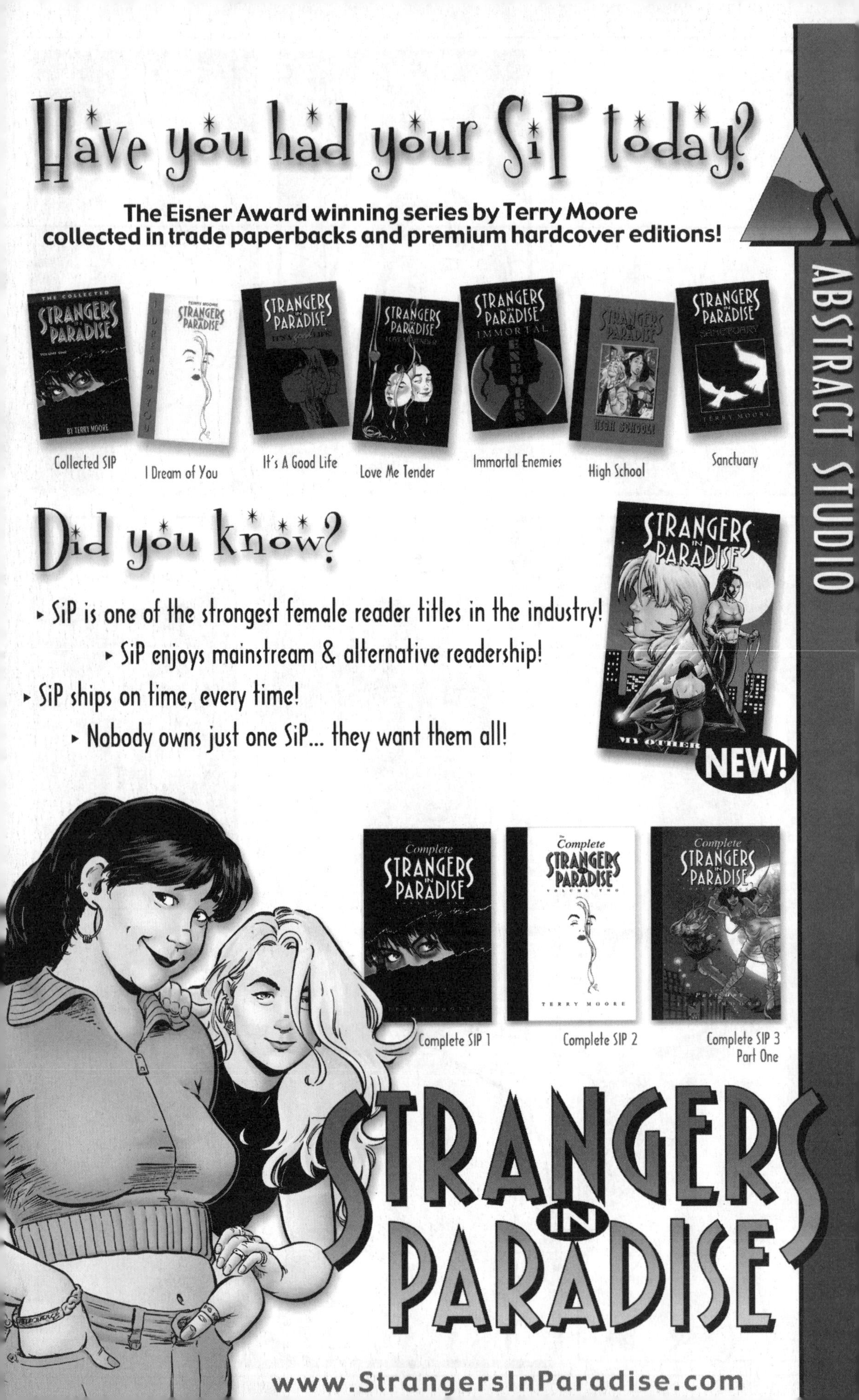

Have you had your SiP today?
The Eisner Award winning series by Terry Moore
collected in trade paperbacks and premium hardcover editions!
Collected SIP
I Dream of You
It's A Good Life
Love Me Tender
Immortal Enemies
High School
Sanctuary
Did you know?
▸ SiP is one of the strongest female reader titles in the industry!
▸ SiP enjoys mainstream & alternative readership!
▸ SiP ships on time, every time!
▸ Nobody owns just one SiP... they want them all!
NEW!
Complete SIP 1
Complete SIP 2
Complete SIP 3
Part One
ABSTRACT STUDIO
STRANGERS IN PARADISE
www.StrangersInParadise.com